I0465540

AutoGen Reference Manual

A catalogue record for this book is available from the Hong Kong Public Libraries.

Published in Hong Kong by Samurai Media Limited.

Email: info@samuraimedia.org

ISBN 978-988-8381-68-5

This manual is for GNU AutoGen version 5.18, updated August 2015.

Minor modifications for publication Copyright 2015 Samurai Media Limited.

Background Cover Image by https://www.flickr.com/people/webtreatsetc/

The Automated Program Generator

This file documents AutoGen version 5.18. It is a tool designed for generating program files that contain repetitive text with varied substitutions. This document is very long because it is intended as a reference document. For a quick start example, See Section 1.2 [Example Usage], page 3.

The AutoGen distribution includes the basic generator engine and several add-on libraries and programs. Of the most general interest would be Automated Option processing, See Chapter 7 [AutoOpts], page 83, which also includes stand-alone support for configuration file parsing, See Section 7.1 [Features], page 83. See Chapter 8 [Add-Ons], page 185, section for additional programs and libraries associated with AutoGen.

This edition documents version 5.18, August 2015.

1 Introduction

AutoGen is a tool designed for generating program files that contain repetitive text with varied substitutions. Its goal is to simplify the maintenance of programs that contain large amounts of repetitious text. This is especially valuable if there are several blocks of such text that must be kept synchronized in parallel tables.

An obvious example is the problem of maintaining the code required for processing program options and configuration settings. Processing options requires a minimum of four different constructs be kept in proper order in different places in your program. You need at least:

1. The flag character in the flag string,

2. code to process the flag when it is encountered,

3. a global state variable or two, and

4. a line in the usage text.

You will need more things besides this if you choose to implement long option names, configuration (rc/ini) file processing, environment variable settings and keep all the documentation for these up to date. This can be done mechanically; with the proper templates and this program. In fact, it has already been done and AutoGen itself uses it See Chapter 7 [AutoOpts], page 83. For a simple example of Automated Option processing, See Section 7.4 [Quick Start], page 88. For a full list of the Automated Option features, See Section 7.1 [Features], page 83. Be forewarned, though, the feature list is ridiculously extensive.

1.1 The Purpose of AutoGen

The idea of this program is to have a text file, a template if you will, that contains the general text of the desired output file. That file includes substitution expressions and sections of text that are replicated under the control of separate definition files.

AutoGen was designed with the following features:

1. The definitions are completely separate from the template. By completely isolating the definitions from the template it greatly increases the flexibility of the template implementation. A secondary goal is that a template user only needs to specify those data that are necessary to describe his application of a template.

2. Each datum in the definitions is named. Thus, the definitions can be rearranged, augmented and become obsolete without it being necessary to go back and clean up older definition files. Reduce incompatibilities!

3. Every definition name defines an array of values, even when there is only one entry. These arrays of values are used to control the replication of sections of the template.

4. There are named collections of definitions. They form a nested hierarchy. Associated values are collected and associated with a group name. These associated data are used collectively in sets of substitutions.

5. The template has special markers to indicate where substitutions are required, much like the `${VAR}` construct in a shell **here doc**. These markers are not fixed strings. They are specified at the start of each template. Template designers know best what fits into their syntax and can avoid marker conflicts.

We did this because it is burdensome and difficult to avoid conflicts using either M4 tokenization or C preprocessor substitution rules. It also makes it easier to specify expressions that transform the value. Of course, our expressions are less cryptic than the shell methods.

6. These same markers are used, in conjunction with enclosed keywords, to indicate sections of text that are to be skipped and for sections of text that are to be repeated. This is a major improvement over using C preprocessing macros. With the C preprocessor, you have no way of selecting output text because it is an *un*varying, mechanical substitution process.

7. Finally, we supply methods for carefully controlling the output. Sometimes, it is just simply easier and clearer to compute some text or a value in one context when its application needs to be later. So, functions are available for saving text or values for later use.

1.2 A Simple Example

This is just one simple example that shows a few basic features. If you are interested, you also may run "make check" with the VERBOSE environment variable set and see a number of other examples in the agen5/test directory.

Assume you have an enumeration of names and you wish to associate some string with each name. Assume also, for the sake of this example, that it is either too complex or too large to maintain easily by hand. We will start by writing an abbreviated version of what the result is supposed to be. We will use that to construct our output templates.

In a header file, list.h, you define the enumeration and the global array containing the associated strings:

```
typedef enum {
        IDX_ALPHA,
        IDX_BETA,
        IDX_OMEGA }  list_enum;

extern char const* az_name_list[ 3 ];
```

Then you also have list.c that defines the actual strings:

```
#include "list.h"
char const* az_name_list[] = {
        "some alpha stuff",
        "more beta stuff",
        "final omega stuff" };
```

First, we will define the information that is unique for each enumeration name/string pair. This would be placed in a file named, list.def, for example.

```
autogen definitions list;
list = { list_element = alpha;
         list_info    = "some alpha stuff"; };
list = { list_info    = "more beta stuff";
         list_element = beta; };
list = { list_element = omega;
```

```
              list_info    = "final omega stuff"; };
```

The `autogen definitions list;` entry defines the file as an AutoGen definition file that uses a template named `list`. That is followed by three `list` entries that define the associations between the enumeration names and the strings. The order of the differently named elements inside of list is unimportant. They are reversed inside of the `beta` entry and the output is unaffected.

Now, to actually create the output, we need a template or two that can be expanded into the files you want. In this program, we use a single template that is capable of multiple output files. The definitions above refer to a `list` template, so it would normally be named, `list.tpl`.

It looks something like this. (For a full description, See Chapter 3 [Template File], page 21.)

```
[+ AutoGen5 template h c +]
[+ CASE (suffix) +] [+
   ==  h  +]
typedef enum {[+
   FOR list "," +]
          IDX_[+ (string-upcase! (get "list_element")) +] [+
   ENDFOR list +] }  list_enum;

extern char const* az_name_list[ [+ (count "list") +] ];
[+

   ==  c  +]
#include "list.h"
char const* az_name_list[] = {[+
   FOR list "," +]
          "[+list_info+]"[+
   ENDFOR list +] };[+

ESAC +]
```

The `[+ AutoGen5 template h c +]` text tells AutoGen that this is an AutoGen version 5 template file; that it is to be processed twice; that the start macro marker is `[+`; and the end marker is `+]`. The template will be processed first with a suffix value of `h` and then with `c`. Normally, the suffix values are appended to the `base-name` to create the output file name.

The `[+ == h +]` and `[+ == c +]` CASE selection clauses select different text for the two different passes. In this example, the output is nearly disjoint and could have been put in two separate templates. However, sometimes there are common sections and this is just an example.

The `[+FOR list "," +]` and `[+ ENDFOR list +]` clauses delimit a block of text that will be repeated for every definition of `list`. Inside of that block, the definition name-value pairs that are members of each `list` are available for substitutions.

The remainder of the macros are expressions. Some of these contain special expression functions that are dependent on AutoGen named values; others are simply Scheme expressions, the result of which will be inserted into the output text. Other expressions are names of AutoGen values. These values will be inserted into the output text. For example, [+list_info+] will result in the value associated with the name list_info being inserted between the double quotes and (string-upcase! (get "list_element")) will first "get" the value associated with the name list_element, then change the case of all the letters to upper case. The result will be inserted into the output document.

If you have compiled AutoGen, you can copy out the template and definitions as described above and run autogen list.def. This will produce exactly the hypothesized desired output.

One more point, too. Lets say you decided it was too much trouble to figure out how to use AutoGen, so you created this enumeration and string list with thousands of entries. Now, requirements have changed and it has become necessary to map a string containing the enumeration name into the enumeration number. With AutoGen, you just alter the template to emit the table of names. It will be guaranteed to be in the correct order, missing none of the entries. If you want to do that by hand, well, good luck.

1.3 csh/zsh caveat

AutoGen tries to use your normal shell so that you can supply shell code in a manner you are accustomed to using. If, however, you use csh or zsh, you cannot do this. Csh is sufficiently difficult to program that it is unsupported. Zsh, though largely programmable, also has some anomalies that make it incompatible with AutoGen usage. Therefore, when invoking AutoGen from these environments, you must be certain to set the SHELL environment variable to a Bourne-derived shell, e.g., sh, ksh or bash.

Any shell you choose for your own scripts need to follow these basic requirements:

1. It handles trap ":" $sig without output to standard out. This is done when the server shell is first started. If your shell does not handle this, then it may be able to by loading functions from its start up files.

2. At the beginning of each scriptlet, the command \\cd $PWD is inserted. This ensures that cd is not aliased to something peculiar and each scriptlet starts life in the execution directory.

3. At the end of each scriptlet, the command echo mumble is appended. The program you use as a shell must emit the single argument mumble on a line by itself.

1.4 A User's Perspective

Alexandre wrote:
>
> I'd appreciate opinions from others about advantages, disadvantages of
> each of these macro packages.

I am using AutoGen in my pet project, and find one of its best points to be that it separates the operational data from the implementation.

Indulge me for a few paragraphs, and all will be revealed: In the manual, Bruce cites the example of maintaining command line flags inside the source code; traditionally spreading usage information, flag names, letters and processing across several functions (if not files). Investing the time in writing a sort of boiler plate (a template in AutoGen terminology) pays by moving all of the option details (usage, flags names etc.) into a well structured table (a definition file if you will), so that adding a new command line option becomes a simple matter of adding a set of details to the table.

So far so good! Of course, now that there is a template, writing all of that tedious optargs processing and usage functions is no longer an issue. Creating a table of the options needed for the new project and running AutoGen generates all of the option processing code in C automatically from just the tabular data. AutoGen in fact already ships with such a template... AutoOpts.

One final consequence of the good separation in the design of AutoGen is that it is retargetable to a greater extent. The egcs/gcc/fixinc/inclhack.def can equally be used (with different templates) to create a shell script (inclhack.sh) or a c program (fixincl.c).

This is just the tip of the iceberg. AutoGen is far more powerful than these examples might indicate, and has many other varied uses. I am certain Bruce or I could supply you with many and varied examples, and I would heartily recommend that you try it for your project and see for yourself how it compares to m4.

As an aside, I would be interested to see whether someone might be persuaded to rationalise autoconf with AutoGen in place of m4... Ben, are you listening? autoconf-3.0! 'kay? =)O|

Sincerely,

    Gary V. Vaughan

2 Definitions File

This chapter describes the syntax and semantics of the AutoGen definition file. In order to instantiate a template, you normally must provide a definitions file that identifies itself and contains some value definitions. Consequently, we keep it very simple. For "advanced" users, there are preprocessing directives, sparse arrays, named indexes and comments that may be used as well.

The definitions file is used to associate values with names. Every value is implicitly an array of values, even if there is only one value. Values may be either simple strings or compound collections of name-value pairs. An array may not contain both simple and compound members. Fundamentally, it is as simple as:

```
prog-name = "autogen";
flag = {
    name      = templ_dirs;
    value     = L;
    descrip   = "Template search directory list";
};
```

For purposes of commenting and controlling the processing of the definitions, C-style comments and most C preprocessing directives are honored. The major exception is that the `#if` directive is ignored, along with all following text through the matching `#endif` directive. The C preprocessor is not actually invoked, so C macro substitution is **not** performed.

2.1 The Identification Definition

The first definition in this file is used to identify it as a AutoGen file. It consists of the two keywords, 'autogen' and '**definitions**' followed by the default template name and a terminating semi-colon (;). That is:

AutoGen Definitions *template-name*;

Note that, other than the name *template-name*, the words 'AutoGen' and 'Definitions' are searched for without case sensitivity. Most lookups in this program are case insensitive.

Also, if the input contains more identification definitions, they will be ignored. This is done so that you may include (see Section 2.5 [Directives], page 12) other definition files without an identification conflict.

AutoGen uses the name of the template to find the corresponding template file. It searches for the file in the following way, stopping when it finds the file:

1. It tries to open `./template-name`. If it fails,

2. it tries `./template-name.tpl`.

3. It searches for either of these files in the directories listed in the templ-dirs command line option.

If AutoGen fails to find the template file in one of these places, it prints an error message and exits.

2.2 Named Definitions

A name is a sequence of characters beginning with an alphabetic character (a through z) followed by zero or more alpha-numeric characters and/or separator characters: hyphen (-), underscore (_) or carat (^). Names are case insensitive.

Any name may have multiple values associated with it. Every name may be considered a sparse array of one or more elements. If there is more than one value, the values my be accessed by indexing the value with [index] or by iterating over them using the FOR (see Section 3.6.16 [FOR], page 60) AutoGen macro on it, as described in the next chapter. Sparse arrays are specified by specifying an index when defining an entry (see Section 2.3 [Assigning an Index to a Definition], page 11).

There are two kinds of definitions, 'simple' and 'compound'. They are defined thus (see Section 2.9 [Full Syntax], page 15):

```
compound_name '=' '{' definition-list '}' ';'

simple-name[2] '=' string ';'

no^text^name ';'
```

simple-name has the third index (index number 2) defined here. No^text^name is a simple definition with a shorthand empty string value. The string values for definitions may be specified in any of several formation rules.

2.2.1 Definition List

definition-list is a list of definitions that may or may not contain nested compound definitions. Any such definitions may **only** be expanded within a FOR block iterating over the containing compound definition. See Section 3.6.16 [FOR], page 60.

Here is, again, the example definitions from the previous chapter, with three additional name value pairs. Two with an empty value assigned (*first* and *last*), and a "global" *group_name*.

```
autogen definitions list;
group_name = example;
list = { list_element = alpha;  first;
         list_info    = "some alpha stuff"; };
list = { list_info    = "more beta stuff";
         list_element = beta; };
list = { list_element = omega;  last;
         list_info    = "final omega stuff"; };
```

2.2.2 Double Quote String

The string follows the C-style escaping, using the backslash to quote (escape) the following character(s). Certain letters are translated to various control codes (e.g. \n, \f, \t, etc.). x introduces a two character hex code. 0 (the digit zero) introduces a one to three character octal code (note: an octal byte followed by a digit must be represented with three octal digits, thus: "\0001" yielding a NUL byte followed by the ASCII digit 1). Any other character following the backslash escape is simply inserted, without error, into the string being formed.

Like ANSI "C", a series of these strings, possibly intermixed with single quote strings, will be concatenated together.

2.2.3 Single Quote String

This is similar to the shell single-quote string. However, escapes \ are honored before another escape, single quotes ' and hash characters #. This latter is done specifically to disambiguate lines starting with a hash character inside of a quoted string. In other words,

```
fumble = '
#endif
';
```

could be misinterpreted by the definitions scanner, whereas this would not:

```
fumble = '
\#endif
';
```

As with the double quote string, a series of these, even intermixed with double quote strings, will be concatenated together.

2.2.4 An Unquoted String

A simple string that does not contain white space *may* be left unquoted. The string must not contain any of the characters special to the definition text (i.e., ", #, ', (,), ,, ;, <, =, >, [,], ', {, or }). This list is subject to change, but it will never contain underscore (_), period (.), slash (/), colon (:), hyphen (-) or backslash (\\). Basically, if the string looks like it is a normal DOS or UNIX file or variable name, and it is not one of two keywords ('autogen' or 'definitions') then it is OK to not quote it, otherwise you should.

2.2.5 Shell Output String

This is assembled according to the same rules as the double quote string, except that there is no concatenation of strings and the resulting string is written to a shell server process. The definition takes on the value of the output string.

NB The text is interpreted by a server shell. There may be left over state from previous server shell processing. This scriptlet may also leave state for subsequent processing. However, a cd to the original directory is always issued before the new command is issued.

2.2.6 Scheme Result String

A scheme result string must begin with an open parenthesis (. The scheme expression will be evaluated by Guile and the value will be the result. The AutoGen expression functions are **dis**abled at this stage, so do not use them.

2.2.7 A Here String

A 'here string' is formed in much the same way as a shell here doc. It is denoted with two less than characters(<<) and, optionally, a hyphen. This is followed by optional horizontal white space and an ending marker-identifier. This marker must follow the syntax rules for identifiers. Unlike the shell version, however, you must not quote this marker.

The resulting string will start with the first character on the next line and continue up to but not including the newline that precedes the line that begins with the marker token. The characters are copied directly into the result string. Mostly.

If a hyphen follows the less than characters, then leading tabs will be stripped and the terminating marker will be recognized even if preceded by tabs. Also, if the first character on the line (after removing tabs) is a backslash and the next character is a tab or space, then the backslash will be removed as well. No other kind of processing is done on this string.

Here are three examples:

```
str1 = <<-  STR_END
        $quotes = " ' `
        STR_END;

str2 = <<   STR_END
        $quotes = " ' `
        STR_END;
STR_END;

str3 = <<-  STR_END
        \ $quotes = " ' `
        STR_END;
```

The first string contains no new line characters. The first character is the dollar sign, the last the back quote.

The second string contains one new line character. The first character is the tab character preceding the dollar sign. The last character is the semicolon after the STR_END. That STR_END does not end the string because it is not at the beginning of the line. In the preceding case, the leading tab was stripped.

The third string is almost identical to the first, except that the first character is a tab. That is, it exactly matches the first line of the second string.

2.2.8 Concatenated Strings

If single or double quote characters are used, then you also have the option, a la ANSI-C syntax, of implicitly concatenating a series of them together, with intervening white space ignored.

NB You **cannot** use directives to alter the string content. That is,

```
str = "fumble"
#ifdef LATER
        "stumble"
#endif
        ;
```

will result in a syntax error. The preprocessing directives are not carried out by the C preprocessor. However,

```
str = '"fumble\n"
#ifdef LATER
```

```
"       stumble\n"
#endif
';
```

Will work. It will enclose the '#ifdef LATER' and '#endif' in the string. But it may also wreak havoc with the definition processing directives. The hash characters in the first column should be disambiguated with an escape \ or join them with previous lines: "fumble\n#ifdef LATER....

2.3 Assigning an Index to a Definition

In AutoGen, every name is implicitly an array of values. When assigning values, they are usually implicitly assigned to the next highest slot. They can also be specified explicitly:

```
mumble[9] = stumble;
mumble[0] = grumble;
```

If, subsequently, you assign a value to **mumble** without an index, its index will be 10, not 1. If indexes are specified, they must not cause conflicts.

#define-d names may also be used for index values. This is equivalent to the above:

```
#define FIRST 0
#define LAST  9
mumble[LAST]  = stumble;
mumble[FIRST] = grumble;
```

All values in a range do **not** have to be filled in. If you leave gaps, then you will have a sparse array. This is fine (see Section 3.6.16 [FOR], page 60). You have your choice of iterating over all the defined values, or iterating over a range of slots. This:

```
[+ FOR mumble +] [+ ENDFOR +]
```

iterates over all and only the defined entries, whereas this:

```
[+ FOR mumble (for-by 1) +] [+ ENDFOR +]
```

will iterate over all 10 "slots". Your template will likely have to contain something like this:

```
[+ IF (exist? (sprintf "mumble[%d]" (for-index))) +]
```

or else "mumble" will have to be a compound value that, say, always contains a "grumble" value:

```
[+ IF (exist? "grumble") +]
```

2.4 Dynamic Text

There are several methods for including dynamic content inside a definitions file. Three of them are mentioned above (Section 2.2.5 [shell-generated], page 9 and see Section 2.2.6 [scheme-generated], page 9) in the discussion of string formation rules. Another method uses the **#shell** processing directive. It will be discussed in the next section (see Section 2.5 [Directives], page 12). Guile/Scheme may also be used to yield to create definitions.

When the Scheme expression is preceded by a backslash and single quote, then the expression is expected to be an alist of names and values that will be used to create AutoGen definitions.

This method can be be used as follows:

```
\'( (name  (value-expression))
      (name2 (another-expr))  )
```

This is entirely equivalent to:

```
name  = (value-expression);
name2 = (another-expr);
```

Under the covers, the expression gets handed off to a Guile function named `alist->autogen-def` in an expression that looks like this:

```
(alist->autogen-def
      ( (name (value-expression))  (name2 (another-expr)) ) )
```

2.5 Controlling What Gets Processed

Definition processing directives can **only** be processed if the '#' character is the first character on a line. Also, if you want a '#' as the first character of a line in one of your string assignments, you should either escape it by preceding it with a backslash '\', or by embedding it in the string as in `"\n#"`.

All of the normal C preprocessing directives are recognized, though several are ignored. There is also an additional `#shell` - `#endshell` pair. Another minor difference is that AutoGen directives must have the hash character (#) in column 1. Unrecognized directives produce an error.

The final tweak is that `#!` is treated as a comment line. Using this feature, you can use: '`#! /usr/local/bin/autogen`' as the first line of a definitions file, set the mode to executable and "run" the definitions file as if it were a direct invocation of AutoGen. This was done for its hack value.

The AutoGen recognized directives are:

`#assert`   This directive *is* processed, but only if the expression begins with either a back quote (`) or an open parenthesis ((). Text within the back quotes are handed off to the shell for processing and parenthesized text is handed off to Guile. Multiple line expressions must be joined with backslashes.

   If the **shell-script** or **scheme-expr** do not yield **true** valued results, autogen will be aborted. If **<anything else>** or nothing at all is provided, then this directive is ignored.

   The result is **false** (and fails) if the result is empty, the number zero, or a string that starts with the letters 'n' or 'f' ("no" or "false").

`#define`   Will add the name to the define list as if it were a DEFINE program argument. Its value will be the first non-whitespace token following the name. Quotes are **not** processed.

   After the definitions file has been processed, any remaining entries in the define list will be added to the environment.

`#elif`   Marks a transition in the #if directive. Error when out of context. #if blocks are always ignored.

`#else`   This must follow an `#if`, `#ifdef` or `#ifndef`. If it follows the `#if`, then it will be ignored. Otherwise, it will change the processing state to the reverse of what it was.

#endif   This must follow an **#if**, **#ifdef** or **#ifndef**. In all cases, this will resume normal processing of text.

#endmac   Marks the end of the #macdef directive. Error when out of context.

#endshell
           Marks the end of the #shell directive. Error when out of context.

#error   This directive will cause AutoGen to stop processing and exit with a status of EXIT_FAILURE.

#ident   Ignored directive.

#if   **#if** expressions are not analyzed. **Everything** from here to the matching **#endif** is skipped.

#ifdef   The definitions that follow, up to the matching **#endif** will be processed only if there is a corresponding **-Dname** command line option or if a **#define** of that name has been previously encountered.

#ifndef   The definitions that follow, up to the matching **#endif** will be processed only if the named value has **not** been defined.

#include   This directive will insert definitions from another file into the current collection. If the file name is adorned with double quotes or angle brackets (as in a C program), then the include is ignored.

#let   Ignored directive.

#line   Alters the current line number and/or file name. You may wish to use this directive if you extract definition source from other files. **getdefs** uses this mechanism so AutoGen will report the correct file and approximate line number of any errors found in extracted definitions.

#macdef   This is a new AT&T research preprocessing directive. Basically, it is a multi-line #define that may include other preprocessing directives. Text between this line and a #endmac directive are ignored.

#option   This directive will pass the option name and associated text to the AutoOpts optionLoadLine routine (see Section 7.6.32.8 [libopts-optionLoadLine], page 137). The option text may span multiple lines by continuing them with a backslash. The backslash/newline pair will be replaced with two space characters. This directive may be used to set a search path for locating template files For example, this:

           #option templ-dirs $ENVVAR/dirname

           will direct autogen to use the **ENVVAR** environment variable to find a directory named **dirname** that (may) contain templates. Since these directories are searched in most recently supplied first order, search directories supplied in this way will be searched before any supplied on the command line.

#pragma   Ignored directive.

#shell   Invokes $SHELL or /bin/sh on a script that should generate AutoGen definitions. It does this using the same server process that handles the back-quoted

      ‘ text. The block of text handed to the shell is terminated with the #endshell directive.

      CAUTION let not your $SHELL be `csh`.

`#undef`   Will remove any entries from the define list that match the undef name pattern.

2.6 Pre-defined Names

When AutoGen starts, it tries to determine several names from the operating environment and put them into environment variables for use in both #ifdef tests in the definitions files and in shell scripts with environment variable tests. `__autogen__` is always defined. For other names, AutoGen will first try to use the POSIX version of the `sysinfo(2)` system call. Failing that, it will try for the POSIX `uname(2)` call. If neither is available, then only `"__autogen__"` will be inserted into the environment. In all cases, the associated names are converted to lower case, surrounded by doubled underscores and non-symbol characters are replaced with underscores.

    With Solaris on a sparc platform, `sysinfo(2)` is available. The following strings are used:

- `SI_SYSNAME` (e.g., `"__sunos__"`)
- `SI_HOSTNAME` (e.g., `"__ellen__"`)
- `SI_ARCHITECTURE` (e.g., `"__sparc__"`)
- `SI_HW_PROVIDER` (e.g., `"__sun_microsystems__"`)
- `SI_PLATFORM` (e.g., `"__sun_ultra_5_10__"`)
- `SI_MACHINE` (e.g., `"__sun4u__"`)

For Linux and other operating systems that only support the `uname(2)` call, AutoGen will use these values:

- `sysname` (e.g., `"__linux__"`)
- `machine` (e.g., `"__i586__"`)
- `nodename` (e.g., `"__bach__"`)

By testing these pre-defines in my definitions, you can select pieces of the definitions without resorting to writing shell scripts that parse the output of `uname(1)`. You can also segregate real C code from autogen definitions by testing for `"__autogen__"`.

```
#ifdef __bach__
  location = home;
#else
  location = work;
#endif
```

2.7 Commenting Your Definitions

The definitions file may contain C and C++ style comments.

```
/*
 * This is a comment.  It continues for several lines and closes
 * when the characters '*' and '/' appear together.
 */
// this comment is a single line comment
```

2.8 What it all looks like.

This is an extended example:

```
autogen definitions 'template-name';
/*
 *  This is a comment that describes what these
 *  definitions are all about.
 */
global = "value for a global text definition.";


/*
 *  Include a standard set of definitions
 */
#include standards.def

a_block = {
    a_field;
    a_subblock = {
        sub_name  = first;
        sub_field = "sub value.";
    };

#ifdef FEATURE
    a_subblock = {
        sub_name  = second;
    };
#endif

};
```

2.9 Finite State Machine Grammar

The preprocessing directives and comments are not part of the grammar. They are handled by the scanner/lexer. The following was extracted directly from the generated defParse-fsm.c source file. The "EVT:" is the token seen, the "STATE:" is the current state and the entries in this table describe the next state and the action to take. Invalid transitions were removed from the table.

```
dp_trans_table[ DP_STATE_CT ][ DP_EVENT_CT ] = {

  /* STATE 0:  DP_ST_INIT */
  { { DP_ST_NEED_DEF, NULL },                    /* EVT:  AUTOGEN */
    { DP_ST_INVALID, dp_do_invalid },            /* EVT:  DEFINITIONS */
    { DP_ST_INVALID, dp_do_invalid },            /* EVT:  End-Of-File */
    { DP_ST_INVALID, dp_do_invalid },            /* EVT:  VAR_NAME */
    { DP_ST_INVALID, dp_do_invalid },            /* EVT:  OTHER_NAME */
    { DP_ST_INVALID, dp_do_invalid },            /* EVT:  STRING */
    { DP_ST_INVALID, dp_do_invalid },            /* EVT:  HERE_STRING */
```

```
    { DP_ST_INVALID, dp_do_invalid },          /* EVT:   DELETE_ENT */
    { DP_ST_INVALID, dp_do_invalid },          /* EVT:   NUMBER */
    { DP_ST_INVALID, dp_do_invalid },          /* EVT:   ; */
    { DP_ST_INVALID, dp_do_invalid },          /* EVT:   = */
    { DP_ST_INVALID, dp_do_invalid },          /* EVT:   , */
    { DP_ST_INVALID, dp_do_invalid },          /* EVT:   { */
    { DP_ST_INVALID, dp_do_invalid },          /* EVT:   } */
    { DP_ST_INVALID, dp_do_invalid },          /* EVT:   [ */
    { DP_ST_INVALID, dp_do_invalid }           /* EVT:   ] */

/* STATE 1:   DP_ST_NEED_DEF */
{ { DP_ST_INVALID, dp_do_invalid },            /* EVT:   AUTOGEN */
    { DP_ST_NEED_TPL, NULL },                  /* EVT:   DEFINITIONS */
    { DP_ST_INVALID, dp_do_invalid },          /* EVT:   End-Of-File */
    { DP_ST_INVALID, dp_do_invalid },          /* EVT:   VAR_NAME */
    { DP_ST_INVALID, dp_do_invalid },          /* EVT:   OTHER_NAME */
    { DP_ST_INVALID, dp_do_invalid },          /* EVT:   STRING */
    { DP_ST_INVALID, dp_do_invalid },          /* EVT:   HERE_STRING */
    { DP_ST_INVALID, dp_do_invalid },          /* EVT:   DELETE_ENT */
    { DP_ST_INVALID, dp_do_invalid },          /* EVT:   NUMBER */
    { DP_ST_INVALID, dp_do_invalid },          /* EVT:   ; */
    { DP_ST_INVALID, dp_do_invalid },          /* EVT:   = */
    { DP_ST_INVALID, dp_do_invalid },          /* EVT:   , */
    { DP_ST_INVALID, dp_do_invalid },          /* EVT:   { */
    { DP_ST_INVALID, dp_do_invalid },          /* EVT:   } */
    { DP_ST_INVALID, dp_do_invalid },          /* EVT:   [ */
    { DP_ST_INVALID, dp_do_invalid }           /* EVT:   ] */

/* STATE 2:   DP_ST_NEED_TPL */
{ { DP_ST_INVALID, dp_do_invalid },            /* EVT:   AUTOGEN */
    { DP_ST_INVALID, dp_do_invalid },          /* EVT:   DEFINITIONS */
    { DP_ST_INVALID, dp_do_invalid },          /* EVT:   End-Of-File */
    { DP_ST_NEED_SEMI, dp_do_tpl_name },       /* EVT:   VAR_NAME */
    { DP_ST_NEED_SEMI, dp_do_tpl_name },       /* EVT:   OTHER_NAME */
    { DP_ST_NEED_SEMI, dp_do_tpl_name },       /* EVT:   STRING */
    { DP_ST_INVALID, dp_do_invalid },          /* EVT:   HERE_STRING */
    { DP_ST_INVALID, dp_do_invalid },          /* EVT:   DELETE_ENT */
    { DP_ST_INVALID, dp_do_invalid },          /* EVT:   NUMBER */
    { DP_ST_INVALID, dp_do_invalid },          /* EVT:   ; */
    { DP_ST_INVALID, dp_do_invalid },          /* EVT:   = */
    { DP_ST_INVALID, dp_do_invalid },          /* EVT:   , */
    { DP_ST_INVALID, dp_do_invalid },          /* EVT:   { */
    { DP_ST_INVALID, dp_do_invalid },          /* EVT:   } */
    { DP_ST_INVALID, dp_do_invalid },          /* EVT:   [ */
    { DP_ST_INVALID, dp_do_invalid }           /* EVT:   ] */

/* STATE 3:   DP_ST_NEED_SEMI */
```

```
{ { DP_ST_INVALID, dp_do_invalid },                        /* EVT:  AUTOGEN */
  { DP_ST_INVALID, dp_do_invalid },                        /* EVT:  DEFINITIONS */
  { DP_ST_INVALID, dp_do_invalid },                        /* EVT:  End-Of-File */
  { DP_ST_INVALID, dp_do_invalid },                        /* EVT:  VAR_NAME */
  { DP_ST_INVALID, dp_do_invalid },                        /* EVT:  OTHER_NAME */
  { DP_ST_INVALID, dp_do_invalid },                        /* EVT:  STRING */
  { DP_ST_INVALID, dp_do_invalid },                        /* EVT:  HERE_STRING */
  { DP_ST_INVALID, dp_do_invalid },                        /* EVT:  DELETE_ENT */
  { DP_ST_INVALID, dp_do_invalid },                        /* EVT:  NUMBER */
  { DP_ST_NEED_NAME, NULL },                                /* EVT:  ; */
  { DP_ST_INVALID, dp_do_invalid },                        /* EVT:  = */
  { DP_ST_INVALID, dp_do_invalid },                        /* EVT:  , */
  { DP_ST_INVALID, dp_do_invalid },                        /* EVT:  { */
  { DP_ST_INVALID, dp_do_invalid },                        /* EVT:  } */
  { DP_ST_INVALID, dp_do_invalid },                        /* EVT:  [ */
  { DP_ST_INVALID, dp_do_invalid }                         /* EVT:  ] */

/* STATE 4:  DP_ST_NEED_NAME */
{ { DP_ST_NEED_DEF, NULL },                                /* EVT:  AUTOGEN */
  { DP_ST_INVALID, dp_do_invalid },                        /* EVT:  DEFINITIONS */
  { DP_ST_DONE, dp_do_need_name_end },                     /* EVT:  End-Of-File */
  { DP_ST_HAVE_NAME, dp_do_need_name_var_name },           /* EVT:  VAR_NAME */
  { DP_ST_INVALID, dp_do_invalid },                        /* EVT:  OTHER_NAME */
  { DP_ST_INVALID, dp_do_invalid },                        /* EVT:  STRING */
  { DP_ST_INVALID, dp_do_invalid },                        /* EVT:  HERE_STRING */
  { DP_ST_INVALID, dp_do_invalid },                        /* EVT:  DELETE_ENT */
  { DP_ST_INVALID, dp_do_invalid },                        /* EVT:  NUMBER */
  { DP_ST_INVALID, dp_do_invalid },                        /* EVT:  ; */
  { DP_ST_INVALID, dp_do_invalid },                        /* EVT:  = */
  { DP_ST_INVALID, dp_do_invalid },                        /* EVT:  , */
  { DP_ST_INVALID, dp_do_invalid },                        /* EVT:  { */
  { DP_ST_HAVE_VALUE, dp_do_end_block },                   /* EVT:  } */
  { DP_ST_INVALID, dp_do_invalid },                        /* EVT:  [ */
  { DP_ST_INVALID, dp_do_invalid }                         /* EVT:  ] */

/* STATE 5:  DP_ST_HAVE_NAME */
{ { DP_ST_INVALID, dp_do_invalid },                        /* EVT:  AUTOGEN */
  { DP_ST_INVALID, dp_do_invalid },                        /* EVT:  DEFINITIONS */
  { DP_ST_INVALID, dp_do_invalid },                        /* EVT:  End-Of-File */
  { DP_ST_INVALID, dp_do_invalid },                        /* EVT:  VAR_NAME */
  { DP_ST_INVALID, dp_do_invalid },                        /* EVT:  OTHER_NAME */
  { DP_ST_INVALID, dp_do_invalid },                        /* EVT:  STRING */
  { DP_ST_INVALID, dp_do_invalid },                        /* EVT:  HERE_STRING */
  { DP_ST_INVALID, dp_do_invalid },                        /* EVT:  DELETE_ENT */
  { DP_ST_INVALID, dp_do_invalid },                        /* EVT:  NUMBER */
  { DP_ST_NEED_NAME, dp_do_empty_val },                    /* EVT:  ; */
  { DP_ST_NEED_VALUE, dp_do_have_name_lit_eq },            /* EVT:  = */
```

```
    { DP_ST_INVALID, dp_do_invalid },              /* EVT:  , */
    { DP_ST_INVALID, dp_do_invalid },              /* EVT:  { */
    { DP_ST_INVALID, dp_do_invalid },              /* EVT:  } */
    { DP_ST_NEED_IDX, NULL },                       /* EVT:  [ */
    { DP_ST_INVALID, dp_do_invalid }               /* EVT:  ] */

/* STATE 6:  DP_ST_NEED_VALUE */
{ { DP_ST_INVALID, dp_do_invalid },                /* EVT:  AUTOGEN */
    { DP_ST_INVALID, dp_do_invalid },              /* EVT:  DEFINITIONS */
    { DP_ST_INVALID, dp_do_invalid },              /* EVT:  End-Of-File */
    { DP_ST_HAVE_VALUE, dp_do_str_value },         /* EVT:  VAR_NAME */
    { DP_ST_HAVE_VALUE, dp_do_str_value },         /* EVT:  OTHER_NAME */
    { DP_ST_HAVE_VALUE, dp_do_str_value },         /* EVT:  STRING */
    { DP_ST_HAVE_VALUE, dp_do_str_value },         /* EVT:  HERE_STRING */
    { DP_ST_NEED_NAME, dp_do_need_value_delete_ent }, /* EVT:  DELETE_ENT */
    { DP_ST_HAVE_VALUE, dp_do_str_value },         /* EVT:  NUMBER */
    { DP_ST_INVALID, dp_do_invalid },              /* EVT:  ; */
    { DP_ST_INVALID, dp_do_invalid },              /* EVT:  = */
    { DP_ST_INVALID, dp_do_invalid },              /* EVT:  , */
    { DP_ST_NEED_NAME, dp_do_start_block },        /* EVT:  { */
    { DP_ST_INVALID, dp_do_invalid },              /* EVT:  } */
    { DP_ST_INVALID, dp_do_invalid },              /* EVT:  [ */
    { DP_ST_INVALID, dp_do_invalid }               /* EVT:  ] */

/* STATE 7:  DP_ST_NEED_IDX */
{ { DP_ST_INVALID, dp_do_invalid },                /* EVT:  AUTOGEN */
    { DP_ST_INVALID, dp_do_invalid },              /* EVT:  DEFINITIONS */
    { DP_ST_INVALID, dp_do_invalid },              /* EVT:  End-Of-File */
    { DP_ST_NEED_CBKT, dp_do_indexed_name },       /* EVT:  VAR_NAME */
    { DP_ST_INVALID, dp_do_invalid },              /* EVT:  OTHER_NAME */
    { DP_ST_INVALID, dp_do_invalid },              /* EVT:  STRING */
    { DP_ST_INVALID, dp_do_invalid },              /* EVT:  HERE_STRING */
    { DP_ST_INVALID, dp_do_invalid },              /* EVT:  DELETE_ENT */
    { DP_ST_NEED_CBKT, dp_do_indexed_name },       /* EVT:  NUMBER */
    { DP_ST_INVALID, dp_do_invalid },              /* EVT:  ; */
    { DP_ST_INVALID, dp_do_invalid },              /* EVT:  = */
    { DP_ST_INVALID, dp_do_invalid },              /* EVT:  , */
    { DP_ST_INVALID, dp_do_invalid },              /* EVT:  { */
    { DP_ST_INVALID, dp_do_invalid },              /* EVT:  } */
    { DP_ST_INVALID, dp_do_invalid },              /* EVT:  [ */
    { DP_ST_INVALID, dp_do_invalid }               /* EVT:  ] */

/* STATE 8:  DP_ST_NEED_CBKT */
{ { DP_ST_INVALID, dp_do_invalid },                /* EVT:  AUTOGEN */
    { DP_ST_INVALID, dp_do_invalid },              /* EVT:  DEFINITIONS */
    { DP_ST_INVALID, dp_do_invalid },              /* EVT:  End-Of-File */
    { DP_ST_INVALID, dp_do_invalid },              /* EVT:  VAR_NAME */
```

```
        { DP_ST_INVALID, dp_do_invalid },        /* EVT:  OTHER_NAME */
        { DP_ST_INVALID, dp_do_invalid },        /* EVT:  STRING */
        { DP_ST_INVALID, dp_do_invalid },        /* EVT:  HERE_STRING */
        { DP_ST_INVALID, dp_do_invalid },        /* EVT:  DELETE_ENT */
        { DP_ST_INVALID, dp_do_invalid },        /* EVT:  NUMBER */
        { DP_ST_INVALID, dp_do_invalid },        /* EVT:  ; */
        { DP_ST_INVALID, dp_do_invalid },        /* EVT:  = */
        { DP_ST_INVALID, dp_do_invalid },        /* EVT:  , */
        { DP_ST_INVALID, dp_do_invalid },        /* EVT:  { */
        { DP_ST_INVALID, dp_do_invalid },        /* EVT:  } */
        { DP_ST_INVALID, dp_do_invalid },        /* EVT:  [ */
        { DP_ST_INDX_NAME, NULL }                 /* EVT:  ] */

/* STATE 9:  DP_ST_INDX_NAME */
{ { DP_ST_INVALID, dp_do_invalid },              /* EVT:  AUTOGEN */
  { DP_ST_INVALID, dp_do_invalid },              /* EVT:  DEFINITIONS */
  { DP_ST_INVALID, dp_do_invalid },              /* EVT:  End-Of-File */
  { DP_ST_INVALID, dp_do_invalid },              /* EVT:  VAR_NAME */
  { DP_ST_INVALID, dp_do_invalid },              /* EVT:  OTHER_NAME */
  { DP_ST_INVALID, dp_do_invalid },              /* EVT:  STRING */
  { DP_ST_INVALID, dp_do_invalid },              /* EVT:  HERE_STRING */
  { DP_ST_INVALID, dp_do_invalid },              /* EVT:  DELETE_ENT */
  { DP_ST_INVALID, dp_do_invalid },              /* EVT:  NUMBER */
  { DP_ST_NEED_NAME, dp_do_empty_val },          /* EVT:  ; */
  { DP_ST_NEED_VALUE, NULL },                    /* EVT:  = */
  { DP_ST_INVALID, dp_do_invalid },              /* EVT:  , */
  { DP_ST_INVALID, dp_do_invalid },              /* EVT:  { */
  { DP_ST_INVALID, dp_do_invalid },              /* EVT:  } */
  { DP_ST_INVALID, dp_do_invalid },              /* EVT:  [ */
  { DP_ST_INVALID, dp_do_invalid }               /* EVT:  ] */

/* STATE 10:  DP_ST_HAVE_VALUE */
{ { DP_ST_INVALID, dp_do_invalid },              /* EVT:  AUTOGEN */
  { DP_ST_INVALID, dp_do_invalid },              /* EVT:  DEFINITIONS */
  { DP_ST_INVALID, dp_do_invalid },              /* EVT:  End-Of-File */
  { DP_ST_INVALID, dp_do_invalid },              /* EVT:  VAR_NAME */
  { DP_ST_INVALID, dp_do_invalid },              /* EVT:  OTHER_NAME */
  { DP_ST_INVALID, dp_do_invalid },              /* EVT:  STRING */
  { DP_ST_INVALID, dp_do_invalid },              /* EVT:  HERE_STRING */
  { DP_ST_INVALID, dp_do_invalid },              /* EVT:  DELETE_ENT */
  { DP_ST_INVALID, dp_do_invalid },              /* EVT:  NUMBER */
  { DP_ST_NEED_NAME, NULL },                     /* EVT:  ; */
  { DP_ST_INVALID, dp_do_invalid },              /* EVT:  = */
  { DP_ST_NEED_VALUE, dp_do_next_val },          /* EVT:  , */
  { DP_ST_INVALID, dp_do_invalid },              /* EVT:  { */
  { DP_ST_INVALID, dp_do_invalid },              /* EVT:  } */
  { DP_ST_INVALID, dp_do_invalid },              /* EVT:  [ */
```

```
        { DP_ST_INVALID, dp_do_invalid }                /* EVT:  ] */
```

2.10 Alternate Definition Forms

There are several methods for supplying data values for templates.

'no definitions'

> It is entirely possible to write a template that does not depend upon external definitions. Such a template would likely have an unvarying output, but be convenient nonetheless because of an external library of either AutoGen or Scheme functions, or both. This can be accommodated by providing the --override-tpl and --no-definitions options on the command line. See Chapter 5 [autogen Invocation], page 67.

'CGI'

> AutoGen behaves as a CGI server if the definitions input is from stdin and the environment variable REQUEST_METHOD is defined and set to either "GET" or "POST", See Section 6.2 [AutoGen CGI], page 81. Obviously, all the values are constrained to strings because there is no way to represent nested values.

'XML'

> AutoGen comes with a program named, xml2ag. Its output can either be redirected to a file for later use, or the program can be used as an AutoGen wrapper. See Section 8.7 [xml2ag Invocation], page 207.
>
> The introductory template example (see Section 1.2 [Example Usage], page 3) can be rewritten in XML as follows:
>
> ```
> <EXAMPLE  template="list.tpl">
> <LIST list_element="alpha"
>       list_info="some alpha stuff"/>
> <LIST list_info="more beta stuff"
>       list_element="beta"/>
> <LIST list_element="omega"
>       list_info="final omega stuff"/>
> </EXAMPLE>
> ```
>
> A more XML-normal form might look like this:
>
> ```
> <EXAMPLE  template="list.tpl">
> <LIST list_element="alpha">some alpha stuff</LIST>
> <LIST list_element="beta" >more beta stuff</LIST>
> <LIST list_element="omega">final omega stuff</LIST>
> </EXAMPLE>
> ```
>
> but you would have to change the template list-info references into text references.

'standard AutoGen definitions'

> Of course. :-)

3 Template File

The AutoGen template file defines the content of the output text. It is composed of two parts. The first part consists of a pseudo macro invocation and commentary. It is followed by the template proper.

This pseudo macro is special. It is used to identify the file as a AutoGen template file, fixing the starting and ending marks for the macro invocations in the rest of the file, specifying the list of suffixes to be generated by the template and, optionally, the shell to use for processing shell commands embedded in the template.

AutoGen-ing a file consists of copying text from the template to the output file until a start macro marker is found. The text from the start marker to the end marker constitutes the macro text. AutoGen macros may cause sections of the template to be skipped or processed several times. The process continues until the end of the template is reached. The process is repeated once for each suffix specified in the pseudo macro.

This chapter describes the format of the AutoGen template macros and the usage of the AutoGen native macros. Users may augment these by defining their own macros, See Section 3.6.7 [DEFINE], page 58.

3.1 Format of the Pseudo Macro

The pseudo macro is used to tell AutoGen how to process a template. It tells autogen:

1. The start macro marker. It consists of punctuation characters used to demarcate the start of a macro. It may be up to seven characters long and must be the first non-whitespace characters in the file.

   It is generally a good idea to use some sort of opening bracket in the starting macro and closing bracket in the ending macro (e.g. {, (, [, or even < in the starting macro). It helps both visually and with editors capable of finding a balancing parenthesis.

2. That start marker must be immediately followed by the identifier strings "AutoGen5" and then "template", though capitalization is not important.

The next several components may be intermingled:

3. Zero, one or more suffix specifications tell AutoGen how many times to process the template file. No suffix specifications mean that it is to be processed once and that the generated text is to be written to stdout. The current suffix for each pass can be determined with the (suffix) scheme function (see Section 3.4.53 [SCM suffix], page 36).

   The suffix specification consists of a sequence of POSIX compliant file name characters and, optionally, an equal sign and a file name formatting specification. That specification may be either an ordinary sequence of file name characters with zero, one or two "%s" formatting sequences in it, or else it may be a Scheme expression that, when evaluated, produces such a string. The Scheme result may not be empty. The two string arguments allowed for that string are the base name of the definition file, and the current suffix (that being the text to the left of the equal sign). (Note: 'POSIX compliant file name characters" consist of alphanumerics plus the period (.), hyphen (-) and underscore (_) characters.)

If the suffix begins with one of these three latter characters and a formatting string is not specified, then that character is presumed to be the suffix separator. Otherwise, without a specified format string, a single period will separate the suffix from the base name in constructing the output file name.

4. Shell specification: to specify that the template was written expecting a particular shell to run the shell commands. By default, the shell used is the autoconf-ed `CONFIG_SHELL`. This will usually be `/bin/sh`. The shell is specified by a hash mark (#) followed by an exclamation mark (!) followed by a full-path file name (e.g. `/usr/xpg4/bin/sh` on Solaris):

```
[= Autogen5 Template c
#!/usr/xpg4/bin/sh
=]
```

5. Comments: blank lines, lines starting with a hash mark (#) and not specifying a shell, and edit mode markers (text between pairs of -*- strings) are all treated as comments.

6. Some scheme expressions may be inserted in order to make configuration changes before template processing begins. *before template processing begins* means that there is no current output file, no current suffix and, basically, none of the AutoGen specific functions (see Section 3.4 [AutoGen Functions], page 26) may be invoked.

The scheme expression can also be used, for example, to save a pre-existing output file for later text extraction (see Section 3.5.5 [SCM extract], page 39).

```
(shellf "mv -f %1$s.c %1$s.sav" (base-name))
```

After these must come the end macro marker:

6. The punctuation characters used to demarcate the end of a macro. Like the start marker, it must consist of seven or fewer punctuation characters.

The ending macro marker has a few constraints on its content. Some of them are just advisory, though. There is no special check for advisory restrictions.

- It must not begin with a POSIX file name character (hyphen -, underscore _ or period .), the backslash (\) or open parenthesis ((). These are used to identify a suffix specification, indicate Scheme code and trim white space.

- If it begins with an equal sign, then it must be separated from any suffix specification by white space.

- The closing marker may not begin with an open parenthesis, as that is used to enclose a scheme expression.

- It cannot begin with a backslash, as that is used to indicate white space trimming after the end macro mark. If, in the body of the template, you put the backslash character (\) before the end macro mark, then any white space characters after the mark and through the newline character are trimmed.

- It is also helpful to avoid using the comment marker (#). It might be seen as a comment within the pseudo macro.

- You should avoid using any of the quote characters double, single or back-quote. It won't confuse AutoGen, but it might well confuse you and/or your editor.

As an example, assume we want to use [+ and +] as the start and end macro markers, and we wish to produce a .c and a .h file, then the pseudo macro might look something like this:

```
[+ AutoGen5 template -*- Mode: emacs-mode-of-choice -*-
h=chk-%s.h
c
# make sure we don't use csh:
(setenv "SHELL" "/bin/sh")   +]
```

The template proper starts after the pseudo-macro. The starting character is either the first non-whitespace character or the first character after the newline that follows the end macro marker.

3.2 Naming a value

When an AutoGen value is specified in a template, it is specified by name. The name may be a simple name, or a compound name of several components. Since each named value in AutoGen is implicitly an array of one or more values, each component may have an index associated with it.

It looks like this:

```
comp-name-1 . comp-name-2 [ 2 ]
```

Note that if there are multiple components to a name, each component name is separated by a dot (.). Indexes follow a component name, enclosed in square brackets ([and]) The index may be either an integer or an integer-valued define name. The first component of the name is searched for in the current definition level. If not found, higher levels will be searched until either a value is found, or there are no more definition levels. Subsequent components of the name must be found within the context of the newly-current definition level. Also, if the named value is prefixed by a dot (.), then the value search is started in the current context only. Backtracking into other definition levels is prevented.

If someone rewrites this, I'll incorporate it. :-)

3.3 Macro Expression Syntax

AutoGen has two types of expressions: full expressions and basic ones. A full AutoGen expression can appear by itself, or as the argument to certain AutoGen built-in macros: CASE, IF, ELIF, INCLUDE, INVOKE (explicit invocation, see Section 3.6.19 [INVOKE], page 62), and WHILE. If it appears by itself, the result is inserted into the output. If it is an argument to one of these macros, the macro code will act on it sensibly.

You are constrained to basic expressions only when passing arguments to user defined macros, See Section 3.6.7 [DEFINE], page 58.

The syntax of a full AutoGen expression is:

```
[[ <apply-code> ] <value-name> ] [ <basic-expr-1> [ <basic-expr-2> ]]
```

How the expression is evaluated depends upon the presence or absence of the apply code and value name. The "value name" is the name of an AutoGen defined value, or not. If it does not name such a value, the expression result is generally the empty string. All expressions must contain either a *value-name* or a *basic-expr*.

3.3.1 Apply Code

The "apply code" selected determines the method of evaluating the expression. There are five apply codes, including the non-use of an apply code.

`'no apply code'`

> This is the most common expression type. Expressions of this sort come in three flavors:
>
> > `'<value-name>'`
> >
> > > The result is the value of *value-name*, if defined. Otherwise it is the empty string.
> >
> > `'<basic-expr>'`
> >
> > > The result of the basic expression is the result of the full expression, See Section 3.3.2 [basic expression], page 24.
> >
> > `'<value-name> <basic-expr>'`
> >
> > > If there is a defined value for *value-name*, then the *basic-expr* is evaluated. Otherwise, the result is the empty string.

`'% <value-name> <basic-expr>'`

> If *value-name* is defined, use *basic-expr* as a format string for sprintf. Then, if the *basic-expr* is either a back-quoted string or a parenthesized expression, then hand the result to the appropriate interpreter for further evaluation. Otherwise, for single and double quote strings, the result is the result of the sprintf operation. Naturally, if *value-name* is not defined, the result is the empty string.
>
> For example, assume that 'fumble' had the string value, 'stumble':
>
> > `[+ % fumble 'printf '%%x\\n' $%s' +]`
>
> This would cause the shell to evaluate `"printf '%x\n' $stumble'"`. Assuming that the shell variable 'stumble' had a numeric value, the expression result would be that number, in hex. Note the need for doubled percent characters and backslashes.

`'? <value-name> <basic-expr-1> <basic-expr-2>'`

> Two *basic-expr*-s are required. If the *value-name* is defined, then the first *basic-expr-1* is evaluated, otherwise *basic-expr-2* is.

`'- <value-name> <basic-expr>'`

> Evaluate *basic-expr* only if *value-name* is *not* defined.

`'?% <value-name> <basic-expr-1> <basic-expr-2>'`

> This combines the functions of '?' and '%'. If *value-name* is defined, it behaves exactly like '%', above, using *basic-expr-1*. If not defined, then *basic-expr-2* is evaluated.
>
> For example, assume again that 'fumble' had the string value, 'stumble':
>
> > `[+ ?% fumble 'cat $%s' 'pwd' +]`
>
> This would cause the shell to evaluate `"'cat $stumble'"`. If 'fumble' were not defined, then the result would be the name of our current directory.

3.3.2 Basic Expression

A basic expression can have one of the following forms:

`''STRING''`

> A single quoted string. Backslashes can be used to protect single quotes ('), hash characters (#), or backslashes (\) in the string. All other characters of

STRING are output as-is when the single quoted string is evaluated. Backslashes are processed before the hash character for consistency with the definition syntax. It is needed there to avoid preprocessing conflicts.

'"STRING"'

A double quoted string. This is a cooked text string as in C, except that they are not concatenated with adjacent strings. Evaluating "'STRING'" will output STRING with all backslash sequences interpreted.

''STRING''

A back quoted string. When this expression is evaluated, STRING is first interpreted as a cooked string (as in '"STRING"') and evaluated as a shell expression by the AutoGen server shell. This expression is replaced by the **stdout** output of the shell.

'(STRING)'

A parenthesized expression. It will be passed to the Guile interpreter for evaluation and replaced by the resulting value. If there is a Scheme error in this expression, Guile 1.4 and Guile 1.6 will report the template line number where the error occurs. Guile 1.7 has lost this capability.

Guile has the capability of creating and manipulating variables that can be referenced later on in the template processing. If you define such a variable, it is invisible to AutoGen. To reference its value, you must use a Guile expression. For example,

        [+ (define my-var "some-string-value") +]

can have that string inserted later, but only as in:

        [+ (. my-var) +]

Additionally, other than in the % and ?% expressions, the Guile expressions may be introduced with the Guile comment character (;) and you may put a series of Guile expressions within a single macro. They will be implicitly evaluated as if they were arguments to the (**begin** ...) expression. The result will be the result of the last Guile expression evaluated.

3.4 AutoGen Scheme Functions

AutoGen uses Guile to interpret Scheme expressions within AutoGen macros. All of the normal Guile functions are available, plus several extensions (see Section 3.5 [Common Functions], page 38) have been added to augment the repertoire of string manipulation functions and manage the state of AutoGen processing.

This section describes those functions that are specific to AutoGen. Please take note that these AutoGen specific functions are not loaded and thus not made available until after the command line options have been processed and the AutoGen definitions have been loaded. They may, of course, be used in Scheme functions that get defined at those times, but they cannot be invoked.

3.4.1 `ag-fprintf` - format to autogen stream

Usage: (ag-fprintf ag-diversion format [format-arg ...])
Format a string using arguments from the alist. Write to a specified AutoGen diversion. That may be either a specified suspended output stream (see Section 3.4.46 [SCM out-suspend], page 35) or an index into the output stack (see Section 3.4.44 [SCM out-push-new], page 35). (`ag-fprintf 0 ...`) is equivalent to (`emit (sprintf ...)`), and (`ag-fprintf 1 ...`) sends output to the most recently suspended output stream.

Arguments:
ag-diversion - AutoGen diversion name or number
format - formatting string
format-arg - Optional - list of arguments to formatting string

3.4.2 `ag-function?` - test for function

Usage: (ag-function? ag-name)
return SCM_BOOL_T if a specified name is a user-defined AutoGen macro, otherwise return SCM_BOOL_F.

Arguments:
ag-name - name of AutoGen macro

3.4.3 `base-name` - base output name

Usage: (base-name)
Returns a string containing the base name of the output file(s). Generally, this is also the base name of the definitions file.

This Scheme function takes no arguments.

3.4.4 `chdir` - Change current directory

Usage: (chdir dir)
Sets the current directory for AutoGen. Shell commands will run from this directory as well. This is a wrapper around the Guile native function. It returns its directory name argument and fails the program on failure.

Arguments:
dir - new directory name

3.4.5 `count` - definition count

Usage: (count ag-name)
Count the number of entries for a definition. The input argument must be a string containing the name of the AutoGen values to be counted. If there is no value associated with the name, the result is an SCM immediate integer value of zero.

Arguments:
ag-name - name of AutoGen value

3.4.6 `def-file` - definitions file name

Usage: (def-file)
Get the name of the definitions file. Returns the name of the source file containing the AutoGen definitions.

This Scheme function takes no arguments.

3.4.7 `def-file-line` - get a definition file+line number

Usage: (def-file-line ag-name [msg-fmt])
Returns the file and line number of a AutoGen defined value, using either the default format, "from %s line %d", or else the format you supply. For example, if you want to insert a "C" language file-line directive, you would supply the format "# %2$d \"%1$s\"", but that is also already supplied with the scheme variable See Section 3.4.59 [SCM c-file-line-fmt], page 37. You may use it thus:

```
(def-file-line "ag-def-name" c-file-line-fmt)
```

It is also safe to use the formatting string, "%2$d". AutoGen uses an argument vector version of printf: See Section 8.8 [snprintfv], page 213.

Arguments:
ag-name - name of AutoGen value
msg-fmt - Optional - formatting for line message

3.4.8 `dne` - "Do Not Edit" warning

Usage: (dne prefix [first_prefix] [optpfx])
Generate a "DO NOT EDIT" or "EDIT WITH CARE" warning string. Which depends on whether or not the `--writable` command line option was set.

The first argument may be an option: '-D' or '-d', causing the second and (potentially) third arguments to be interpreted as the first and second arguments. The only useful option is '-D':

'-D'   will add date, timestamp and version information.

'-d'   is ignored, but still accepted for compatibility with older versions of the "dne" function where emitting the date was the default.

If one of these options is specified, then the "prefix" and "first" arguments are obtained from the following arguments. The presence (or absence) of this option can be overridden with the environment variable, 'AUTOGEN_DNE_DATE'. The date is disabled if the value is empty or starts with one of the characters, 'OnNfF' – zero or the first letter of "no" or "false".

The **prefix** argument is a per-line string prefix. The optional second argument is a prefix for the first line only and, in read-only mode, activates editor hints.

```
-*- buffer-read-only: t -*- vi: set ro:
```

The warning string also includes information about the template used to construct the file and the definitions used in its instantiation.

Arguments:
prefix - string for starting each output line
first_prefix - Optional - for the first output line
optpfx - Optional - shifted prefix

3.4.9 `emit` - emit the text for each argument

Usage: (emit alist ...)
Walk the tree of arguments, displaying the values of displayable SCM types. EXCEPTION: if the first argument is a number, then that number is used to index the output stack. "0" is the default, the current output.

Arguments:
alist - list of arguments to stringify and emit

3.4.10 `emit-string-table` - output a string table

Usage: (emit-string-table st-name)
Emit into the current output stream a **static char const** array named **st-name** that will have **NUL** bytes between each inserted string.

Arguments:
st-name - the name of the array of characters

3.4.11 `error` - display message and exit

Usage: (error message)
The argument is a string that printed out as part of an error message. The message is formed from the formatting string:

```
DEFINITIONS ERROR in %s line %d for %s:  %s\n
```

The first three arguments to this format are provided by the routine and are: The name of the template file, the line within the template where the error was found, and the current output file name.

After displaying the message, the current output file is removed and autogen exits with the EXIT_FAILURE error code. IF, however, the argument begins with the number 0 (zero), or the string is the empty string, then processing continues with the next suffix.

Arguments:
message - message to display before exiting

3.4.12 `exist?` - test for value name

Usage: (exist? ag-name)
return SCM_BOOL_T iff a specified name has an AutoGen value. The name may include indexes and/or member names. All but the last member name must be an aggregate definition. For example:

```
(exist? "foo[3].bar.baz")
```
will yield true if all of the following is true:
There is a member value of either group or string type named `baz` for some group value `bar` that is a member of the `foo` group with index 3. There may be multiple entries of `bar` within `foo`, only one needs to contain a value for `baz`.

Arguments:
ag-name - name of AutoGen value

3.4.13 `find-file` - locate a file in the search path

Usage: (find-file file-name [suffix])
AutoGen has a search path that it uses to locate template and definition files. This function will search the same list for `file-name`, both with and without the `.suffix`, if provided.

Arguments:
file-name - name of file with text
suffix - Optional - file suffix to try, too

3.4.14 `first-for?` - detect first iteration

Usage: (first-for? [for_var])
Returns `SCM_BOOL_T` if the named FOR loop (or, if not named, the current innermost loop) is on the first pass through the data. Outside of any FOR loop, it returns `SCM_UNDEFINED`, see Section 3.6.16 [FOR], page 60.

Arguments:
for_var - Optional - which for loop

3.4.15 `for-by` - set iteration step

Usage: (for-by by)
This function records the "step by" information for an AutoGen FOR function. Outside of the FOR macro itself, this function will emit an error. See Section 3.6.16 [FOR], page 60.

Arguments:
by - the iteration increment for the AutoGen FOR macro

3.4.16 `for-from` - set initial index

Usage: (for-from from)
This function records the initial index information for an AutoGen FOR function. Outside of the FOR macro itself, this function will emit an error. See Section 3.6.16 [FOR], page 60.

Arguments:
from - the initial index for the AutoGen FOR macro

3.4.17 `for-index` - get current loop index

Usage: (for-index [for_var])
Returns the current index for the named FOR loop. If not named, then the index for the innermost loop. Outside of any FOR loop, it returns `SCM_UNDEFINED`, See Section 3.6.16 [FOR], page 60.

Arguments:
for_var - Optional - which for loop

3.4.18 `for-sep` - set loop separation string

Usage: (for-sep separator)
This function records the separation string that is to be inserted between each iteration of an AutoGen FOR function. This is often nothing more than a comma. Outside of the FOR macro itself, this function will emit an error.

   Arguments:
separator - the text to insert between the output of each FOR iteration

3.4.19 `for-to` - set ending index

Usage: (for-to to)
This function records the terminating value information for an AutoGen FOR function. Outside of the FOR macro itself, this function will emit an error. See Section 3.6.16 [FOR], page 60.

   Arguments:
to - the final index for the AutoGen FOR macro

3.4.20 `found-for?` - is current index in list?

Usage: (found-for? [for_var])
Returns SCM_BOOL_T if the currently indexed value is present, otherwise SCM_BOOL_F. Outside of any FOR loop, it returns SCM_UNDEFINED. See Section 3.6.16 [FOR], page 60.

   Arguments:
for_var - Optional - which for loop

3.4.21 `get` - get named value

Usage: (get ag-name [alt-val])
Get the first string value associated with the name. It will either return the associated string value (if the name resolves), the alternate value (if one is provided), or else the empty string.

   Arguments:
ag-name - name of AutoGen value
alt-val - Optional - value if not present

3.4.22 `get-c-name` - get named value, mapped to C name syntax

Usage: (get-c-name ag-name)
Get the first string value associated with the name. It will either return the associated string value (if the name resolves), the alternate value (if one is provided), or else the empty string. The result is passed through "string->c-name!".

   Arguments:
ag-name - name of AutoGen value

3.4.23 `get-down-name` - get lower cased named value, mapped to C name syntax

Usage: (get-down-name ag-name)
Get the first string value associated with the name. It will either return the associated string value (if the name resolves), the alternate value (if one is provided), or else the empty string. The result is passed through "string->c-name!" and "string->down-case!".

Arguments:
ag-name - name of AutoGen value

3.4.24 `get-up-name` - get upper cased named value, mapped to C name syntax

Usage: (get-up-name ag-name)
Get the first string value associated with the name. It will either return the associated string value (if the name resolves), the alternate value (if one is provided), or else the empty string. The result is passed through "string->c-name!" and "string->up-case!".

Arguments:
ag-name - name of AutoGen value

3.4.25 `high-lim` - get highest value index

Usage: (high-lim ag-name)
Returns the highest index associated with an array of definitions. This is generally, but not necessarily, one less than the `count` value. (The indexes may be specified, rendering a non-zero based or sparse array of values.)

This is very useful for specifying the size of a zero-based array of values where not all values are present. For example:

```
tMyStruct myVals[ [+ (+ 1 (high-lim "my-val-list")) +] ];
```

Arguments:
ag-name - name of AutoGen value

3.4.26 `insert-file` - insert the contents of a (list of) files.

Usage: (insert-file alist ...)
Insert the contents of one or more files.

Arguments:
alist - list of files to emit

3.4.27 `insert-suspended` - insert a named suspension in current output

Usage: (insert-suspended susp-name)
Emit into the current output the output suspended under a given diversion name.

Arguments:
susp-name - the name of the suspended output

3.4.28 `last-for?` - detect last iteration

Usage (last-for? [for_var])
Returns SCM_BOOL_T if the named FOR loop (or, if not named, the current innermost loop) is on the last pass through the data. Outside of any FOR loop, it returns SCM_UNDEFINED. See Section 3.6.16 [FOR], page 60.

Arguments:
for_var - Optional - which for loop

3.4.29 `len` - get count of values

Usage: (len ag-name)
If the named object is a group definition, then "len" is the same as "count". Otherwise, if it is one or more text definitions, then it is the sum of their string lengths. If it is a single text definition, then it is equivalent to (`string-length` (get "ag-name")).

Arguments:
ag-name - name of AutoGen value

3.4.30 `low-lim` - get lowest value index

Usage: (low-lim ag-name)
Returns the lowest index associated with an array of definitions.

Arguments:
ag-name - name of AutoGen value

3.4.31 `make-header-guard` - make self-inclusion guard

Usage: (make-header-guard name)
This function will create a `#ifndef`/`#define` sequence for protecting a header from multiple evaluation. It will also set the Scheme variable `header-file` to the name of the file being protected and it will set `header-guard` to the name of the `#define` being used to protect it. It is expected that this will be used as follows:

```
[+ (make-header-guard "group_name") +]
...
#endif /* [+ (. header-guard) +] */

#include "[+ (. header-file)  +]"
```

The `#define` name is composed as follows:

1. The first element is the string argument and a separating underscore.
2. That is followed by the name of the header file with illegal characters mapped to underscores.
3. The end of the name is always, "`_GUARD`".
4. Finally, the entire string is mapped to upper case.

The final `#define` name is stored in an SCM symbol named `header-guard`. Consequently, the concluding `#endif` for the file should read something like:

```
#endif /* [+ (. header-guard) +] */
```

The name of the header file (the current output file) is also stored in an SCM symbol, `header-file`. Therefore, if you are also generating a C file that uses the previously generated header file, you can put this into that generated file:

```
#include "[+ (. header-file) +]"
```

Obviously, if you are going to produce more than one header file from a particular template, you will need to be careful how these SCM symbols get handled.

Arguments:
name - header group name

3.4.32 `make-tmp-dir` - create a temporary directory

Usage: (make-tmp-dir)
Create a directory that will be cleaned up upon exit.

This Scheme function takes no arguments.

3.4.33 `match-value?` - test for matching value

Usage: (match-value? op ag-name test-str)
This function answers the question, "Is there an AutoGen value named **ag-name** with a value that matches the pattern **test-str** using the match function **op**?" Return SCM_BOOL_T iff at least one occurrence of the specified name has such a value. The operator can be any function that takes two string arguments and yields a boolean. It is expected that you will use one of the string matching functions provided by AutoGen.
The value name must follow the same rules as the **ag-name** argument for **exist?** (see Section 3.4.12 [SCM exist?], page 28).

Arguments:
op - boolean result operator
ag-name - name of AutoGen value
test-str - string to test against

3.4.34 `max-file-time` - get the maximum input file modification time

Usage: (max-file-time)
returns the time stamp of the most recently modified sourc file as the number of seconds since the epoch. If any input is dynamic (a shell command), then it will be the current time.

This Scheme function takes no arguments.

3.4.35 `mk-gettextable` - print a string in a gettext-able format

Usage: (mk-gettextable string)
Returns SCM_UNDEFINED. The input text string is printed to the current output as one puts() call per paragraph.

Arguments:
string - a multi-paragraph string

3.4.36 `out-delete` - delete current output file

Usage: (out-delete)
Remove the current output file. Cease processing the template for the current suffix. It is an error if there are **push**-ed output files. Use the (**error "0"**) scheme function instead. See Section 3.7 [output controls], page 63.

This Scheme function takes no arguments.

3.4.37 `out-depth` - output file stack depth

Usage: (out-depth)
Returns the depth of the output file stack. See Section 3.7 [output controls], page 63.

This Scheme function takes no arguments.

3.4.38 `out-emit-suspended` - emit the text of suspended output

Usage: (out-emit-suspended susp_nm)
This function is equivalent to (`begin` (`out-resume` <name>) (`out-pop` #t))

   Arguments:
susp_nm - A name tag of suspended output

3.4.39 `out-line` - output file line number

Usage: (out-line)
Returns the current line number of the output file. It rewinds and reads the file to count newlines.

   This Scheme function takes no arguments.

3.4.40 `out-move` - change name of output file

Usage: (out-move new-name)
Rename current output file. See Section 3.7 [output controls], page 63. Please note: changing the name will not save a temporary file from being deleted. It *may*, however, be used on the root output file.

   Arguments:
new-name - new name for the current output file

3.4.41 `out-name` - current output file name

Usage: (out-name)
Returns the name of the current output file. If the current file is a temporary, unnamed file, then it will scan up the chain until a real output file name is found. See Section 3.7 [output controls], page 63.

   This Scheme function takes no arguments.

3.4.42 `out-pop` - close current output file

Usage: (out-pop [disp])
If there has been a **push** on the output, then close that file and go back to the previously open file. It is an error if there has not been a **push**. See Section 3.7 [output controls], page 63.

   If there is no argument, no further action is taken. Otherwise, the argument should be #t and the contents of the file are returned by the function.

   Arguments:
disp - Optional - return contents of the file

3.4.43 `out-push-add` - append output to file

Usage: (out-push-add file-name)
Identical to **push-new**, except the contents are **not** purged, but appended to. See Section 3.7 [output controls], page 63.

   Arguments:
file-name - name of the file to append text to

3.4.44 out-push-new - purge and create output file

Usage: (out-push-new [file-name])
Leave the current output file open, but purge and create a new file that will remain open until a **pop delete** or **switch** closes it. The file name is optional and, if omitted, the output will be sent to a temporary file that will be deleted when it is closed. See Section 3.7 [output controls], page 63.

Arguments:
file-name - Optional - name of the file to create

3.4.45 out-resume - resume suspended output file

Usage: (out-resume susp_nm)
If there has been a suspended output, then make that output descriptor current again. That output must have been suspended with the same tag name given to this routine as its argument.

Arguments:
susp_nm - A name tag for reactivating

3.4.46 out-suspend - suspend current output file

Usage: (out-suspend suspName)
If there has been a **push** on the output, then set aside the output descriptor for later reactiviation with (**out-resume "xxx"**). The tag name need not reflect the name of the output file. In fact, the output file may be an anonymous temporary file. You may also change the tag every time you suspend output to a file, because the tag names are forgotten as soon as the file has been "resumed".

Arguments:
suspName - A name tag for reactivating

3.4.47 out-switch - close and create new output

Usage: (out-switch file-name)
Switch output files - close current file and make the current file pointer refer to the new file. This is equivalent to **out-pop** followed by **out-push-new**, except that you may not pop the base level output file, but you may **switch** it. See Section 3.7 [output controls], page 63.

Arguments:
file-name - name of the file to create

3.4.48 output-file-next-line - print the file name and next line number

Usage: (output-file-next-line [line_off] [alt_fmt])
Returns a string with the current output file name and line number. The default format is: # <line+1> "<output-file-name>' The argument may be either a number indicating an offset from the current output line number or an alternate formatting string. If both are provided, then the first must be a numeric offset.

Be careful that you are directing output to the final output file. Otherwise, you will get the file name and line number of the temporary file. That won't be what you want.

Arguments:

line_off - Optional - offset to line number

alt_fmt - Optional - alternate format string

3.4.49 `set-option` - Set a command line option

Usage: (set-option opt)

The text argument must be an option name followed by any needed option argument. Returns SCM_UNDEFINED.

Arguments:

opt - AutoGen option name + its argument

3.4.50 `set-writable` - Make the output file be writable

Usage: (set-writable [set?])

This function will set the current output file to be writable (or not). This is only effective if neither the `--writable` nor `--not-writable` have been specified. This state is reset when the current suffix's output is complete.

Arguments:

set? - Optional - boolean arg, false to make output non-writable

3.4.51 `stack` - make list of AutoGen values

Usage: (stack ag-name)

Create a scheme list of all the strings that are associated with a name. They must all be text values or we choke.

Arguments:

ag-name - AutoGen value name

3.4.52 `stack-join` - stack values then join them

Usage: (stack-join join ag-name)

This function will collect all the values named `ag-name` (see the see Section 3.4.51 [SCM stack], page 36) and join them separated by the `join` string (see the see Section 3.5.14 [SCM join], page 42).

Arguments:

join - string between each element

ag-name - name of autogen values to stack

3.4.53 `suffix` - get the current suffix

Usage: (suffix)

Returns the current active suffix (see Section 3.1 [pseudo macro], page 21).

This Scheme function takes no arguments.

3.4.54 `tpl-file` - get the template file name

Usage: (tpl-file [full_path])

Returns the name of the current template file. If `#t` is passed in as an argument, then the template file is hunted for in the template search path. Otherwise, just the unadorned name.

Arguments:
full_path - Optional - include full path to file

3.4.55 `tpl-file-line` - get the template file+line number

Usage: (tpl-file-line [msg-fmt])
Returns the file and line number of the current template macro using either the default
format, "from %s line %d", or else the format you supply. For example, if you want to
insert a "C" language file-line directive, you would supply the format "# %2$d \"%1$s\"",
but that is also already supplied with the scheme variable See Section 3.4.59 [SCM c-file-
line-fmt], page 37. You may use it thus:

```
(tpl-file-line c-file-line-fmt)
```

It is also safe to use the formatting string, "%2$d". AutoGen uses an argument vector
version of printf: See Section 8.8 [snprintfv], page 213, and it does not need to know the
types of each argument in order to skip forward to the second argument.

Arguments:
msg-fmt - Optional - formatting for line message

3.4.56 `tpl-file-next-line` - get the template file plus next line number

Usage: (tpl-file-next-line [msg-fmt])
This is almost the same as See Section 3.4.55 [SCM tpl-file-line], page 37, except that the
line referenced is the next line, per C compiler conventions, and consequently defaults to
the format: # <line-no+1> "<file-name>"

Arguments:
msg-fmt - Optional - formatting for line message

3.4.57 `warn` - display warning message and continue

Usage: (warn message)
The argument is a string that printed out to stderr. The message is formed from the
formatting string:

```
WARNING:  %s\n
```

The template processing resumes after printing the message.

Arguments:
message - message to display

3.4.58 `autogen-version` - autogen version number

This is a symbol defining the current AutoGen version number string. It was first defined
in AutoGen-5.2.14. It is currently "5.18.6pre15".

3.4.59 format file info as, "#line nn "file""

This is a symbol that can easily be used with the functions See Section 3.4.55 [SCM tpl-file-
line], page 37, and See Section 3.4.7 [SCM def-file-line], page 27. These will emit C program
`#line` directives pointing to template and definitions text, respectively.

3.5 Common Scheme Functions

This section describes a number of general purpose functions that make the kind of string processing that AutoGen does a little easier. Unlike the AutoGen specific functions (see Section 3.4 [AutoGen Functions], page 26), these functions are available for direct use during definition load time. The equality test (see Section 3.5.45 [SCM =], page 50) is "overloaded" to do string equivalence comparisons. If you are looking for inequality, the Scheme/Lisp way of spelling that is, "(not (= ...))".

3.5.1 `agpl` - GNU Affero General Public License

Usage: (agpl prog-name prefix)
Emit a string that contains the GNU Affero General Public License. This function is now deprecated. Please See Section 3.5.18 [SCM license-description], page 43.

Arguments:
prog-name - name of the program under the GPL
prefix - String for starting each output line

3.5.2 `bsd` - BSD Public License

Usage: (bsd prog_name owner prefix)
Emit a string that contains the Free BSD Public License. This function is now deprecated. Please See Section 3.5.18 [SCM license-description], page 43.

Arguments:
prog_name - name of the program under the BSD
owner - Grantor of the BSD License
prefix - String for starting each output line

3.5.3 `c-string` - emit string for ANSI C

Usage: (c-string string)
Reform a string so that, when printed, the C compiler will be able to compile the data and construct a string that contains exactly what the current string contains. Many non-printing characters are replaced with escape sequences. Newlines are replaced with a backslash, an n, a closing quote, a newline, seven spaces and another re-opening quote. The compiler will implicitly concatenate them. The reader will see line breaks.

A K&R compiler will choke. Use **kr-string** for that compiler.

Arguments:
string - string to reformat

3.5.4 `error-source-line` - display of file & line

Usage: (error-source-line)
This function is only invoked just before Guile displays an error message. It displays the file name and line number that triggered the evaluation error. You should not need to invoke this routine directly. Guile will do it automatically.

This Scheme function takes no arguments.

3.5.5 extract - extract text from another file

Usage: (extract file-name marker-fmt [caveat] [default])
This function is used to help construct output files that may contain text that is carried
from one version of the output to the next.

The first two arguments are required, the second are optional:

- The `file-name` argument is used to name the file that contains the demarcated text.

- The `marker-fmt` is a formatting string that is used to construct the starting and ending
  demarcation strings. The sprintf function is given the `marker-fmt` with two arguments.
  The first is either "START" or "END". The second is either "DO NOT CHANGE
  THIS COMMENT" or the optional `caveat` argument.

- `caveat` is presumed to be absent if it is the empty string (""). If absent, "DO NOT
  CHANGE THIS COMMENT" is used as the second string argument to the `marker-`
  `fmt`.

- When a `default` argument is supplied and no pre-existing text is found, then this text
  will be inserted between the START and END markers.

The resulting strings are presumed to be unique within the subject file. As a simplified
example:

```
[+ (extract "fname" "// %s - SOMETHING - %s" ""
"example default") +]
```

will result in the following text being inserted into the output:

```
// START - SOMETHING - DO NOT CHANGE THIS COMMENT
example default
// END   - SOMETHING - DO NOT CHANGE THIS COMMENT
```

The "example default" string can then be carried forward to the next generation of the
output, *provided* the output is not named "fname" *and* the old output is renamed to
"fname" before AutoGen-eration begins.

NB: You can set aside previously generated source files inside the pseudo macro with
              a Guile/scheme function, extract the text you want to keep with this extract
              function. Just remember you should delete it at the end, too. Here is an
              example from my Finite State Machine generator:

```
[+ AutoGen5 Template  -*- Mode: text -*-
h=%s-fsm.h   c=%s-fsm.c
(shellf
"test -f %1$s-fsm.h && mv -f %1$s-fsm.h .fsm.head
test -f %1$s-fsm.c && mv -f %1$s-fsm.c .fsm.code" (base-name))
+]
```

              This code will move the two previously produced output files to files named
              ".fsm.head" and ".fsm.code". At the end of the 'c' output processing, I delete
              them.

also NB: This function presumes that the output file ought to be editable so that the
              code between the **START** and **END** marks can be edited by the template user.
              Consequently, when the (extract ...) function is invoked, if the `writable`
              option has not been specified, then it will be set at that point. If this is not the

desired behavior, the `--not-writable` command line option will override this. Also, you may use the guile function (`chmod "file" mode-value`) to override whatever AutoGen is using for the result mode.

Arguments:
file-name - name of file with text
marker-fmt - format for marker text
caveat - Optional - warn about changing marker
default - Optional - default initial text

3.5.6 `format-arg-count` - count the args to a format

Usage: (format-arg-count format)
Sometimes, it is useful to simply be able to figure out how many arguments are required by a format string. For example, if you are extracting a format string for the purpose of generating a macro to invoke a printf-like function, you can run the formatting string through this function to determine how many arguments to provide for in the macro. e.g. for this extraction text:

```
/*=fumble bumble
 * fmt: 'stumble %s: %d\n'
=*/
```

You may wish to generate a macro:

```
#define BUMBLE(a1,a2) printf_like(something,(a1),(a2))
```

You can do this by knowing that the format needs two arguments.

Arguments:
format - formatting string

3.5.7 `fprintf` - format to a file

Usage: (fprintf port format [format-arg ...])
Format a string using arguments from the alist. Write to a specified port. The result will NOT appear in your output. Use this to print information messages to a template user.

Arguments:
port - Guile-scheme output port
format - formatting string
format-arg - Optional - list of arguments to formatting string

3.5.8 `gperf` - perform a perfect hash function

Usage: (gperf name str)
Perform the perfect hash on the input string. This is only useful if you have previously created a gperf program with the `make-gperf` function See Section 3.5.22 [SCM make-gperf], page 44. The `name` you supply here must match the name used to create the program and the string to hash must be one of the strings supplied in the `make-gperf` string list. The result will be a perfect hash index.

See the documentation for `gperf(1GNU)` for more details.

Arguments:
name - name of hash list
str - string to hash

3.5.9 `gperf-code` - emit the source of the generated gperf program

Usage: (gperf-code st-name)
Returns the contents of the emitted code, suitable for inclusion in another program. The interface contains the following elements:

'struct <*st-name*>_index'
> containg the fields: {char const * name, int const id; };

'<*st-name*>_hash()'
> This is the hashing function with local only scope (static).

'<*st-name*>_find()'
> This is the searching and validation function. The first argument is the string to look up, the second is its length. It returns a pointer to the corresponding <*st-name*>_index entry.

Use this in your template as follows where "<*st-name*>" was set to be "lookup":

```
[+ (make-gperf "lookup' (join "\n" (stack "name_list")))
(gperf-code "lookup") +]
void my_fun(char * str) {
struct lookup_index * li = lookup_find(str, strlen(str));
if (li != NULL) printf("%s yields %d\n", str, li->idx);
```

Arguments:
st-name - the name of the gperf hash list

3.5.10 `gpl` - GNU General Public License

Usage: (gpl prog-name prefix)
Emit a string that contains the GNU General Public License. This function is now deprecated. Please See Section 3.5.18 [SCM license-description], page 43.

Arguments:
prog-name - name of the program under the GPL
prefix - String for starting each output line

3.5.11 `hide-email` - convert eaddr to javascript

Usage: (hide-email display eaddr)
Hides an email address as a java scriptlett. The 'mailto:' tag and the email address are coded bytes rather than plain text. They are also broken up.

Arguments:
display - display text
eaddr - email address

3.5.12 `html-escape-encode` - encode html special characters

Usage: (html-escape-encode str)
This function will replace replace the characters '&', '<' and '>' characters with the HTML/XML escape-encoded strings ("&", "<", and ">", respectively).

Arguments:
str - string to make substitutions in

3.5.13 `in?` - test for string in list

Usage: (in? test-string string-list ...)
Return SCM_BOOL_T if the first argument string is found in one of the entries in the second (list-of-strings) argument.

Arguments:
test-string - string to look for
string-list - list of strings to check

3.5.14 `join` - join string list with separator

Usage: (join separator list ...)
With the first argument as the separator string, joins together an a-list of strings into one long string. The list may contain nested lists, partly because you cannot always control that.

Arguments:
separator - string to insert between entries
list - list of strings to join

3.5.15 `kr-string` - emit string for K&R C

Usage: (kr-string string)
Reform a string so that, when printed, a K&R C compiler will be able to compile the data and construct a string that contains exactly what the current string contains. Many non-printing characters are replaced with escape sequences. New-lines are replaced with a backslash-n-backslash and newline sequence,

Arguments:
string - string to reformat

3.5.16 `lgpl` - GNU Library General Public License

Usage: (lgpl prog_name owner prefix)
Emit a string that contains the GNU Library General Public License. This function is now deprecated. Please See Section 3.5.18 [SCM license-description], page 43.

Arguments:
prog_name - name of the program under the LGPL
owner - Grantor of the LGPL
prefix - String for starting each output line

3.5.17 `license` - an arbitrary license

Usage: (license lic_name prog_name owner prefix)
Emit a string that contains the named license. This function is now deprecated. Please See Section 3.5.18 [SCM license-description], page 43.

Arguments:
lic_name - file name of the license
prog_name - name of the licensed program or library

owner - Grantor of the License
prefix - String for starting each output line

3.5.18 `license-description` - Emit a license description

Usage: (license-description license prog-name prefix [owner])
Emit a string that contains a detailed license description, with substitutions for program name, copyright holder and a per-line prefix. This is the text typically used as part of a source file header. For more details, See Section 3.5.19 [SCM license-full], page 43.

   Arguments:
license - name of license type
prog-name - name of the program under the GPL
prefix - String for starting each output line
owner - Optional - owner of the program

3.5.19 `license-full` - Emit the licensing information and description

Usage: (license-full license prog-name prefix [owner] [years])
Emit all the text that `license-info` and `license-description` would emit (see Section 3.5.20 [SCM license-info], page 44, and see Section 3.5.18 [SCM license-description], page 43), with all the same substitutions.

   All of these depend upon the existence of a license file named after the `license` argument with a `.lic` suffix. That file should contain three blocks of text, each separated by two or more consecutive newline characters (at least one completely blank line).

   The first section describes copyright attribution and the name of the usage licence. For GNU software, this should be the text that is to be displayed with the program version. Four text markers can be replaced: <PFX>, <program>, <years> and <owner>.

   The second section is a short description of the terms of the license. This is typically the kind of text that gets displayed in the header of source files. Only the <PFX>, <owner> and <program> markers are substituted.

   The third section is strictly the name of the license. No marker substitutions are performed.

```
<PFX>Copyright (C) <years> <owner>, all rights reserved.
<PFX>
<PFX>This is free software. It is licensed for use,
<PFX>modification and redistribution under the terms
<PFX>of the GNU General Public License, version 3 or later
<PFX>    <http://gnu.org/licenses/gpl.html>

<PFX><program> is free software: you can redistribute it
<PFX>and/or modify it under the terms of the GNU General
<PFX>Public License as published by the Free Software ...

the GNU General Public License, version 3 or later
```

   Arguments:
license - name of license type

prog-name - name of the program under the GPL
prefix - String for starting each output line
owner - Optional - owner of the program
years - Optional - copyright years

3.5.20 `license-info` - Emit the licensing information and copyright years

Usage: (license-info license prog-name prefix [owner] [years])
Emit a string that contains the licensing description, with some substitutions for program name, copyright holder, a list of years when the source was modified, and a per-line prefix. This text typically includes a brief license description and is often printed out when a program starts running or as part of the `--version` output. For more details, See Section 3.5.19 [SCM license-full], page 43.

  Arguments:
license - name of license type
prog-name - name of the program under the GPL
prefix - String for starting each output line
owner - Optional - owner of the program
years - Optional - copyright years

3.5.21 `license-name` - Emit the name of the license

Usage: (license-name license)
Emit a string that contains the full name of the license.

  Arguments:
license - name of license type

3.5.22 `make-gperf` - build a perfect hash function program

Usage: (make-gperf name strings ...)
Build a program to perform perfect hashes of a known list of input strings. This function produces no output, but prepares a program named, `gperf_<name>` for use by the gperf function See Section 3.5.8 [SCM gperf], page 40.

  This program will be obliterated as AutoGen exits. However, you may incorporate the generated hashing function into your C program with commands something like the following:

```
[+ (shellf "sed '/^int main(/,$d;/^#line/d' ${gpdir}/%s.c"
name ) +]
```

  where `name` matches the name provided to this `make-perf` function. `gpdir` is the variable used to store the name of the temporary directory used to stash all the files.

  Arguments:
name - name of hash list
strings - list of strings to hash

3.5.23 `makefile-script` - create makefile script

Usage: (makefile-script text)
This function will take ordinary shell script text and reformat it so that it will work properly

inside of a makefile shell script. Not every shell construct can be supported; the intent is to have most ordinary scripts work without much, if any, alteration.

The following transformations are performed on the source text:

1. Trailing whitespace on each line is stripped.

2. Except for the last line, the string, " ; \\" is appended to the end of every line that does not end with certain special characters or keywords. Note that this will mutilate multi-line quoted strings, but **make** renders it impossible to use multi-line constructs anyway.

3. If the line ends with a backslash, it is left alone.

4. If the line ends with a semi-colon, conjunction operator, pipe (vertical bar) or one of the keywords "then", "else" or "in", then a space and a backslash is added, but no semi-colon.

5. The dollar sign character is doubled, unless it immediately precedes an opening parenthesis or the single character make macros '*', '<', '@', '?' or '%'. Other single character make macros that do not have enclosing parentheses will fail. For shell usage of the "$@", "$?" and "$*" macros, you must enclose them with curly braces, e.g., "${?}". The ksh construct $(<command>) will not work. Though some **makes** accept ${var} constructs, this function will assume it is for shell interpretation and double the dollar character. You must use $(var) for all **make** substitutions.

6. Double dollar signs are replaced by four before the next character is examined.

7. Every line is prefixed with a tab, unless the first line already starts with a tab.

8. The newline character on the last line, if present, is suppressed.

9. Blank lines are stripped.

10. Lines starting with "@ifdef", "@ifndef", "@else" and "@endif" are presumed to be autoconf "sed" expression tags. These lines will be emitted as-is, with no tab prefix and no line splicing backslash. These lines can then be processed at configure time with **AC_CONFIG_FILES** sed expressions, similar to:

```
sed "/^@ifdef foo/d;/^@endif foo/d;/^@ifndef foo/,/^@endif foo/d'
```

This function is intended to be used approximately as follows:

```
$(TARGET) : $(DEPENDENCIES)
<+ (out-push-new) +>
....mostly arbitrary shell script text....
<+ (makefile-script (out-pop #t)) +>
```

Arguments:
text - the text of the script

3.5.24 max - maximum value in list

Usage: (max list ...)
Return the maximum value in the list

Arguments:
list - list of values. Strings are converted to numbers

3.5.25 `min` - minimum value in list

Usage: (min list ...)
Return the minimum value in the list

    Arguments:
list - list of values. Strings are converted to numbers

3.5.26 `prefix` - prefix lines with a string

Usage: (prefix prefix text)
Prefix every line in the second string with the first string. This includes empty lines, though trailing white space will be removed if the line consists only of the "prefix". Also, if the last character is a newline, then *two* prefixes will be inserted into the result text.

    For example, if the first string is "# " and the second contains:

```
"two\nlines\n"
```

The result string will contain:

```
# two
# lines
#
```

    The last line will be incomplete: no newline and no space after the hash character, either.

    Arguments:
prefix - string to insert at start of each line
text - multi-line block of text

3.5.27 `printf` - format to stdout

Usage: (printf format [format-arg ...])
Format a string using arguments from the alist. Write to the standard out port. The result will NOT appear in your output. Use this to print information messages to a template user. Use "(sprintf ...)" to add text to your document.

    Arguments:
format - formatting string
format-arg - Optional - list of arguments to formatting string

3.5.28 `raw-shell-str` - single quote shell string

Usage: (raw-shell-str string)
Convert the text of the string into a singly quoted string that a normal shell will process into the original string. (It will not do macro expansion later, either.) Contained single quotes become tripled, with the middle quote escaped with a backslash. Normal shells will reconstitute the original string.

    Notice: some shells will not correctly handle unusual non-printing characters. This routine works for most reasonably conventional ASCII strings.

    Arguments:
string - string to transform

3.5.29 `shell` - invoke a shell script

Usage: (shell command ...)
Generate a string by writing the value to a server shell and reading the output back in. The template programmer is responsible for ensuring that it completes within 10 seconds. If it does not, the server will be killed, the output tossed and a new server started.

Please note: This is the same server process used by the '#shell' definitions directive and backquoted ` definitions. There may be left over state from previous shell expressions and the ` processing in the declarations. However, a `cd` to the original directory is always issued before the new command is issued.

Also note: When initializing, autogen will set the environment variable "AGexe" to the full path of the autogen executable.

Arguments:
command - shell command - the result is from stdout

3.5.30 `shell-str` - double quote shell string

Usage: (shell-str string)
Convert the text of the string into a double quoted string that a normal shell will process into the original string, almost. It will add the escape character \\ before two special characters to accomplish this: the backslash \\ and double quote ".

Notice: some shells will not correctly handle unusual non-printing characters. This routine works for most reasonably conventional ASCII strings.

WARNING:
This function omits the extra backslash in front of a backslash, however, if it is followed by either a backquote or a dollar sign. It must do this because otherwise it would be impossible to protect the dollar sign or backquote from shell evaluation. Consequently, it is not possible to render the strings "\\$" or "\\`" . The lesser of two evils.

All others characters are copied directly into the output.

The **sub-shell-str** variation of this routine behaves identically, except that the extra backslash is omitted in front of " instead of `. You have to think about it. I'm open to suggestions.

Meanwhile, the best way to document is with a detailed output example. If the backslashes make it through the text processing correctly, below you will see what happens with three example strings. The first example string contains a list of quoted foos, the second is the same with a single backslash before the quote characters and the last is with two backslash escapes. Below each is the result of the **raw-shell-str**, **shell-str** and **sub-shell-str** functions.

```
foo[0]             ''foo'' 'foo' "foo" `foo` $foo
raw-shell-str -> \'\''foo'\'\'' '\''foo'\'' 'foo" `foo` $foo'
shell-str     -> "''foo'' 'foo' \"foo\" `foo` $foo"
sub-shell-str -> '''foo'' 'foo' "foo" \`foo\` $foo`

foo[1]             \'bar\' \'bar\" \'bar\` \$bar
raw-shell-str -> '\'\''bar'\'\'' \"bar\" \`bar\` \$bar'
shell-str     -> "\\'bar\\' \\\"bar\\\" \`bar\` \$bar"
```

```
sub-shell-str -> '\\'bar\\' \"bar\" \\\'bar\\\' \$bar'

foo[2]          \\'BAZ\\' \\"BAZ\\" \\'BAZ\\' \\$BAZ
raw-shell-str -> '\\'\''BAZ\\'\'' \\"BAZ\\" \\'BAZ\\' \\$BAZ'
shell-str    -> "\\\\'BAZ\\\\' \\\\\\"BAZ\\\\\\" \\\'BAZ\\\' \\\$BAZ"
sub-shell-str -> '\\\\'BAZ\\\\' \\\"BAZ\\\" \\\\\'BAZ\\\\\' \\\$BAZ'
```

There should be four, three, five and three backslashes for the four examples on the last line, respectively. The next to last line should have four, five, three and three backslashes. If this was not accurately reproduced, take a look at the agen5/test/shell.test test. Notice the backslashes in front of the dollar signs. It goes from zero to one to three for the "cooked" string examples.

Arguments:
string - string to transform

3.5.31 shellf - format a string, run shell

Usage: (shellf format [format-arg ...])
Format a string using arguments from the alist, then send the result to the shell for interpretation.

Arguments:
format - formatting string
format-arg - Optional - list of arguments to formatting string

3.5.32 sprintf - format a string

Usage: (sprintf format [format-arg ...])
Format a string using arguments from the alist.

Arguments:
format - formatting string
format-arg - Optional - list of arguments to formatting string

3.5.33 string-capitalize - capitalize a new string

Usage: (string-capitalize str)
Create a new SCM string containing the same text as the original, only all the first letter of each word is upper cased and all other letters are made lower case.

Arguments:
str - input string

3.5.34 string-capitalize! - capitalize a string

Usage: (string-capitalize! str)
capitalize all the words in an SCM string.

Arguments:
str - input/output string

3.5.35 string-contains-eqv? - caseless substring

Usage: (*=* text match)
string-contains-eqv?: Test to see if a string contains an equivalent string. 'equivalent' means

the strings match, but without regard to character case and certain characters are considered 'equivalent'. Viz., '-', '_' and '^' are equivalent.

Arguments:
text - text to test for pattern
match - pattern/substring to search for

3.5.36 `string-contains?` - substring match

Usage: (*==* text match)
string-contains?: Test to see if a string contains a substring. "strstr(3)" will find an address.

Arguments:
text - text to test for pattern
match - pattern/substring to search for

3.5.37 `string-downcase` - lower case a new string

Usage: (string-downcase str)
Create a new SCM string containing the same text as the original, only all the upper case letters are changed to lower case.

Arguments:
str - input string

3.5.38 `string-downcase!` - make a string be lower case

Usage: (string-downcase! str)
Change to lower case all the characters in an SCM string.

Arguments:
str - input/output string

3.5.39 `string-end-eqv-match?` - caseless regex ending

Usage: (*~ text match)
string-end-eqv-match?: Test to see if a string ends with a pattern. Case is not significant.

Arguments:
text - text to test for pattern
match - pattern/substring to search for

3.5.40 `string-end-match?` - regex match end

Usage: (*~~ text match)
string-end-match?: Test to see if a string ends with a pattern. Case is significant.

Arguments:
text - text to test for pattern
match - pattern/substring to search for

3.5.41 `string-ends-eqv?` - caseless string ending

Usage: (*= text match)
string-ends-eqv?: Test to see if a string ends with an equivalent string.

Arguments:

text - text to test for pattern

match - pattern/substring to search for

3.5.42 `string-ends-with?` - string ending

Usage: (*== text match)

string-ends-with?: Test to see if a string ends with a substring. strcmp(3) returns zero for comparing the string ends.

Arguments:

text - text to test for pattern

match - pattern/substring to search for

3.5.43 `string-equals?` - string matching

Usage: (== text match)

string-equals?: Test to see if two strings exactly match.

Arguments:

text - text to test for pattern

match - pattern/substring to search for

3.5.44 `string-eqv-match?` - caseless regex match

Usage: (~ text match)

string-eqv-match?: Test to see if a string fully matches a pattern. Case is not significant, but any character equivalences must be expressed in your regular expression.

Arguments:

text - text to test for pattern

match - pattern/substring to search for

3.5.45 `string-eqv?` - caseless match

Usage: (= text match)

string-eqv?: Test to see if two strings are equivalent. 'equivalent' means the strings match, but without regard to character case and certain characters are considered 'equivalent'. Viz., '-', '_' and '^' are equivalent. If the arguments are not strings, then the result of the numeric comparison is returned.

This is an overloaded operation. If the arguments are both numbers, then the query is passed through to `scm_num_eq_p()`, otherwise the result depends on the SCMs being strictly equal.

Arguments:

text - text to test for pattern

match - pattern/substring to search for

3.5.46 `string-has-eqv-match?` - caseless regex contains

Usage: (*~* text match)

string-has-eqv-match?: Test to see if a string contains a pattern. Case is not significant.

Arguments:

text - text to test for pattern

match - pattern/substring to search for

3.5.47 `string-has-match?` - contained regex match

Usage: (*~* text match)
string-has-match?: Test to see if a string contains a pattern. Case is significant.

Arguments:
text - text to test for pattern
match - pattern/substring to search for

3.5.48 `string-match?` - regex match

Usage: (~~ text match)
string-match?: Test to see if a string fully matches a pattern. Case is significant.

Arguments:
text - text to test for pattern
match - pattern/substring to search for

3.5.49 `string-start-eqv-match?` - caseless regex start

Usage: (~* text match)
string-start-eqv-match?: Test to see if a string starts with a pattern. Case is not significant.

Arguments:
text - text to test for pattern
match - pattern/substring to search for

3.5.50 `string-start-match?` - regex match start

Usage: (~~* text match)
string-start-match?: Test to see if a string starts with a pattern. Case is significant

Arguments:
text - text to test for pattern
match - pattern/substring to search for

3.5.51 `string-starts-eqv?` - caseless string start

Usage: (=* text match)
string-starts-eqv?: Test to see if a string starts with an equivalent string.

Arguments:
text - text to test for pattern
match - pattern/substring to search for

3.5.52 `string-starts-with?` - string starting

Usage: (==* text match)
string-starts-with?: Test to see if a string starts with a substring.

Arguments:
text - text to test for pattern
match - pattern/substring to search for

3.5.53 `string-substitute` - multiple global replacements

Usage: (string-substitute source match repl)
`match` and `repl` may be either a single string or a list of strings. Either way, they must

have the same structure and number of elements. For example, to replace all amphersands, less than and greater than characters, do something like this:

```
(string-substitute source
(list "&"      "<"     ">")
(list "&amp;" "&lt;" "&gt;"))
```

Arguments:
source - string to transform
match - substring or substring list to be replaced
repl - replacement strings or substrings

3.5.54 `string-table-add` - Add an entry to a string table

Usage: (string-table-add st-name str-val)
Check for a duplicate string and, if none, then insert a new string into the string table. In all cases, returns the character index of the beginning of the string in the table.

The returned index can be used in expressions like:

```
string_array + <returned-value>
```

that will yield the address of the first byte of the inserted string. See the `strtable.test` AutoGen test for a usage example.

Arguments:
st-name - the name of the array of characters
str-val - the (possibly) new value to add

3.5.55 `string-table-add-ref` - Add an entry to a string table, get reference

Usage: (string-table-add-ref st-name str-val)
Identical to string-table-add, except the value returned is the string "st-name" '+' and the index returned by string-table-add.

Arguments:
st-name - the name of the array of characters
str-val - the (possibly) new value to add

3.5.56 `string-table-new` - create a string table

Usage: (string-table-new st-name)
This function will create an array of characters. The companion functions, (See Section 3.5.54 [SCM string-table-add], page 52, See Section 3.5.55 [SCM string-table-add-ref], page 52, and see Section 3.4.10 [SCM emit-string-table], page 28) will insert text and emit the populated table.

With these functions, it should be much easier to construct structures containing string offsets instead of string pointers. That can be very useful when transmitting, storing or sharing data with different address spaces.

Here is a brief example copied from the strtable.test test:

```
[+ (string-table-new "scribble")
   (out-push-new) ;; redirect output to temporary
   (define ct 1)  +][+
```

```
FOR str IN that was the week that was +][+
  (set! ct (+ ct 1))
+]
    [+ (string-table-add-ref "scribble" (get "str")) +],[+
ENDFOR  +]
[+ (out-suspend "main")
   (emit-string-table "scribble")
   (ag-fprintf 0 "\nchar const *ap[%d] = {" ct)
   (out-resume "main")
   (out-pop #t) ;; now dump out the redirected output +]
    NULL };
```

Some explanation:

I added the (out-push-new) because the string table text is diverted into an output stream named, "scribble" and I want to have the string table emitted before the string table references. The string table references are also emitted inside the FOR loop. So, when the loop is done, the current output is suspended under the name, "main" and the "scribble" table is then emitted into the primary output. (emit-string-table inserts its output directly into the current output stream. It does not need to be the last function in an AutoGen macro block.) Next I ag-fprintf the array-of-pointer declaration directly into the current output. Finally I restore the "main" output stream and (out-pop #t) it into the main output stream.

Here is the result. Note that duplicate strings are not repeated in the string table:

```
static char const scribble[18] =
    "that\0" "was\0" 'the\0"  "week\0";

char const *ap[7] = {
    scribble+0,
    scribble+5,
    scribble+9,
    scribble+13,
    scribble+0,
    scribble+5,
    NULL };
```

These functions use the global name space stt-* in addition to the function names.

If you utilize this in your programming, it is recommended that you prevent printf format usage warnings with the GCC option -Wno-format-contains-nul

Arguments:
st-name - the name of the array of characters

3.5.57 string-table-size - print the current size of a string table

Usage: (string-table-size st-name)
Returns the current byte count of the string table.

Arguments:
st-name - the name of the array of characters

3.5.58 `string->c-name!` - map non-name chars to underscore

Usage: (string->c-name! str)
Change all the graphic characters that are invalid in a C name token into underscores. Whitespace characters are ignored. Any other character type (i.e. non-graphic and non-white) will cause a failure.

    Arguments:
str - input/output string

3.5.59 `string->camelcase` - make a string be CamelCase

Usage: (string->camelcase str)
Capitalize the first letter of each block of letters and numbers, and stripping out characters that are not alphanumerics. For example, "alpha-beta0gamma" becomes "Alpha-Beta0gamma".

    Arguments:
str - input/output string

3.5.60 `string-tr` - convert characters with new result

Usage: (string-tr source match translation)
This is identical to **string-tr!**, except that it does not over-write the previous value.

    Arguments:
source - string to transform
match - characters to be converted
translation - conversion list

3.5.61 `string-tr!` - convert characters

Usage: (string-tr! source match translation)
This is the same as the **tr(1)** program, except the string to transform is the first argument. The second and third arguments are used to construct mapping arrays for the transformation of the first argument.

    It is too bad this little program has so many different and incompatible implementations!

    Arguments:
source - string to transform
match - characters to be converted
translation - conversion list

3.5.62 `string-upcase` - upper case a new string

Usage: (string-upcase str)
Create a new SCM string containing the same text as the original, only all the lower case letters are changed to upper case.

    Arguments:
str - input string

3.5.63 `string-upcase!` - make a string be upper case

Usage: (string-upcase! str)
Change to upper case all the characters in an SCM string.

Arguments:
str - input/output string

3.5.64 `sub-shell-str` - back quoted (sub-)shell string

Usage: (sub-shell-str string)
This function is substantially identical to `shell-str`, except that the quoting character is
' and the "leave the escape alone" character is ".

Arguments:
string - string to transform

3.5.65 `sum` - sum of values in list

Usage: (sum list ...)
Compute the sum of the list of expressions.

Arguments:
list - list of values. Strings are converted to numbers

3.5.66 `time-string->number` - duration string to seconds

Usage: (time-string->number time_spec)
Convert the argument string to a time period in seconds. The string may use multiple parts
consisting of days, hours minutes and seconds. These are indicated with a suffix of `d`, `h`. `m`
and `s` respectively. Hours, minutes and seconds may also be represented with `HH:MM:SS` or,
without hours, as `MM:SS`.

Arguments:
time_spec - string to parse

3.5.67 `version-compare` - compare two version numbers

Usage: (version-compare op v1 v2)
Converts v1 and v2 strings into 64 bit values and returns the result of running 'op' on those
values. It assumes that the version is a 1 to 4 part dot-separated series of numbers. Suffixes
like, "5pre4" or "5-pre4" will be interpreted as two numbers. The first number ("5" in
this case) will be decremented and the number after the "pre" will be added to 0xC000.
(Unless your platform is unable to support 64 bit integer arithmetic. Then it will be added
to 0xC0.) Consequently, these yield true:

```
(version-compare > "5.8.5"      "5.8.5-pre4")
(version-compare > "5.8.5-pre10" "5.8.5-pre4")
```

Arguments:
op - comparison operator
v1 - first version
v2 - compared-to version

3.6 AutoGen Native Macros

This section describes the various AutoGen natively defined macros. Unlike the Scheme
functions, some of these macros are "block macros" with a scope that extends through a
terminating macro. Block macros must not overlap. That is to say, a block macro started

within the scope of an encompassing block macro must have its matching end macro appear before the encompassing block macro is either ended or subdivided.

The block macros are these:

CASE   This macro has scope through the ESAC macro. The scope is subdivided by SELECT macros. You must have at least one SELECT macro.

DEFINE   This macro has scope through the ENDDEF macro. The defined user macro can never be a block macro. This macro is extracted from the template *before* the template is processed. Consequently, you cannot select a definition based on context. You can, however, place them all at the end of the file.

FOR   This macro has scope through the ENDFOR macro.

IF   This macro has scope through the ENDIF macro. The scope may be subdivided by ELIF and ELSE macros. Obviously, there may be only one ELSE macro and it must be the last of these subdivisions.

INCLUDE   This macro has the scope of the included file. It is a block macro in the sense that the included file must not contain any incomplete block macros.

WHILE   This macro has scope through the ENDWHILE macro.

3.6.1 AutoGen Macro Syntax

The general syntax is:

    [{ <native-macro-name> | <user-defined-name> }] [<arg> ...]

The syntax for <arg> depends on the particular macro, but is generally a full expression (see Section 3.3 [expression syntax], page 23). Here are the exceptions to that general rule:

1. INVOKE macros, implicit or explicit, must be followed by a list of name/string value pairs. The string values are *simple expressions*, as described above.

   That is, the INVOKE syntax is one of these two:

        <user-macro-name> [<name> [= <expression>] ...]

        INVOKE <name-expression> [<name> [= <expression>] ...]

2. AutoGen FOR macros must be in one of three forms:

        FOR <name> [<separator-string>]

        FOR <name> (...Scheme expression list)

        FOR <name> IN <string-entry> [...]

   where:

   '<name>'   must be a simple name.

   '<separator-string>'
                   is inserted between copies of the enclosed block. Do not try to use "IN" as your separator string. It won't work.

   '<string-entry>'
                   is an entry in a list of strings. "<name>" is assigned each value from the "IN" list before expanding the FOR block.

'(...Scheme expression list)'
     is expected to contain one or more of the `for-from`, `for-to`, `for-by`, and `for-sep` functions. (See Section 3.6.15 [FOR], page 60, and Section 3.4 [AutoGen Functions], page 26)

The first two forms iterate over the `FOR` block if `<name>` is found in the AutoGen values. The last form will create the AutoGen value named `<name>`.

3. AutoGen `DEFINE` macros must be followed by a simple name. Anything after that is ignored. Consequently, that "comment space" may be used to document any named values the macro expects to have set up as arguments. See Section 3.6.7 [DEFINE], page 58.

4. The AutoGen `COMMENT`, `ELSE`, `ESAC` and the `END*` macros take no arguments and ignore everything after the macro name (e.g. see Section 3.6.4 [COMMENT], page 58)

3.6.2 BREAK - Leave a FOR or WHILE macro

This will unwind the loop context and resume after ENDFOR/ENDWHILE. Note that unless this happens to be the last iteration anyway, the (last-for?) function will never yield `"#t"`.

3.6.3 CASE - Select one of several template blocks

The arguments are evaluated and converted to a string. if necessary. A simple name will be interpreted as an AutoGen value name and its value will be used by the `SELECT` macros (see the example below and the expression evaluation function, see Section 3.6.15 [EXPR], page 60). The scope of the macro is up to the matching `ESAC` macro. Within the scope of a `CASE`, this string is matched against case selection macros. There are sixteen match macros that are derived from four different ways matches may be performed, plus an "always true", "true if the AutoGen value was found", and "true if no AutoGen value was found" matches. The codes for the nineteen match macros are formed as follows:

1. Must the match start matching from the beginning of the string? If not, then the match macro code starts with an asterisk (*).

2. Must the match finish matching at the end of the string? If not, then the match macro code ends with an asterisk (*).

3. Is the match a pattern match or a string comparison? If a comparison, use an equal sign (=). If a pattern match, use a tilde (~).

4. Is the match case sensitive? If alphabetic case is important, double the tilde or equal sign.

5. Do you need a default match when none of the others match? Use a single asterisk (*).

6. Do you need to distinguish between an empty string value and a value that was not found? Use the non-existence test (!E) before testing a full match against an empty string (== ''). There is also an existence test (+E), more for symmetry than for practical use.

For example:

```
[+ CASE <full-expression> +]
[+ ~~*  "[Tt]est" +]reg exp must match at start, not at end
[+ ==   "TeSt"    +]a full-string, case sensitive compare
```

```
[+ =     "TEST"    +]a full-string, case insensitive compare
[+ !E              +]not exists - matches if no AutoGen value found
[+ ==    ""        +]expression yielded a zero-length string
[+ +E              +]exists - matches if there is any value result
[+ *               +]always match - no testing
[+ ESAC +]
```

<full-expression> (see Section 3.3 [expression syntax], page 23) may be any expression, including the use of apply-codes and value-names. If the expression yields a number, it is converted to a decimal string.

These case selection codes have also been implemented as Scheme expression functions using the same codes. They are documented in this texi doc as "string-*?" predicates (see Section 3.5 [Common Functions], page 38).

3.6.4 COMMENT - A block of comment to be ignored

This function can be specified by the user, but there will never be a situation where it will be invoked at emit time. The macro is actually removed from the internal representation.

If the native macro name code is #, then the entire macro function is treated as a comment and ignored.

```
[+ # say what you want, but no '+' before any ']' chars +]
```

3.6.5 CONTINUE - Skip to end of a FOR or WHILE macro.

This will skip the remainder of the loop and start the next.

3.6.6 DEBUG - Print debug message to trace output

If the tracing level is at "debug-message" or above (see [autogen trace], page 72), this macro prints a debug message to trace output. This message is not evaluated. This macro can also be used to set useful debugger breakpoints. By inserting [+DEBUG n+] into your template, you can set a debugger breakpoint on the #n case element below (in the AutoGen source) and step through the processing of interesting parts of your template.

To be useful, you have to have access to the source tree where autogen was built and the template being processed. The definitions are also helpful, but not crucial. Please contact the author if you think you might actually want to use this.

3.6.7 DEFINE - Define a user AutoGen macro

This function will define a new macro. You must provide a name for the macro. You do not specify any arguments, though the invocation may specify a set of name/value pairs that are to be active during the processing of the macro.

```
[+ define foo +]
... macro body with macro functions ...
[+ enddef +]
... [+ foo bar='raw text' baz=<<text expression>> +]
```

Once the macro has been defined, this new macro can be invoked by specifying the macro name as the first token after the start macro marker. Alternatively, you may make the invocation explicitly invoke a defined macro by specifying INVOKE (see Section 3.6.19 [INVOKE], page 62) in the macro invocation. If you do that, the macro name can be computed with an expression that gets evaluated every time the INVOKE macro is encountered.

Any remaining text in the macro invocation will be used to create new name/value pairs that only persist for the duration of the processing of the macro. The expressions are evaluated the same way basic expressions are evaluated. See Section 3.3 [expression syntax], page 23.

The resulting definitions are handled much like regular definitions, except:

1. The values may not be compound. That is, they may not contain nested name/value pairs.

2. The bindings go away when the macro is complete.

3. The name/value pairs are separated by whitespace instead of semi-colons.

4. Sequences of strings are not concatenated.

> **NB:** The macro is extracted from the template as the template is scanned. You cannot conditionally define a macro by enclosing it in an IF/ENDIF (see Section 3.6.17 [IF], page 61) macro pair. If you need to dynamically select the format of a DEFINEd macro. then put the flavors into separate template files that simply define macros. INCLUDE (see Section 3.6.18 [INCLUDE], page 61) the appropriate template when you have computed which you need.

Due to this, it is acceptable and even a good idea to place all the DEFINE macros at the end of the template. That puts the main body of the template at the beginning of the file.

3.6.8 ELIF - Alternate Conditional Template Block

This macro must only appear after an IF function, and before any associated ELSE or ENDIF functions. It denotes the start of an alternate template block for the IF function. Its expression argument is evaluated as are the arguments to IF. For a complete description See Section 3.6.17 [IF], page 61.

3.6.9 ELSE - Alternate Template Block

This macro must only appear after an IF function, and before the associated ENDIF function. It denotes the start of an alternate template block for the IF function. For a complete description See Section 3.6.17 [IF], page 61.

3.6.10 ENDDEF - Ends a macro definition.

This macro ends the DEFINE function template block. For a complete description See Section 3.6.7 [DEFINE], page 58.

3.6.11 ENDFOR - Terminates the FOR function template block

This macro ends the FOR function template block. For a complete description See Section 3.6.16 [FOR], page 60.

3.6.12 ENDIF - Terminate the IF Template Block

This macro ends the IF function template block. For a complete description See Section 3.6.17 [IF], page 61.

3.6.13 ENDWHILE - Terminate the `WHILE` Template Block

This macro ends the `WHILE` function template block. For a complete description See Section 3.6.23 [WHILE], page 62.

3.6.14 ESAC - Terminate the `CASE` Template Block

This macro ends the `CASE` function template block. For a complete description, See Section 3.6.3 [CASE], page 57.

3.6.15 EXPR - Evaluate and emit an Expression

This macro does not have a name to cause it to be invoked explicitly, though if a macro starts with one of the apply codes or one of the simple expression markers, then an expression macro is inferred. The result of the expression evaluation (see Section 3.3 [expression syntax], page 23) is written to the current output.

3.6.16 FOR - Emit a template block multiple times

This macro has a slight variation on the standard syntax:

```
FOR <value-name> [ <separator-string> ]

FOR <value-name> (...Scheme expression list)

FOR <value-name> IN "string" [ ... ]
```

Other than for the last form, the first macro argument must be the name of an AutoGen value. If there is no value associated with the name, the `FOR` template block is skipped entirely. The scope of the `FOR` macro extends to the corresponding ENDFOR macro. The last form will create an array of string values named `<value-name>` that only exists within the context of this `FOR` loop. With this form, in order to use a `separator-string`, you must code it into the end of the template block using the `(last-for?)` predicate function (see Section 3.4.28 [SCM last-for?], page 31).

If there are any arguments after the `value-name`, the initial characters are used to determine the form. If the first character is either a semi-colon (`;`) or an opening parenthesis (`(`), then it is presumed to be a Scheme expression containing the FOR macro specific functions `for-from`, `for-by`, `for-to`, and/or `for-sep`. See Section 3.4 [AutoGen Functions], page 26. If it consists of an 'i' an 'n' and separated by white space from more text, then the `FOR x IN` form is processed. Otherwise, the remaining text is presumed to be a string for inserting between each iteration of the loop. This string will be emitted one time less than the number of iterations of the loop. That is, it is emitted after each loop, excepting for the last iteration.

If the from/by/to functions are invoked, they will specify which copies of the named value are to be processed. If there is no copy of the named value associated with a particular index, the `FOR` template block will be instantiated anyway. The template must use found-for? (see Section 3.4.20 [SCM found-for?], page 30) or other methods for detecting missing definitions and emitting default text. In this fashion, you can insert entries from a sparse or non-zero based array into a dense, zero based array.

NB: the `for-from`, `for-to`, `for-by` and `for-sep` functions are disabled outside of the context of the `FOR` macro. Likewise, the `first-for?`, `last-for?` `for-index`, and `found-for?` functions are disabled outside of the range of a `FOR` block.

Also: the `<value-name>` must be a single level name, not a compound name (see Section 3.2 [naming values], page 23).

```
[+FOR var (for-from 0) (for-to <number>) (for-sep ",") +]
... text with various substitutions ...[+
ENDFOR var+]
```

this will repeat the `... text with various substitutions ...` `<number>`+1 times. Each repetition, except for the last, will have a comma , after it.

```
[+FOR var ",\n" +]
... text with various substitutions ...[+
ENDFOR var +]
```

This will do the same thing, but only for the index values of **var** that have actually been defined.

3.6.17 IF - Conditionally Emit a Template Block

Conditional block. Its arguments are evaluated (see Section 3.6.15 [EXPR], page 60) and if the result is non-zero or a string with one or more bytes, then the condition is true and the text from that point until a matched `ELIF`, `ELSE` or `ENDIF` is emitted. `ELIF` introduces a conditional alternative if the `IF` clause evaluated FALSE and `ELSE` introduces an unconditional alternative.

```
[+IF <full-expression> +]
emit things that are for the true condition[+

ELIF <full-expression-2> +]
emit things that are true maybe[+

ELSE "This may be a comment" +]
emit this if all but else fails[+

ENDIF "This may *also* be a comment" +]
```

`<full-expression>` may be any expression described in the EXPR expression function, including the use of apply-codes and value-names. If the expression yields an empty string, it is interpreted as *false*.

3.6.18 INCLUDE - Read in and emit a template block

The entire contents of the named file is inserted at this point. The contents of the file are processed for macro expansion. The arguments are eval-ed, so you may compute the name of the file to be included. The included file must not contain any incomplete function blocks. Function blocks are template text beginning with any of the macro functions 'CASE', 'DEFINE', 'FOR', 'IF' and 'WHILE'; extending through their respective terminating macro functions.

3.6.19 INVOKE - Invoke a User Defined Macro

User defined macros may be invoked explicitly or implicitly. If you invoke one implicitly, the macro must begin with the name of the defined macro. Consequently, this may **not** be a computed value. If you explicitly invoke a user defined macro, the macro begins with the macro name **INVOKE** followed by a *basic expression* that must yield a known user defined macro. A macro name _must_ be found, or AutoGen will issue a diagnostic and exit.

Arguments are passed to the invoked macro by name. The text following the macro name must consist of a series of names each of which is followed by an equal sign (=) and a *basic expression* that yields a string.

The string values may contain template macros that are parsed the first time the macro is processed and evaluated again every time the macro is evaluated.

3.6.20 RETURN - Leave an INVOKE-d (DEFINE) macro

This will unwind looping constructs inside of a DEFINE-d macro and return to the invocation point. The output files and diversions *are left alone*. This means it is unwise to start diversions in a DEFINEd macro and RETURN from it before you have handled the diversion. Unless you are careful. Here is some rope for you. Please be careful using it.

3.6.21 SELECT - Selection block for CASE function

This macro selects a block of text by matching an expression against the sample text expression evaluated in the **CASE** macro. See Section 3.6.3 [CASE], page 57.

You do not specify a **SELECT** macro with the word "select". Instead, you must use one of the 19 match operators described in the **CASE** macro description.

3.6.22 UNKNOWN - Either a user macro or a value name.

The macro text has started with a name not known to AutoGen. If, at run time, it turns out to be the name of a defined macro, then that macro is invoked. If it is not, then it is a conditional expression that is evaluated only if the name is defined at the time the macro is invoked.

You may not specify UNKNOWN explicitly.

3.6.23 WHILE - Conditionally loop over a Template Block

Conditionally repeated block. Its arguments are evaluated (see Section 3.6.15 [EXPR], page 60) and as long as the result is non-zero or a string with one or more bytes, then the condition is true and the text from that point until a matched ENDWHILE is emitted.

```
[+WHILE <full-expression> +]
emit things that are for the true condition[+

ENDWHILE +]
```

<full-expression> may be any expression described in the EXPR expression function, including the use of apply-codes and value-names. If the expression yields an empty string, it is interpreted as *false*.

3.6.24 Inserting text from a shell script

If the text between the start and end macro markers starts with an opening curly brace
('{') or is surrounded by back quotes (''), then the text is handed off to the server shell
for evaluation. The output to standard out is inserted into the document. If the text starts
with the curly brace, all the text is passed off as is to the shell. If surrounded by back
quotes, then the string is "cooked" before being handed off to the shell.

3.6.25 Inserting text from a scheme script

If the text between the start and end macro markers starts with a semi-colon or an opening
parenthesis, all the text is handed off to the Guile/scheme processor. If the last result is
text or a number, it is added (as text) to the output document.

3.7 Redirecting Output

AutoGen provides a means for redirecting the template output to different files or, in M4
parlance, to various diversions. It is accomplished by providing a set of Scheme functions
named out-* (see Section 3.4 [AutoGen Functions], page 26).

'out-push-new (see Section 3.4.44 [SCM out-push-new], page 35)'
> This allows you to logically "push" output files onto a stack. If you supply a
> string name, then a file by that name is created to hold the output. If you
> do not supply a name, then the text is written to a scratch pad and retrieved
> by passing a #t argument to the out-pop (see Section 3.4.42 [SCM out-pop],
> page 34) function.

'out-pop (see Section 3.4.42 [SCM out-pop], page 34)'
> This function closes the current output file and resumes output to the next
> one in the stack. At least one output must have been pushed onto the output
> stack with the cut-push-new (see Section 3.4.44 [SCM out-push-new], page 35)
> function. If #t is passed in as an argument, then the entire contents of the
> diversion (or file) is returned.

'out-suspend (see Section 3.4.46 [SCM out-suspend], page 35)'
> This function does not close the current output, but instead sets it aside for
> resumption by the given name with out-resume. The current output must have
> been pushed on the output queue with out-push-new (see Section 3.4.44 [SCM
> out-push-new], page 35).

'out-resume (see Section 3.4.45 [SCM out-resume], page 35)'
> This will put a named file descriptor back onto the top of stack so that it
> becomes the current output again.

'out-switch (see Section 3.4.47 [SCM out-switch], page 35)'
> This closes the current output and creates a new file, purging any preexisting
> one. This is a shortcut for "pop" followed by "push", but this can also be done
> at the base level.

'out-move (see Section 3.4.40 [SCM out-move], page 34)'
> Renames the current output file without closing it.

There are also several functions for determining the output status. See Section 3.4 [AutoGen Functions], page 26.

4 Augmenting AutoGen Features

AutoGen was designed to be simple to enhance. You can do it by providing shell commands, Guile/Scheme macros or callout functions that can be invoked as a Guile macro. Here is how you do these.

4.1 Shell Output Commands

Shell commands are run inside of a server process. This means that, unlike **make**, context is kept from one command to the next. Consequently, you can define a shell function in one place inside of your template and invoke it in another. You may also store values in shell variables for later reference. If you load functions from a file containing shell functions, they will remain until AutoGen exits.

If your shell script should determine that AutoGen should stop processing, the recommended method for stopping AutoGen is:

```
die "some error text"
```

That is a shell function added by AutoGen. It will send a SIGTERM to autogen and exit from the "persistent" shell.

4.2 Guile Macros

Guile also maintains context from one command to the next. This means you may define functions and variables in one place and reference them elsewhere. If your Scheme script should determine that AutoGen should stop processing, the recommended method for stopping AutoGen is:

```
(error "some error text")
```

4.3 Guile Callout Functions

Callout functions must be registered with Guile to work. This can be accomplished either by putting your routines into a shared library that contains a **void scm_init(void)** routine that registers these routines, or by building them into AutoGen.

To build them into AutoGen, you must place your routines in the source directory and name the files **exp*.c**. You also must have a stylized comment that **getdefs** can find that conforms to the following:

```
/*=gfunc <function-name>
 *
 *  what:     <short one-liner>
 *  general_use:
 *  string:   <invocation-name-string>
 *  exparg:   <name>, <description> [, ['optional'] [, 'list']]
 *  doc:      A long description telling people how to use
 *            this function.
=*/
SCM
ag_scm_<function-name>( SCM arg_name[, ...] )
{ <code> }
```

'gfunc'   You must have this exactly thus.

'<function-name>'
             This must follow C syntax for variable names

'<short one-liner>'
             This should be about a half a line long. It is used as a subsection title in this
             document.

'general_use:'
             You must supply this unless you are an AutoGen maintainer and are writing a
             function that queries or modifies the state of AutoGen.

'<invocation-name-string>'
             Normally, the *function-name* string will be transformed into a reasonable invo-
             cation name. However, that is not always true. If the result does not suit your
             needs, then supply an alternate string.

'exparg:'   You must supply one for each argument to your function. All optional argu-
             ments must be last. The last of the optional arguments may be a list, if you
             choose.

'doc:'   Please say something meaningful.

'[, ...]'   Do not actually specify an ANSI ellipsis here. You must provide for all the
             arguments you specified with *exparg*.

See the Guile documentation for more details. More information is also available in a
large comment at the beginning of the **agen5/snarf.tpl** template file.

4.4 AutoGen Macros

There are two kinds those you define yourself and AutoGen native. The user-defined macros
may be defined in your templates, See Section 3.6.7 [DEFINE], page 58.

As for AutoGen native macros, do not add any. It is easy to do, but I won't like it. The
basic functions needed to accomplish looping over and selecting blocks of text have proved
to be sufficient over a period of several years. New text transformations can be easily added
via any of the AutoGen extension methods, as discussed above.

5 Invoking autogen

AutoGen creates text files from templates using external definitions.

AutoGen is designed for generating program files that contain repetitive text with varied substitutions. The goal is to simplify the maintenance of programs that contain large amounts of repetitious text. This is especially valuable if there are several blocks of such text that must be kept synchronized.

One common example is the problem of maintaining the code required for processing program options. Processing options requires a minimum of four different constructs be kept in proper order in different places in your program. You need at least: The flag character in the flag string, code to process the flag when it is encountered, a global state variable or two, and a line in the usage text. You will need more things besides this if you choose to implement long option names, configuration file processing, environment variables and so on.

All of this can be done mechanically; with the proper templates and this program.

This chapter was generated by **AutoGen**, using the `agtexi-cmd` template and the option descriptions for the `autogen` program. This software is released under the GNU General Public License, version 3 or later.

5.1 autogen help/usage (--help)

This is the automatically generated usage text for autogen.

The text printed is the same whether selected with the `help` option (`--help`) or the `more-help` option (`--more-help`). `more-help` will print the usage text by passing it through a pager program. `more-help` is disabled on platforms without a working `fork(2)` function. The `PAGER` environment variable is used to select the program, defaulting to `more`. Both will exit with a status code of 0.

```
autogen (GNU AutoGen) - The Automated Program Generator - Ver. 5.18.6pre2
Usage:  autogen [ -<flag> [<val>] | --<name>[{=| }<val>] ]... [ <def-file> ]

The following options select definitions, templates and scheme functions
to use:

   Flg Arg Option-Name    Description
    -L Str templ-dirs      Search for templates in DIR
                                - may appear multiple times
    -T Str override-tpl    Use TPL-FILE for the template
                                - may not be preset
       Str definitions     Read definitions from FILE
                                - disabled as '--no-definitions'
                                - enabled by default
                                - may not be preset
       Str shell           name or path name of shell to use
    -m no  no-fmemopen     Do not use in-mem streams
       Str equate          characters considered equivalent
```

The following options modify how output is handled:

```
Flg Arg Option-Name    Description
 -b Str base-name      Specify NAME as the base name for output
                         - may not be preset
    no  source-time    set mod times to latest source
                         - disabled as '--no-source-time'
    no  writable       Allow output files to be writable
                         - disabled as '--not-writable'
```

The following options are often useful while debugging new templates:

```
Flg Arg Option-Name    Description
    Num loop-limit     Limit on increment loops
                         - is scalable with a suffix: k/K/m/M/g/G/t/T
                         - it must lie in one of the ranges:
                           -1 exactly, or
                           1 to 16777216
 -t Num timeout        Limit server shell operations to SECONDS
                         - it must be in the range:
                           0 to 3600
    KWd trace          tracing level of detail
    Str trace-out      tracing output file or filter
    no  show-defs      Show the definition tree
                         - may not be preset
    no  used-defines   Show the definitions used
                         - may not be preset
 -C no  core           Leave a core dump on a failure exit
```

These options can be used to control what gets processed in the
definitions files and template files:

```
Flg Arg Option-Name    Description
 -s Str skip-suffix    Skip the file with this SUFFIX
                         - prohibits the option 'select-suffix'
                         - may not be preset
                         - may appear multiple times
 -o Str select-suffix  specify this output suffix
                         - may not be preset
                         - may appear multiple times
 -D Str define         name to add to definition list
                         - may appear multiple times
 -U Str undefine       definition list removal pattern
                         - an alternate for 'define'
```

This option is used to automate dependency tracking:

```
Flg Arg Option-Name    Description
 -M opt make-dep        emit make dependency file
                            - may not be preset
                            - may appear multiple times
```

help, version and option handling:

```
Flg Arg Option-Name    Description
 -R Str reset-option    reset an option's state
 -v opt version         output version information and exit
 -? no  help            display extended usage information and exit
 -! no  more-help       extended usage information passed thru pager
 -u no  usage           abbreviated usage to stdout
 -> opt save-opts       save the option state to a config file
 -< Str load-opts       load options from a config file
                            - disabled as '--no-load-opts'
                            - may appear multiple times
```

Options are specified by doubled hyphens and their name or by a single
hyphen and the flag character.
AutoGen creates text files from templates using external definitions.

The following option preset mechanisms are supported:
 - reading file $HOME
 - reading file ./.autogenrc
 - examining environment variables named AUTOGEN_*

The valid "trace" option keywords are:
  nothing   debug-message server-shell templates   block-macros
  expressions   everything
  or an integer from 0 through 6
AutoGen is a tool designed for generating program files that contain
repetitive text with varied substitutions.
Packaged by Bruce (2015-08-08)
Report autogen bugs to bkorb@gnu.org

5.2 input-select options

The following options select definitions, templates and scheme functions to use.

templ-dirs option (-L).

This is the "search for templates in dir" option. This option takes a string argument DIR.

This option has some usage constraints. It:

- may appear an unlimited number of times.

Add a directory to the list of directories `autogen` searches when opening a template, either as the primary template or an included one. The last entry has the highest priority in the search list. That is to say, they are searched in reverse order.

override-tpl option (-T).

This is the "use `tpl-file` for the template" option. This option takes a string argument `TPL-FILE`.

This option has some usage constraints. It:

- may not be preset with environment variables or configuration (rc/ini) files.

Definition files specify the standard template that is to be expanded. This option will override that name and expand a different template.

lib-template option (-l).

This is the "load autogen macros from `tpl-file`" option. This option takes a string argument `TPL-FILE`.

This option has some usage constraints. It:

- may appear an unlimited number of times.

DEFINE macros are saved from this template file for use in processing the main macro file. Template text aside from the DEFINE macros is is ignored.

Do not use this. Instead, use the INCLUDE macro in your template.

NOTE: THIS OPTION IS DEPRECATED

definitions option.

This is the "read definitions from `file`" option. This option takes a string argument `FILE`. This option has some usage constraints. It:

- can be disabled with –no-definitions.
- It is enabled by default.
- may not be preset with environment variables or configuration (rc/ini) files.

Use this argument to specify the input definitions file with a command line option. If you do not specify this option, then there must be a command line argument that specifies the file, even if only to specify stdin with a hyphen (-). Specify, `--no-definitions` when you wish to process a template without any active AutoGen definitions.

shell option.

This is the "name or path name of shell to use" option. This option takes a string argument `shell`.

This option has some usage constraints. It:

- must be compiled in by defining `SHELL_ENABLED` during the compilation.

By default, when AutoGen is built, the configuration is probed for a reasonable Bourne-like shell to use for shell script processing. If a particular template needs an alternate shell, it must be specified with this option on the command line, with an environment variable (`SHELL`) or in the configuration/initialization file.

no-fmemopen option (-m).

This is the "do not use in-mem streams" option. If the local C library supports "fopencookie(3GNU)", or "funopen(3BSD)" then AutoGen prefers to use in-memory stream buffer opens instead of anonymous files. This may lead to problems if there is a shortage of virtual memory. If, for a particular application, you run out of memory, then specify this option. This is unlikely in a modern 64-bit virtual memory environment.

On platforms without these functions, the option is accepted but ignored. fmemopen(POSIX) is not adequate because its string buffer is not reallocatable. open_memstream(POSIX) is *also* not adequate because the stream is only opened for output. AutoGen needs a reallocatable buffer available for both reading and writing.

equate option.

This is the "characters considered equivalent" option. This option takes a string argument char-list. This option will alter the list of characters considered equivalent. The default are the three characters, "_-^". (The last is conventional on a Tandem/HP-NonStop and I used to do a lot of work on Tandems.)

5.3 out-handling options

The following options modify how output is handled.

base-name option (-b).

This is the "specify name as the base name for output" option. This option takes a string argument NAME.

This option has some usage constraints. It:

- may not be preset with environment variables or configuration (rc/ini) files.

A template may specify the exact name of the output file. Normally, it does not. Instead, the name is composed of the base name of the definitions file with suffixes appended. This option will override the base name derived from the definitions file name. This is required if there is no definitions file and advisable if definitions are being read from stdin. If the definitions are being read from standard in, the base name defaults to stdin. Any leading directory components in the name will be silently removed. If you wish the output file to appear in a particular directory, it is recommended that you "cd" into that directory first, or use directory names in the format specification for the output suffix lists, See Section 3.1 [pseudo macro], page 21.

source-time option.

This is the "set mod times to latest source" option.

This option has some usage constraints. It:

- can be disabled with –no-source-time.

If you stamp your output files with the DNE macro output, then your output files will always be different, even if the content has not really changed. If you use this option, then the modification time of the output files will change only if the input files change. This will help reduce unneeded builds.

writable option.

This is the "allow output files to be writable" option.

This option has some usage constraints. It:

- can be disabled with –not-writable.

This option will leave output files writable. Normally, output files are read-only.

5.4 debug-tpl options

The following options are often useful while debugging new templates. They specify limits that prevent the template from taking overly long or producing more output than expected.

loop-limit option.

This is the "limit on increment loops" option. This option takes a number argument `lim`. This option prevents runaway loops. For example, if you accidentally specify, "FOR x (for-from 1) (for-to -1) (for-by 1)", it will take a long time to finish. If you do have more than 256 entries in tables, you will need to specify a new limit with this option.

timeout option (-t).

This is the "limit server shell operations to `seconds`" option. This option takes a number argument `SECONDS`.

This option has some usage constraints. It:

- must be compiled in by defining `SHELL_ENABLED` during the compilation.

AutoGen works with a shell server process. Most normal commands will complete in less than 10 seconds. If, however, your commands need more time than this, use this option.

The valid range is 0 to 3600 seconds (1 hour). Zero will disable the server time limit.

trace option.

This is the "tracing level of detail" option. This option takes a keyword argument `level`.

This option has some usage constraints. It:

- This option takes a keyword as its argument. The argument sets an enumeration value that can be tested by comparing the option value macro (OPT_VALUE_TRACE). The available keywords are:

      nothing   debug-message server-shell
      templates   block-macros expressions
      everything

  or their numeric equivalent.

This option will cause AutoGen to display a trace of its template processing. There are six levels, each level including messages from the previous levels:

'`nothing`' Does no tracing at all (default)

‘debug-message’
>	Print messages from the "DEBUG" AutoGen macro (see Section 3.6.6 [DE-BUG], page 58).

‘server-shell’
>	Traces all input and output to the server shell. This includes a shell "independent" initialization script about 30 lines long. Its output is discarded and not inserted into any template.

‘templates’
>	Traces the invocation of DEFINEd macros and INCLUDEs

‘block-macros’
>	Traces all block macros. The above, plus IF, FOR, CASE and WHILE.

‘expressions’
>	Displays the results of expression evaluations.

‘everything’
>	Displays the invocation of every AutoGen macro, even TEXT macros (i.e. the text outside of macro quotes). Additionally, if you rebuild the "expr.ini" file with debugging enabled, then all calls to AutoGen defined scheme functions will also get logged:

```
cd ${top_builddir}/agen5
DEBUG_ENABLED=true bash bootstrap.dir expr.ini
make CFLAGS='-g -DDEBUG_ENABLED=1'
```

>	Be aware that you cannot rebuild this source in this way without first having installed the autogen executable in your search path. Because of this, "expr.ini" is in the distributed source list, and not in the dependencies.

trace-out option.

This is the "tracing output file or filter" option. This option takes a string argument file. The output specified may be a file name, a file that is appended to, or, if the option argument begins with the pipe operator (|), a command that will receive the tracing output as standard in. For example, --traceout='| less' will run the trace output through the less program. Appending to a file is specified by preceding the file name with two greater-than characters (>>).

show-defs option.

This is the "show the definition tree" option.

This option has some usage constraints. It:

- must be compiled in by defining DEBUG_ENABLED during the compilation.
- may not be preset with environment variables or configuration (rc/ini) files.

This will print out the complete definition tree before processing the template.

used-defines option.

This is the "show the definitions used" option.

This option has some usage constraints. It:

- may not be preset with environment variables or configuration (rc/ini) files.

This will print out the names of definition values searched for during the processing of the template, whether actually found or not. There may be other referenced definitions in a template in portions of the template not evaluated. Some of the names listed may be computed names and others AutoGen macro arguments. This is not a means for producing a definitive, all-encompassing list of all and only the values used from a definition file. This is intended as an aid to template documentation only.

core option (-C).

This is the "leave a core dump on a failure exit" option.

This option has some usage constraints. It:

- must be compiled in by defining `HAVE_SYS_RESOURCE_H` during the compilation.

Many systems default to a zero sized core limit. If the system has the sys/resource.h header and if this option is supplied, then in the failure exit path, autogen will attempt to set the soft core limit to whatever the hard core limit is. If that does not work, then an administrator must raise the hard core size limit.

5.5 processing options

These options can be used to control what gets processed in the definitions files and template files. They specify which outputs and parts of outputs to produce.

skip-suffix option (-s).

This is the "skip the file with this `suffix`" option. This option takes a string argument `SUFFIX`.

This option has some usage constraints. It:

- may appear an unlimited number of times.
- may not be preset with environment variables or configuration (rc/ini) files.
- must not appear in combination with any of the following options: select-suffix.

Occasionally, it may not be desirable to produce all of the output files specified in the template. (For example, only the `.h` header file, but not the `.c` program text.) To do this specify `--skip-suffix=c` on the command line.

select-suffix option (-o).

This is the "specify this output suffix" option. This option takes a string argument `SUFFIX`.

This option has some usage constraints. It:

- may appear an unlimited number of times.

- may not be preset with environment variables or configuration (rc/ini) files.

If you wish to override the suffix specifications in the template, you can use one or more copies of this option. See the suffix specification in the Section 3.1 [pseudo macro], page 21 section of the info doc.

define option (-D).

This is the "name to add to definition list" option. This option takes a string argument `value`.

This option has some usage constraints. It:

- may appear an unlimited number of times.

The AutoGen define names are used for the following purposes:

1. Sections of the AutoGen definitions may be enabled or disabled by using C-style #ifdef and #ifndef directives.

2. When defining a value for a name, you may specify the index for a particular value. That index may be a literal value, a define option or a value #define-d in the definitions themselves.

3. The name of a file may be prefixed with `$NAME/`. The `$NAME` part of the name string will be replaced with the define-d value for `NAME`.

4. When AutoGen is finished loading the definitions, the defined values are exported to the environment with, `putenv(3)`. These values can then be used in shell scripts with `${NAME}` references and in templates with (getenv "NAME").

5. While processing a template, you may specify an index to retrieve a specific value. That index may also be a define-d value.

It is entirely equivalent to place this name in the exported environment. Internally, that is what AutoGen actually does with this option.

undefine option (-U).

This is the "definition list removal pattern" option. This option takes a string argument `name-pat`.

This option has some usage constraints. It:

- may appear an unlimited number of times.
- may not be preset with environment variables or configuration (rc/ini) files.

Similar to 'C', AutoGen uses `#ifdef/#ifndef` preprocessing directives. This option will cause the matching names to be removed from the list of defined values.

5.6 dep-track options

This option is used to automate dependency tracking.

make-dep option (-M).

This is the "emit make dependency file" option. This option takes an optional string argument **type**.

This option has some usage constraints. It:

- may appear an unlimited number of times.
- may not be preset with environment variables or configuration (rc/ini) files.

This option behaves fairly closely to the way the `-M` series of options work with the gcc compiler, except that instead of just emitting the predecessor dependencies, this also emits the successor dependencies (output target files). By default, the output dependency information will be placed in `<base-name>.d`, but may also be specified with `-MF<file>`. The time stamp on this file will be manipulated so that it will be one second older than the oldest primary output file.

The target in this dependency file will normally be the dependency file name, but may also be overridden with `-MT<targ-name>`. AutoGen will not alter the contents of that file, but it may create it and it will adjust the modification time to match the start time.

NB: these second letters are part of the option argument, so `-MF <file>` must have the space character quoted or omitted, and `-M "F <file>"` is acceptable because the F is part of the option argument.

`-M` may be followed by any of the letters M, F, P, T, Q, D, or G. However, only F, Q, T and P are meaningful. All but F have somewhat different meanings. `-MT<name>` is interpreted as meaning `<name>` is a sentinel file that will depend on all inputs (templates and definition files) and all the output files will depend on this sentinel file. It is suitable for use as a real make target. Q is treated identically to T, except dollar characters ('$') are doubled. P causes a special clean (clobber) phoney rule to be inserted into the make file fragment. An empty rule is always created for building the list of targets.

This is the recommended usage:

```
-MFwhatever-you-like.dep -MTyour-sentinel-file -MP
```

and then in your `Makefile`, make the `autogen` rule:

```
-include whatever-you-like.dep
clean_targets += clean-your-sentinel-file

your-sentinel-file:
    autogen -MT$@ -MF$*.d .....

local-clean :
    rm -f $(clean_targets)
```

The modification time on the dependency file is adjusted to be one second before the earliest time stamp of any other output file. Consequently, it is suitable for use as the sentinel file testifying to the fact the program was successfully run. (`-include` is the GNU make way of specifying "include it if it exists". Your make must support that feature or your bootstrap process must create the file.)

All of this may also be specified using the `DEPENDENCIES_OUTPUT` or `AUTOGEN_MAKE_DEP` environment variables. If defined, dependency information will be output. If defined with white space free text that is something other than **true**, **false**, **yes**, **no**, **0** or **1**, then the string is taken to be an output file name. If it contains a string of white space characters, the first token is as above and the second token is taken to be the target (sentinel) file as -MT in the paragraphs above. **DEPENDENCIES_OUTPUT** will be ignored if there are multiple sequences of white space characters or if its contents are, specifically, **false**, **no** or **0**.

5.7 presetting/configuring autogen

Any option that is not marked as *not presettable* may be preset by loading values from configuration ("rc" or "ini") files, and values from environment variables named **AUTOGEN** and **AUTOGEN_<OPTION_NAME>**. **<OPTION_NAME>** must be one of the options listed above in upper case and segmented with underscores. The **AUTOGEN** variable will be tokenized and parsed like the command line. The remaining variables are tested for existence and their values are treated like option arguments.

libopts will search in 2 places for configuration files:

- $HOME
- $PWD

The environment variables **HOME**, and **PWD** are expanded and replaced when **autogen** runs. For any of these that are plain files, they are simply processed. For any that are directories, then a file named .autogenrc is searched for within that directory and processed.

Configuration files may be in a wide variety of formats. The basic format is an option name followed by a value (argument) on the same line. Values may be separated from the option name with a colon, equal sign or simply white space. Values may be continued across multiple lines by escaping the newline with a backslash.

Multiple programs may also share the same initialization file. Common options are collected at the top, followed by program specific segments. The segments are separated by lines like:

```
[AUTOGEN]
```

or by

```
<?program autogen>
```

Do not mix these styles within one configuration file.

Compound values and carefully constructed string values may also be specified using XML syntax:

```
<option-name>
    <sub-opt>...&lt;...&gt;...</sub-opt>
</option-name>
```

yielding an **option-name.sub-opt** string value of

```
"...<...>..."
```

AutoOpts does not track suboptions. You simply note that it is a hierarchicly valued option. **AutoOpts** does provide a means for searching the associated name/value pair list (see: optionFindValue).

The command line options relating to configuration and/or usage help are:

version (-v)

Print the program version to standard out, optionally with licensing information, then exit 0. The optional argument specifies how much licensing detail to provide. The default is to print just the version. The licensing infomation may be selected with an option argument. Only the first letter of the argument is examined:

'version'   Only print the version. This is the default.

'copyright'
            Name the copyright usage licensing terms.

'verbose'   Print the full copyright usage licensing terms.

usage (-u)

Print abbreviated usage to standard out, then exit 0.

reset-option (-R)

Resets the specified option to the compiled-in initial state. This will undo anything that may have been set by configuration files. The option argument may be either the option flag character or its long name.

5.8 autogen exit status

One of the following exit values will be returned:

'0 (EXIT_SUCCESS)'
            Successful program execution.

'1 (EXIT_OPTION_ERROR)'
            The command options were misconfigured.

'2 (EXIT_BAD_TEMPLATE)'
            An error was encountered processing the template.

'3 (EXIT_BAD_DEFINITIONS)'
            The definitions could not be deciphered.

'4 (EXIT_LOAD_ERROR)'
            An error was encountered during the load phase.

'5 (EXIT_FS_ERROR)'
            a file system error stopped the program.

'6 (EXIT_NO_MEM)'
            Insufficient memory to operate.

'128 (EXIT_SIGNAL)'
            autogen exited due to catching a signal. If your template includes string formatting, a number argument to a "%s" formatting element will trigger a segmentation fault. Autogen will catch the seg fault signal and exit with AUTOGEN_EXIT_SIGNAL(5). Alternatively, AutoGen may have been interrupted with a kill(2) signal.

            Subtract 128 from the actual exit code to detect the signal number.

'66 (EX_NOINPUT)'
>   A specified configuration file could not be loaded.

'70 (EX_SOFTWARE)'
>   libopts had an internal operational error.   Please report it to autogen-
>   users@lists.sourceforge.net. Thank you.

5.9 autogen Examples

Here is how the man page is produced:

```
autogen -Tagman-cmd.tpl -MFman-dep -MTstamp-man opts.def
```

This command produced this man page from the AutoGen option definition file. It
overrides the template specified in `opts.def` (normally `options.tpl`) and uses `agman-cmd.tpl`. It also sets the make file dependency output to `man-dep` and the sentinel file
(time stamp file) to `man-stamp`. The base of the file name is derived from the defined
`prog-name`.

The texi invocation document is produced via:

```
autogen -Tagtexi-cmd.tpl -MFtexi-dep -MTtexi-stamp opts.def
```

6 Configuring and Installing

6.1 Configuring AutoGen

AutoGen is configured and built using Libtool, Automake and Autoconf. Consequently, you can install it wherever you wish using the '`--prefix`' and other options. To the various configuration options supplied by these tools, AutoGen adds a few of its own:

'`--disable-shell`'

> AutoGen is now capable of acting as a CGI forms server, See Section 6.2 [AutoGen CGI], page 81. As such, it will gather its definitions using either '`GET`' or '`POST`' methods. All you need to do is have a template named `cgi.tpl` handy or specify a different one with a command line option.
>
> However, doing this without disabling the server shell brings considerable risk. If you were to pass user input to a script that contained, say, the classic "'`rm -rf /`'", you might have a problem. This configuration option will cause shell template commands to simply return the command string as the result. No mistakes. Much safer. Strongly recommended. The default is to have server shell scripting enabled.
>
> Disabling the shell will have some build side effects, too.
>
> * Many of the make check tests will fail, since they assume a working server shell.
> * The getdefs and columns programs are not built. The options are distributed as definition files and they cannot be expanded with a shell-disabled AutoGen.
> * Similarly, the documentation cannot be regenerated because the documentation templates depend on subshell functionality.

'`--enable-debug`'

> Turning on AutoGen debugging enables very detailed inspection of the input definitions and monitoring shell script processing. These options are not particularly useful to anyone not directly involved in maintaining AutoGen. If you do choose to enable AutoGen debugging, be aware that the usage page was generated without these options, so when the build process reaches the documentation rebuild, there will be a failure. '`cd`' into the `agen5` build directory, '`make`' the '`autogen.texi`' file and all will be well thereafter.

'`--with-regex-header`'
'`--with-header-path`'
'`--with-regex-lib`'

> These three work together to specify how to compile with and link to a particular POSIX regular expression library. The value for `--with-regex-header=value` must be the name of the relevant header file. The AutoGen sources will attempt to include that source with a `#include <value>` C preprocessing statement. The *path* from the `--with-header-path=path` will be added to `CPPFLAGS` as `-Ipath`. The *lib-specs* from `--with-regex-lib=lib-specs` will be added to `LDFLAGS` without any adornment.

6.2 AutoGen as a CGI server

AutoGen is now capable of acting as a CGI forms server. It behaves as a CGI server if the definitions input is from stdin and the environment variable REQUEST_METHOD is defined and set to either "GET" or "POST". If set to anything else, AutoGen will exit with a failure message. When set to one of those values, the CGI data will be converted to AutoGen definitions (see Chapter 2 [Definitions File], page 7) and the template named "cgi.tpl" will be processed.

This works by including the name of the real template to process in the form data and having the "cgi.tpl" template include that template for processing. I do this for processing the form http://autogen.sourceforge.net/conftest.html. The "cgi.tpl" looks approximately like this:

```
<? AutoGen5 Template ?>
<?
IF (not (exist? "template"))                    ?><?
  form-error                                    ?><?

ELIF (=* (get "template") "/")                  ?><?
  form-error                                    ?><?

ELIF (define tpl-file (string-append "cgi-tpl/"
                    (get "template")))
        (access? tpl-file R_OK)                 ?><?
  INCLUDE (. tpl-file)                          ?><?

ELIF (set! tpl-file (string-append tpl-file ".tpl"))
        (access? tpl-file R_OK)                 ?><?
  INCLUDE (. tpl-file)                          ?><?

ELSE                                            ?><?
  form-error                                    ?><?
ENDIF                                           ?>
```

This forces the template to be found in the "cgi-tpl/" directory. Note also that there is no suffix specified in the pseudo macro (see Section 3.1 [pseudo macro], page 21). That tells AutoGen to emit the output to stdout.

The output is actually spooled until it is complete so that, in the case of an error, the output can be discarded and a proper error message can be written in its stead.

Please also note that it is advisable, *especially* for network accessible machines, to configure AutoGen (see Section 6.1 [configuring], page 80) with shell processing disabled (--disable-shell). That will make it impossible for any referenced template to hand data to a subshell for interpretation.

6.3 Signal Names

When AutoGen is first built, it tries to use psignal(3), sys_siglist, strsigno(3) and strsignal(3) from the host operating system. If your system does not supply these, the AutoGen distribution will. However, it will use the distributed mapping and this mapping is unlikely to match what your system uses. This can be fixed. Once you have installed autogen, the mapping can be rebuilt on the host operating system. To do so, you must perform the following steps:

1. Build and install AutoGen in a place where it will be found in your search path.
2. `cd ${top_srcdir}/compat`
3. 'autogen strsignal.def'
4. Verify the results by examining the `strsignal.h` file produced.
5. Re-build and re-install AutoGen.

If you have any problems or peculiarities that cause this process to fail on your platform, please send me copies of the header files containing the signal names and numbers, along with the full path names of these files. I will endeavor to fix it. There is a shell script inside of `strsignal.def` that tries to hunt down the information.

6.4 Installing AutoGen

There are several files that get installed. The number depend whether or not both shared and archive libraries are to be installed. The following assumes that everything is installed relative to `$prefix`. You can, of course, use `configure` to place these files where you wish.

NB AutoGen does not contain any compiled-in path names. All support directories are located via option processing, the environment variable `HOME` or finding the directory where the executable came from.

The installed files are:

1. The executables in `bin` (autogen, getdefs and columns).
2. The AutoOpts link libraries as `lib/libopts.*`.
3. An include file in `include/options.h`, needed for Automated Option Processing (see next chapter).
4. Several template files and a scheme script in `share/autogen`, needed for Automated Option Processing (see Chapter 7 [AutoOpts], page 83), parsing definitions written with scheme syntax (see Section 2.4 [Dynamic Text], page 11), the templates for producing documentation for your program (see Section 7.5.9 [documentation attributes], page 118), autoconf test macros, and AutoFSM.
5. Info-style help files as `info/autogen.info*`. These files document AutoGen, the option processing library AutoOpts, and several add-on components.
6. The three man pages for the three executables are installed in man/man1.

This program, library and supporting files can be installed with three commands:

- <src-dir>/configure [<configure-options>]
- make
- make install

However, you may wish to insert 'make check' before the 'make install' command.

If you do perform a 'make check' and there are any failures, you will find the results in <module>/test/FAILURES. Needless to say, I would be interested in seeing the contents of those files and any associated messages. If you choose to go on and analyze one of these failures, you will need to invoke the test scripts individually. You may do so by specifying the test (or list of test) in the TESTS make variable, thus:

```
gmake TESTS=test-name.test check
```

I specify **gmake** because most makes will not let you override internal definitions with command line arguments. **gmake** does.

All of the AutoGen tests are written to honor the contents of the **VERBOSE** environment variable. Normally, any commentary generated during a test run is discarded unless the **VERBOSE** environment variable is set. So, to see what is happening during the test, you might invoke the following with *bash* or *ksh*:

```
VERBOSE=1 gmake TESTS="for.test forcomma.test" check
```

Or equivalently with *csh*:

```
env VERBOSE=1 gmake TESTS="for.test forcomma.test" check
```

7 Automated Option Processing

AutoOpts 41.1 is bundled with AutoGen. It is a tool that virtually eliminates the hassle of processing options and keeping man pages, info docs and usage text up to date. This package allows you to specify several program attributes, thousands of option types and many option attributes. From this, it then produces all the code necessary to parse and handle the command line and configuration file options, and the documentation that should go with your program as well.

All the features notwithstanding, some applications simply have well-established command line interfaces. Even still, those programs may use the configuration file parsing portion of the library. See the "AutoOpts Features" and "Configuration File Format" sections.

7.1 AutoOpts Features

AutoOpts supports option processing; option state saving; and program documentation with innumerable features. Here, we list a few obvious ones and some important ones, but the full list is really defined by all the attributes defined in the Section 7.5 [Option Definitions], page 90 section.

1. POSIX-compliant short (flag) option processing.

2. GNU-style long options processing. Long options are recognized without case sensitivity, and they may be abbreviated.

3. Environment variable initializations, See Section 7.10.4 [environrc], page 153.

4. Initialization from configuration files (aka RC or INI files), and saving the option state back into one, See Section 7.10.1 [loading rcfile], page 147.

5. Config files may be partitioned. One config file may be used by several programs by partitioning it with lines containing, [PROGRAM_NAME] or <?program-name>, See Section 7.10.1 [loading rcfile], page 147.

6. Config files may contain AutoOpts directives. <?auto-options [[option-text]]> may be used to set **AutoOpts** option processing options. Viz., GNU usage layout versus **AutoOpts** conventional layout, and **misuse-usage** versus **no-misuse-usage**, See Section 7.5.1.1 [usage attributes], page 91.

7. Options may be marked as `dis-abled` with a disablement prefix. Such options may default to either an enabled or a disabled state. You may also provide an enablement prefix, too, e.g., `--allow-mumble` and `--prevent-mumble` (see Section 7.5.5.2 [Common Attributes], page 106).

8. Verify that required options are present between the minimum and maximum number of times on the command line. Verify that conflicting options do not appear together. Verify that options requiring the presence of other options are, in fact, used in the presence of other options. See See Section 7.5.5.2 [Common Attributes], page 106, and See Section 7.5.5.4 [Option Conflict Attributes], page 108.

9. There are several Section 7.5.10 [automatic options], page 121. They will have short flags if any options have option flags and the flags are not suppressed. The associated flag may be altered or suppressed by specifying no value or an alternate character for `xxx-value;` in the option definition file. `xxx` is the name of the option below:

'`--help`'
'`--more-help`'
> These are always available. '`--more-help`' will pass the full usage text through a pager.

'`--usage`' This is added to the option list if `usage-opt` is specified. It yields the abbreviated usage to `stdout`.

'`--version`'
> This is added to the option list if `version = xxx;` is specified.

'`--load-opts`'
'`--save-opts`'
> These are added to the option list if `homerc` is specified. Mostly. If, `disable-save` is specified, then `--save-opts` is disabled.

10. Various forms of main procedures can be added to the output, See Section 7.5.4 [Generated main], page 100. There are four basic forms:

   a. A program that processes the arguments and writes to standard out portable shell commands containing the digested options.

   b. A program that will generate portable shell commands to parse the defined options. The expectation is that this result will be copied into a shell script and used there.

   c. A `for-each` main that will invoke a named function once for either each non-option argument on the command line or, if there are none, then once for each non-blank, non-comment input line read from stdin.

   d. A main procedure of your own design. Its code can be supplied in the option description template or by incorporating another template.

11. There are several methods for handling option arguments.

   • nothing (see Section 7.6.13 [OPT_ARG], page 128) option argument strings are globally available.

   • user supplied (see Section 7.5.7 [Option Argument Handling], page 115)

   • stack option arguments (see Section 7.5.7 [Option Argument Handling], page 115)

   • integer numbers (see Section 7.5.6.2 [arg-type number], page 111)

- true or false valued (see Section 7.5.6.3 [arg-type boolean], page 111)
- enumerated list of names (see Section 7.5.6.4 [arg-type keyword], page 112)
- an enumeration (membership) set (see Section 7.5.6.5 [arg-type set membership], page 112)
- a list of name/value pairs (option **subopts**) (see Section 7.5.6.6 [arg-type hierarchy], page 113)
- a time duration or a specific time and date
- validated file name (see Section 7.5.6.7 [arg-type file name], page 113)
- optional option argument (see Section 7.5.6.11 [arg-optional], page 115)

12. The generated usage text can be emitted in either AutoOpts standard format (maximizing the information about each option), or GNU-ish normal form. The default form is selected by either specifying or not specifying the **gnu-usage** attribute (see Section 7.5.3 [information attributes], page 98). This can be overridden by the user himself with the **AUTOOPTS_USAGE** environment variable. If it exists and is set to the string 'gnu', it will force GNU-ish style format; if it is set to the string 'autoopts', it will force AutoOpts standard format; otherwise, it will have no effect.

13. The usage text and many other strings are stored in a single character array (see Section 3.5.56 [SCM string-table-new], page 52). This reduces fixup costs when loading the program or library. The downside is that if GCC detects that any of these strings are used in a printf format, you may get the warning, embedded '\0' in format. To eliminate the warning, you must provide GCC with the -Wno-format-contains-nul option.

14. If you compile with **ENABLE_NLS** defined and _() defined to a localization function (e.g. **gettext(3GNU)**), then the option processing code will be localizable (see Section 7.16 [i18n], page 180). Provided also that you do not define the **no-xlate** attribute to *anything* (see Section 7.5.1.4 [presentation attributes], page 96).

    You should also ensure that the **ATTRIBUTE_FORMAT_ARG()** gets #define-ed to something useful. There is an autoconf macro named **AG_COMPILE_FORMAT_ARG** in **ag_macros.m4** that will set it appropriately for you. If you do not do this, then translated formatting strings may trigger GCC compiler warnings.

15. Provides a callable routine to parse a text string as if it were from one of the rc/ini/config files, hereafter referred to as a configuration file.

16. By adding a 'doc' and 'arg-name' attributes to each option, AutoGen will also be able to produce a man page and the 'invoking' section of a texinfo document.

17. Intermingled option processing. AutoOpts options may be intermingled with command line operands and options processed with other parsing techniques. This is accomplished by setting the **allow-errors** (see Section 7.5.1 [program attributes], page 90) attribute. When processing reaches a point where **optionProcess** (see Section 7.6.32.14 [libopts-optionProcess], page 139) needs to be called again, the current option can be set with **RESTART_OPT(n)** (see Section 7.6.19 [RESTART_OPT], page 129) before calling **optionProcess**.

    See: See Section 7.5.2 [library attributes], page 97.

18. Library suppliers can specify command line options that their client programs will accept. They specify option definitions that get #include-d into the client option

definitions and they specify an "anchor" option that has a callback and must be invoked. That will give the library access to the option state for their options.

19. library options. An AutoOpt-ed library may export its options for use in an AutoOpt-ed program. This is done by providing an option definition file that client programs `#include` into their own option definitions. See "AutoOpt-ed Library for AutoOpt-ed Program" (see Section 7.5.2.1 [lib and program], page 97) for more details.

7.2 AutoOpts Licensing

When AutoGen is installed, the AutoOpts project is installed with it. AutoOpts includes various AutoGen templates and a pair of shared libraries. These libraries may be used under the terms of version 3 of the GNU Lesser General Public License (LGPL).

One of these libraries (`libopts`) is needed by programs that are built using AutoOpts generated code. This library is available as a separate "tear-off" source tarball. It is redistributable for use under either of two licenses: The above mentioned GNU Lesser General Public License, and the advertising-clause-free BSD license. Both of these license terms are incorporated into appropriate COPYING files included with the `libopts` source tarball. This source may be incorporated into your package with the following simple commands:

```
rm -rf libopts libopts-*
gunzip -c `autoopts-config libsrc` | \
    tar -xvf -
mv libopts-*.*.* libopts
```

View the `libopts/README` file for further integration information.

7.3 Developer and User Notes

The formatting of the usage message can be controlled with the use of the `AUTOOPTS_USAGE` environment variable. If it contains any of five possible comma separated values, it will affect `libopts` behavior. Any extraneous or conflicting data will cause its value to be ignored.

If the program attributes `long-usage` and `short-usage` have been specified (see Section 7.5.1.1 [usage attributes], page 91), these strings are used for displaying full usage and abbreviated usage. "Full usage" is used when usage is requested, "abbreviated usage" when a usage error is detected. If these strings are not provided, the usage text is computed.

The `AUTOOPTS_USAGE` environment variable may be set to the comma and/or white space separated list of the following strings:

'compute' Ignore the provision of `long-usage` and `short-usage` attributes, and compute the usage strings. This is useful, for example, if you wish to regenerate the basic form of these strings and either tweak them or translate them. The methods used to compute the usage text are not suitable for translation.

'gnu' The format of the usage text will be displayed in GNU-normal form. The default display for `--version` will be to include a note on licensing terms.

'autoopts'

The format of the extended usage will be in AutoOpts' native layout. The default version display will be one line of text with the last token the version. `gnu` and `autoopts` conflict and may not be used together.

'no-misuse-usage'

When an option error is made on the command line, the abbreviated usage text will be suppressed. An error message and the method for getting full usage information will be displayed.

'misuse-usage'

When an option error is made on the command line, the abbreviated usage text will be shown. `misuse-usage` and `no-misuse-usage` conflict and may not be used together.

`misuse-usage` and `autoopts` are the defaults. These defaults may be flipped to `no-misuse-usage` and `gnu` by specifying `gnu-usage` and `no-misuse-usage` program attributes, respectively, in the option definition file.

Note for developers:

The templates used to implement AutoOpts depend heavily upon token pasting. That means that if you name an option, `debug`, for example, the generated header will expect to be able to emit `#define` macros such as this:

```
#define DESC(n) (autogenOptions.pOptDesc[INDEX_OPT_## n])
```

and expect DESC(DEBUG) to expand correctly into (autogenOptions.pOptDesc[INDEX_OPT_DEBUG]). If DEBUG is `#defined` to something else, then that something else will be in the above expansion.

If you discover you are having strange problems like this, you may wish to use some variation of the `guard-option-names` See Section 7.5.1 [program attributes], page 90.

7.4 Quick Start

Since it is generally easier to start with a simple example than it is to look at the options that AutoGen uses itself, here is a very simple AutoOpts example. You can copy this example out of the Info file and into a source file to try it. You can then embellish it into what you really need. For more extensive examples, you can also examine the help output and option definitions for the commands `columns`, `getdefs` and `autogen` itself.

If you are looking for a more extensive example, you may search the autogen sources for files named `*opts.def`. `xml2ag` is ridiculous and `autogen` is very lengthy, but `columns` and `getdefs` are not too difficult. The `sharutils` sources are fairly reasonable, too.

7.4.1 Example option requirements

For our simple example, assume you have a program named `check` that takes two options:

1. A list of directories to check over for whatever it is `check` does. You want this option available as a POSIX-style flag option and a GNU long option. You want to allow as many of these as the user wishes.

2. An option to show or not show the definition tree being used. Only one occurrence is to be allowed, specifying one or the other.

7.4.2 Example option definitions

First, specify your program attributes and its options to AutoOpts, as with the following example.

```
AutoGen Definitions options;
prog-name     = check;
prog-title    = "Checkout Automated Options";
long-opts;
gnu-usage;     /* GNU style preferred to default */

main = { main-type = shell-process; };

flag = {
    name      = check-dirs;
    value     = L;         /* flag style option character */
    arg-type  = string;    /* option argument indication  */
    max       = NOLIMIT;   /* occurrence limit (none)     */
    stack-arg;             /* save opt args in a stack     */
    descrip   = "Checkout directory list";
    doc       = 'name of each directory that is to be "checked out".';
};

flag = {
    name      = show_defs;
    descrip   = "Show the definition tree";
    disable   = dont;      /* mark as enable/disable type */
                           /* option.  Disable as 'dont-' */
    doc       = 'disable, if you do not want to see the tree.';
```

```
};
```

7.4.3 Build the example options

This program will produce a program that digests its options and writes the values as shell script code to stdout. Run the following short script to produce this program:

```
base=check
BASE=`echo $base | tr '[a-z-]' '[A-Z_]'`
cflags="-DTEST_${BASE} `autoopts-config cflags`"
ldflags="`autoopts-config ldflags`"
autogen ${base}.def
cc -o ${base} -g ${cflags} ${base}.c ${ldflags}
./${base} --help
```

7.4.4 Example option help text

Running the build commands yields:

```
exit 0
```

7.4.5 Using the example options

Normally, however, you would not use the **main** clause. Instead, the file would be named something like **checkopt.def**, you would compile **checkopt.c** the usual way, and link the object with the rest of your program.

The options are processed by calling **optionProcess** (see Section 7.6.32.14 [libopts-optionProcess], page 139):

```
main( int argc, char** argv )
{
  {
    int optct = optionProcess( &checkOptions, argc, argv );
    argc -= optct;
    argv += optct;
  }
```

The options are tested and used as in the following fragment. **ENABLED_OPT** is used instead of **HAVE_OPT** for the **--show-defs** option because it is an enabled/disabled option type:

```
if (  ENABLED_OPT( SHOW_DEFS )
   && HAVE_OPT( CHECK_DIRS )) {
  int    dirct = STACKCT_OPT( CHECK_DIRS );
  char** dirs  = STACKLST_OPT( CHECK_DIRS );
  while (dirct-- > 0) {
    char* dir = *dirs++;
    ...
```

7.4.6 Example option documentation

The **doc** clauses are used in the flag stanzas for man pages and texinfo invoking documentation. With the definition file described above, the two following commands will produce the two documentation files `check.1` and `invoke-check.texi`. The latter file will be generated as a chapter, rather than a section or subsection.

```
autogen -Tagman-cmd check.def
autogen -DLEVEL=chapter -Tagtexi-cmd -binvoke-check.texi check.def
```

The result of which is left as an exercise for the reader.

A lot of magic happens to make this happen. The rest of this chapter will describe the myriad of option attributes supported by AutoOpts. However, keep in mind that, in general, you won't need much more than what was described in this "quick start" section.

7.5 Option Definitions

AutoOpts uses an AutoGen definitions file for the definitions of the program options and overall configuration attributes. The complete list of program and option attributes is quite extensive, so if you are reading to understand how to use AutoOpts, I recommend reading the "Quick Start" section (see Section 7.4 [Quick Start], page 88) and paying attention to the following:

1. `prog-name`, `prog-title`, and `argument`, program attributes, See Section 7.5.1 [program attributes], page 90.

2. `name` and `descrip` option attributes, See Section 7.5.5.1 [Required Attributes], page 105.

3. `value` (flag character) and `min` (occurrence counts) option attributes, See Section 7.5.5.2 [Common Attributes], page 106.

4. `arg-type` from the option argument specification section, See Section 7.5.6 [Option Arguments], page 110.

5. Read the overall how to, See Section 7.9 [Using AutoOpts], page 144.

6. Highly recommended, but not required, are the several "man" and "info" documentation attributes, See Section 7.5.9 [documentation attributes], page 118.

Keep in mind that the majority are rarely used and can be safely ignored. However, when you have special option processing requirements, the flexibility is there.

7.5.1 Program Description Attributes

The following global definitions are used to define attributes of the entire program. These generally alter the configuration or global behavior of the AutoOpts option parser. The first two are required of every program. The third is required if there are to be any left over arguments (operands) after option processing. The rest have been grouped below. Except as noted, there may be only one copy of each of these definitions:

'prog-name'

> This attribute is required. Variable names derived from this name are derived using **string->c_name!** (see Section 3.5.58 [SCM string->c-name!], page 54).

'prog-title'

> This attribute is required and may be any descriptive text.

'argument'

> This attribute is required if your program uses operand arguments. It specifies the syntax of the arguments that **follow** the options. It may not be empty, but

if it is not supplied, then option processing must consume all the arguments. If
it is supplied and starts with an open bracket ([), then there is no requirement
on the presence or absence of command line arguments following the options.
Lastly, if it is supplied and does not start with an open bracket, then option
processing must **not** consume all of the command line arguments.

'config-header'

> If your build has a configuration header, it must be included before anything
> else. Specifying the configuration header file name with this attribute will cause
> that to happen.

7.5.1.1 Usage and Version Info Display

These will affect the way usage is seen and whether or not version information gets displayed.

'full-usage'

> If this attribute is provided, it may specify the full length usage text, or a
> variable name assignable to a **char const *** pointer, or it may be empty. The
> meanings are determined by the length.
>
> - If not provided, the text will be computed as normal.
> - If the length is zero, then the usage text will be derived from the current
>   settings and inserted as text into the generated .c file.
> - If the length is 1 to 32 bytes, then it is presumed to be a variable name
>   that either points to or is an array of const chars.
> - If it is longer than that, it is presumed to be the help text itself. This text
>   will be inserted into the generated .c file.
>
> This string should be readily translatable. Provision will be made to translate it
> if this is provided, if the source code is compiled with **ENABLE_NLS** defined, and
> **no-xlate** has not been set to the value *anything*. The untranslated text will be
> handed to **dgettext("libopts",** *txt*) and then **gettext(***txt***)** for translation,
> one paragraph at a time.
>
> To facilitate the creation and maintenance of this text, you can force the string
> to be ignored and recomputed by specifying
>
> > AUTOOPTS_USAGE=compute
>
> in the environment and requesting help or usage information. See See
> Section 7.3 [Caveats], page 87.

'short-usage'

> If this attribute is provided, it is used to specify an abbreviated version of
> the usage text. This text is constructed in the same way as the **full-usage**,
> described above.

'gnu-usage'

> AutoOpts normaly displays usage text in a format that provides more informa-
> tion than the standard GNU layout, but that also means it is not the standard
> GNU layout. This attribute changes the default to GNU layout, with the
> **AUTOOPTS_USAGE** environment variable used to request **autoopts** layout. See
> See Section 7.3 [Caveats], page 87.

'usage-opt'

> I apologize for too many confusing usages of usage. This attribute specifies that --usage and/or -u be supported. The help (usage) text displayed will be abbreviated when compared to the default help text.

'no-misuse-usage'

> When there is a command line syntax error, by default AutoOpts will display the abbreviated usage text, rather than just a one line "you goofed it, ask for usage" message. You can change the default behavior for your program by supplying this attribute. The user may override this choice, again, with the **AUTOOPTS_USAGE** environment variable. See See Section 7.3 [Caveats], page 87.

'prog-group'

> The version text in the **getopt.tpl** template will include this text in parentheses after the program name, when this attribute is specified. For example:
>
> > mumble (stumble) 1.0
>
> says that the '**mumble**' program is version 1.0 and is part of the '**stumble**' group of programs.

'usage'

> If your program has some cleanup work that must be done before exiting on usage mode issues, or if you have to customize the usage message in some way, specify this procedure and it will be called instead of the default **optionUsage()** function. For example, if a program is using the curses library and needs to invoke the usage display, then you must arrange to call **endwin()** before invoking the library function **optionUsage()**. This can be handled by specifying your own usage function, thus:
>
> ```
> void
> my_usage(tOptions * opts, int ex)
> {
>     if (curses_window_active)
>         endwin();
>     optionUsage(opts, ex);
> }
> ```

'version' Specifies the program version and activates the VERSION option, See Section 7.5.10 [automatic options], page 121.

7.5.1.2 Program Configuration

Programs may be "pre-configured" before normal command line options are processed (See see Section 7.5.5.3 [Immediate Action], page 107). How configuration files and environment variables are handled get specified with these attributes.

'disable-load'
'disable-save'

> Indicates that the command line usage of --load-opts and/or --save-opts are disallowed.

'environrc'

> Indicates looking in the environment for values of variables named, **PROGRAM_OPTNAME** or **PROGRAM**, where **PROGRAM** is the upper cased *C-name* of the program

and 'OPTNAME' is the upper cased *C-name* of a specific option. The contents of the PROGRAM variable, if found, are tokenized and processed. The contents of PROGRAM_OPTNAME environment variables are taken as the option argument to the option nameed --optname.

'homerc'   Specifies that option settings may be loaded from and stored into configuration files. Each instance of this attribute is either a directory or a file using a specific path, a path based on an environment variable or a path relative to installation directories. The method used depends on the name. If the one entry is empty, it enables the loading and storing of settings, but no specific files are searched for. Otherwise, a series of configuration files are hunted down and, if found, loaded.

If the first character of the 'homerc' value is not the dollar character (S) then it is presumed to be a path name based on the current directory. Otherwise, the method depends on the second character:

$ The path is relative to the directory where the executable was found.

@   The path is relative to the package data directory, e.g. /usr/local/share/autogen.

[a-zA-Z]   The path is derived from the named environment variable.

Use as many as you like. The presence of this attribute activates the --save-opts and --load-opts options. However, saving into a file may be disabled with the 'disable-save'. See Section 7.10.1 [loading rcfile], page 147. See the optionMakePath(3AGEN) man page for excruciating details.

'rcfile'   Specifies the configuration file name. This is only useful if you have provided at least one homerc attribute.

            default: .<prog-name>rc

'vendor-opt'
            This option implements the -W vendor option command line option.

            For POSIX specified utilities, the options are constrained to the options that are specified by POSIX. Extensions should be handled with -W command line options, the short flag form. Long option name processing must be disabled. In fact, the long-opts attribute must not be provided, and some options must be specified without flag values.

            The -W long-name is processed by looking up the long option name that follows it. It cannot be a short flag because that would conflict with the POSIX flag name space. It will be processed as if long options were accepted and --long-name were found on the command line.

7.5.1.3 Programming Details

These attributes affect some of the ways that the option data are used and made available to the program.

'config-header'
>   The contents of this attribute should be just the name of the configuration
>   file. A "#include" naming this file will be inserted at the top of the generated
>   header.

'exit-name'
'exit-desc'
>   These values should be defined as indexed values, thus:

```
exit-name[0] = success;
exit-desc[0] = 'Successful program execution.';
exit-name[1] = failure;
exit-desc[1] = 'The operation failed or command syntax was not valid
```

>   By default, all programs have these effectively defined for them. They may be
>   overridden by explicitly defining any or all of these values. Additional names
>   and descriptions may be defined. They will cause an enumeration to be emitted,
>   like this one for getdefs:

```
typedef enum {
    GETDEFS_EXIT_SUCCESS = 0,
    GETDEFS_EXIT_FAILURE = 1
} getdefs_exit_code_t;
```

>   which will be augmented by any exit-name definitions beyond '1'.

>   Some of the generated code will exit non-zero if there is an allocation error.
>   This exit will always be code '1', unless there is an exit named 'no_mem' or
>   'nomem'. In that case, that value will be used. Additionally, if there is such
>   a value, and if die-code is specified, then a function nomem_err(size_t len,
>   char const * what) will be emitted as an inline function for reporting out-of-
>   memory conditions.

'usage-message'
>   This attribute will cause two procedures to be added to the code file: usage_
>   message() and vusage_message(), with any applicable prefix (see prefix,
>   below). They are declared in the generated header, thus:

```
extern void vusage_message(char const * fmt, va_list ap);
extern void usage_message(char const * fmt, ...);
```

>   These functions print the message to stderr and invoke the usage function
>   with the exit code set to 1 (EXIT_FAILURE).

'die-code'
>   This tells AutoOpts templates to emit code for vdie(), die(), fserr(), and,
>   possibly the nomem_err() functions. The latter is emitted if an exit name of
>   'no-mem' or 'nomem' is specified. If the die-code is assigned a text value, then
>   that code will be inserted in the vdie function immediately before it prints the
>   death rattle message.

>   The profiles for these functions are:

```
extern void vdie( int exit_code, char const * fmt, va_list);
extern void die(  int exit_code, char const * fmt, ...);
extern void fserr(int exit_code, char const * op, char const * fname
```

```
static inline void
nomem_err(size_t sz, char const * what) {...}
```

'no-return'

If `usage-message` or `die-code` are specified, you may also specify that the generated functions are marked as "noreturn" with this attribute. If this attribute is not empty, then the specified string is used instead of "noreturn". If "noreturn" has not been defined before these functions are declared, then it will be "#define"-d to the empty string. No such protection is made for any non-default value. These functions will be declared "extern noreturn void".

'export'   This string is inserted into the .h interface file. Generally used for global variables or #include directives required by `flag-code` text and shared with other program text. Do not specify your configuration header (`config.h`) in this attribute or the `include` attribute, however. Instead, use `config-header`, above.

'guard-option-names'

AutoOpts generates macros that presume that there are no cpp macros with the same name as the option name. For example, if you have an option named, --debug, then you must not use #ifdef DEBUG in your code. If you specify this attribute, every option name will be guarded. If the name is #define-d, then a warning will be issued and the name undefined. If you do not specify this and there is a conflict, you will get strange error messages.

This attribute may be set to any of four recognized states:

- Not defined. AutoOpts will behave as described above.

- Defined, but set to the empty string. Text will be emitted into the header to undefine (#undef) any conflicting preprocessor macros. The code will include compiler warnings (via #warning). Some compilers are not ANSI-C-99 compliant yet and will error out on those warnings. You may compile with -DNO_OPTION_NAME_WARNINGS to silence or mostly silence them.

- Defined and set to the string, `no-warning`. All of the needed #undefs will be emitted, without any conflict checking #warning directives emitted.

- Defined and set to the string, `full-enum`. The option manipulation preprocessor macros will not token paste the option names to the index enumeration prefix. e.g. you will need to use HAVE_OPT(INDEX_OPT_DEBUG) instead of HAVE_OPT(DEBUG).

'include'   This string is inserted into the .c file. Generally used for global variables required only by `flag-code` program text.

'no-libopts'

If you are going to handle your option processing with the `getopt.tpl` template instead of using libopts, then specify this attribute. It will suppress mention of --more-help in the generated documentation. (getopt_long does not support --more-help.)

'prefix'   This value is inserted into **all** global names. This will disambiguate them if more than one set of options are to be compiled into a single program.

7.5.1.4 User Presentation Attributes

Attributes that affect the user's experience.

`allow-errors`

> The presence of this attribute indicates ignoring any command line option errors. This may also be turned on and off by invoking the macros `ERRSKIP_OPTERR` and `ERRSTOP_OPTERR` from the generated interface file.

`long-opts`

> Presence indicates GNU-standard long option processing. Partial name matches are accepted, if they are at least two characters long and the partial match is unique. The matching is not case sensitive, and the underscore, hyphen and carat characters are all equivalent (they match).
>
> If any options do not have an option value (flag character) specified, and least one does specify such a value, then you must specify `long-opts`. If none of your options specify an option value (flag character) and you do not specify `long-opts`, then command line arguments are processed in "named option mode". This means that:
>
> - Every command line argument must be a long option.
> - The flag markers - and -- are completely optional.
> - The `argument` program attribute is disallowed.
> - One of the options may be specified as the default (as long as it has a required option argument).

`no-xlate`

> Modifies when or whether option names get translated. If provided, it must be assigned one of these values:
>
> `opt-cfg`   to suppress option name translation for configuration file and and environment variable processing.
>
> `opt`   to suppress option name translation completely. The usage text will always be translated if `ENABLE_NLS` is defined and you have translations for that text.
>
> `anything`
> > Specifies disabling all internationalization support for option code, completely.
>
> See also the various `XLAT` interface entries in the AutoOpts Programmatic Interface section (see Section 7.6 [AutoOpts API], page 125).

`reorder-args`

> Normally, POSIX compliant commands do not allow for options to be interleaved with operands. If this is necessary for historical reasons, there are two approaches available:
>
> - Allow `optionProcess` to return the index of the operand like it normally does and process the operand(s). When an operand is encountered that starts with a hyphen, then set the AutoOpts current index with the `RESTART_OPT` macro (see see Section 7.6.19 [RESTART_OPT], page 129),

and re-invoke `optionProcess`. This will also allow you to process the operands in context.

- Specify this attribute. AutoOpts will re-order the command arguments so that the operands appear (in the original order) at the end of the argument list. Differing configuration state is not possible to detect after all options have been processed.

'`resettable`'

> Specifies that the `--reset-option` command line option is to be supported. This makes it possible to suppress any setting that might be found in a configuration file or environment variable.

7.5.2 Options for Library Code

Some libraries provide their own code for processing command line options, and this may be used by programs that utilize AutoOpts. You may also wish to write a library that gets configured with AutoOpts options and config files. Such a library may either supply its own configury routine and process its own options, or it may export its option descriptions to programs that also use AutoOpts. This section will describe how to do all of these different things.

7.5.2.1 AutoOpt-ed Library for AutoOpt-ed Program

The library source code must provide an option definition file that consists of only the attribute `library` and `flag` entries. The `library` attribute does not need any associated value, so it will generally appeary by itself on a line folowed by a semi-colon. The first `flag` entry must contain the following attributes:

'`name`'   This name is used in the construction of a global pointer of type `tOptDesc const*`. It is always required.

'`documentation`'

> It tells `AutoOpts` that this option serves no normal purpose. It will be used to add usage clarity and to locate option descriptors in the library code.

'`descrip`'   This is a string that is inserted in the extended usage display before the options specific to the current library. It is always required.

'`lib-name`'

> This should match the name of the library. This string is also used in the construction of the option descriptor pointer name. In the end, it looks like this:
>
> ```
>         extern tOptDesc const* <<lib-name>>_<<name>>_optDesc_p;
> ```
>
> and is used in the macros generated for the library's `.h` file.

In order to compile this `AutoOpts` using library, you must create a special header that is not used by the client program. This is accomplished by creating an option definition file that contains essentially exactly the following:

```
AutoGen definitions options;
prog-name  = does-not-matter;  // but is always required
prog-title = 'also does not matter';  // also required
```

```
config-header = 'config.h'; // optional, but common
library;
#include library-options-only.def
```

and nothing else. AutoGen will produce only the `.h` file. You may now compile your library, referencing just this `.h` file. The macros it creates will utilize a global variable that will be defined by the `AutoOpts`-using client program. That program will need to have the following `#include` in *its* option definition file:

```
#include library-options-only.def
```

All the right things will magically happen so that the global variables named `<<`*lib-name*`>>_<<`*name*`>>_optDesc_p` are initialized correctly. For an example, please see the `AutoOpts` test script: `autoopts/test/library.test`.

7.5.2.2 AutoOpt-ed Library for Regular Program

In this case, your library must provide an option processing function to a calling program. This is accomplished by setting the `allow-errors` global option attribute. Each time your option handling function is called, you must determine where your scan is to resume and tell the AutoOpts library by invoking:

```
RESTART_OPT(next_arg_index);
```

and then invoke `not_opt_index = optionProcess(...)`. The `not_opt_index` value can be used to set `optind`, if that is the global being used to scan the program argument array.

In this method, do **NOT** utilize the global `library` attribute. Your library must specify its options as if it were a complete program. You may choose to specify an alternate `usage()` function so that usage for other parts of the option interface may be displayed as well. See "Program Information Attributes" (see Section 7.5.3 [information attributes], page 98).

At the moment, there is no method for calling `optionUsage()` telling it to produce just the information about the options and not the program as a whole. Some later revision after somebody asks.

7.5.2.3 AutoOpt-ed Program Calls Regular Library

As with providing an `AutoOpt`-ed library to a non-`AutoOpt`-ed program, you must write the option description file as if you were writing all the options for the program, but you should specify the `allow-errors` global option attribute and you will likely want an alternate `usage()` function (see "Program Information Attributes" see Section 7.5.3 [information attributes], page 98). In this case, though, when `optionProcess()` returns, you need to test to see if there might be library options. If there might be, then call the library's exported routine for handling command line options, set the next-option-to-process with the `RESTART_OPT()` macro, and recall `optionProcess()`. Repeat until done.

7.5.3 Program Information Attributes

These attributes are used to define how and what information is displayed to the user of the program.

`copyright`

> The `copyright` is a structured value containing three to five values. If `copyright` is used, then the first three are required.

1. date - the list of applicable dates for the copyright.

2. owner - the name of the copyright holder.

3. type - specifies the type of distribution license. AutoOpts/AutoGen supports the text of the GNU Public License (gpl), the GNU Lesser General Public License with Library extensions (lgpl), the Modified Free BSD license (mbsd) and a few others. Other licenses may be specified, out you must provide your own license file. The list of license files provided by AutoOpts may be seen by typing:

   ls $(autoopts-config pkgdatadir)/*.lic

4. text - the text of the copyright notice. This must be provided if type is set to NOTE.

5. author - in case the author name is to appear in the documentation and is different from the copyright owner.

6. eaddr - email address for receiving praises and complaints. Typically that of the author or copyright holder.

An example of this might be:

```
copyright = {
    date  = "1992-2015";
    cwner = "Bruce Korb";
    eaddr = 'bkorb@gnu.org';
    type  = GPL;
};
```

'detail'   This string is added to the usage output when the HELP option is selected.

'explain'   Gives additional information whenever the usage routine is invoked.

'package'   The name of the package the program belongs to. This will appear parenthetically after the program name in the version and usage output, e.g.: autogen (GNU autogen) - The Automated Program Generator.

'preserve-case'
             This attribute will not change anything except appearance. Normally, the option names are all documented in lower case. However, if you specify this attribute, then they will display in the case used in their specification. Command line options will still be matched without case sensitivity. This is useful for specifying option names in camel-case.

'prog-desc and'
'opts-ptr'
             These define global pointer variables that point to the program descriptor and the first option descriptor for a library option. This is intended for use by certain libraries that need command line and/or initialization file option processing. These definitions have no effect on the option template output, but are used for creating a library interface file. Normally, the first "option" for a library will be a documentation option that cannot be specified on the command line, but is marked as settable. The library client program will invoke the SET_OPTION

macro which will invoke a handler function that will finally set these global variables.

'usage'   Optionally names the usage procedure, if the library routine `optionUsage()` does not work for you. If you specify `my_usage` as the value of this attribute, for example, you will use a procedure by that name for displaying usage. Of course, you will need to provide that procedure and it must conform to this profile:

```
void my_usage( tOptions* pOptions, int exitCode )
```

'gnu-usage'
                   Normally, the default format produced by the `optionUsage` procedure is *AutoOpts Standard*. By specifying this attribute, the default format will be *GNU-ish style*. Either default may be overridden by the user with the `AUTOOPTS_USAGE` environment variable. If it is set to `gnu` or `autoopts`, it will alter the style appropriately. This attribute will conflict with the `usage` attribute.

'reorder-args'
                   Some applications traditionally require that the command operands be intermixed with the command options. In order to handle that, the arguments must be reordered. If you are writing such an application, specify this global option. All of the options (and any associated option arguments) will be brought to the beginning of the argument list. New applications should not use this feature, if at all possible. This feature is *disabled* if `POSIXLY_CORRECT` is defined in the environment.

7.5.4 Generating main procedures

When AutoOpts generates the code to parse the command line options, it has the ability to produce any of several types of `main()` procedures. This is done by specifying a global structured value for `main`. The values that it contains are dependent on the value set for the one value it must have: `main-type`.

The recognized values for `main-type` are `guile`, `shell-process`, `shell-parser`, `main`, `include`, `invoke`, and `for-each`.

7.5.4.1 guile: main and inner_main procedures

When the `main-type` is specified to be `guile`, a `main()` procedure is generated that calls `gh_enter()`, providing it with a generated `inner_main()` to invoke. If you must perform certain tasks before calling `gh_enter()`, you may specify such code in the value for the `before-guile-boot` attribute.

The `inner_main()` procedure itself will process the command line arguments (by calling `optionProcess()`, see Section 7.6.32.14 [libopts-optionProcess], page 139), and then either invoke the code specified with the `guile-main` attribute, or else export the parsed options to Guile symbols and invoke the `scm_shell()` function from the Guile library. This latter will render the program nearly identical to the stock `guile(1)` program.

7.5.4.2 shell-process: emit Bourne shell results

This will produce a `main()` procedure that parses the command line options and emits to
`stdout` Bourne shell commands that puts the option state into environment variables. This
can be used within a shell script as follows:

```
unset OPTION_CT
eval "`opt_parser \"$@\"`"
test ${OPTION_CT} -gt 0 && shift ${OPTION_CT}
```

If the option parsing code detects an error or a request for usage or version, it will
emit a command to exit with an appropriate exit code to `stdout`. This form of `main` will
cause all messages, including requested usage and version information, to be emitted to
`stderr`. Otherwise, a numeric value for `OPTION_CT` is guaranteed to be emitted, along with
assignments for all the options parsed, something along the lines of the following will be
written to `stdout` for evaluation:

```
OPTION_CT=4
export OPTION_CT
MYPROG_SECOND='first'
export MYPROG_SECOND
MYPROG_ANOTHER=1 # 0x1
export MYPROG_ANOTHER
```

If the arguments are to be reordered, however, then the resulting set of operands will be
emitted and `OPTION_CT` will be set to zero. For example, the following would be appended
to the above:

```
set -- 'operand1' 'operand2' 'operand3'
OPTION_CT=0
```

`OPTION_CT` is set to zero since it is not necessary to shift off any options.

7.5.4.3 shell-parser: emit Bourne shell script

This will produce a `main()` procedure that emits a shell script that will parse the command
line options. That script can be emitted to `stdout` or inserted or substituted into a pre-
existing shell script file. Improbable markers are used to identify previously inserted parsing
text:

```
# # # # # # # # # # -- do not modify this marker --
```

The program is also pretty insistent upon starting its parsing script on the second line.

7.5.4.4 main: user supplied main procedure

You must supply a value for the `main-text` attribute. You may also supply a value for
`option-code`. If you do, then the `optionProcess` invocation will not be emitted into the
code. AutoOpts will wrap the `main-text` inside of:

```
int
main( int argc, char** argv )
{
    int res = <<success-exit-code>>;
    { // replaced by option-code, if that exists
        int ct = optionProcess( &<<prog-name>>Options, argc, argv);
```

```
            argc -= ct;
            argv += ct;
        }
    <<main-text>>
        return res;
    }
```

so you can most conveniently set the value with a **here string** (see Section 2.2.7 [here-string], page 9):

```
    code = <<- _EndOfMainProc_
    <<your text goes here>>
    _EndOfMainProc_;
```

7.5.4.5 include: code emitted from included template

You must write a template to produce your main procedure. You specify the name of the template with the **tpl** attribute and it will be incorporated at the point where AutoOpts is ready to emit the **main()** procedure.

This can be very useful if, in your working environment, you have many programs with highly similar **main()** procedures. All you need to do is parameterize the variations and specify which variant is needed within the **main** AutoOpts specification. Since you are coding the template for this, the attributes needed for this variation would be dictated by your template.

Here is an example of an **include** variation:

```
    main = {
      main-type = include;
      tpl       = "main-template.tpl";
    };
```

7.5.4.6 invoke: code emitted from AutoGen macro

You must write a template to produce your main procedure. That template must contain a definition for the function specified with the **func** attribute to this **main()** procedure specification. This variation operates in much the same way as **include** (see Section 7.5.4.5 [main include], page 102) method.

7.5.4.7 for-each: perform function on each operand

This produces a main procedure that invokes a procedure once for each operand on the command line (non-option arguments), **OR** once for each non-blank, non-comment **stdin** input line. Leading and trailing white space is trimmed from the input line and comment lines are lines that are empty or begin with a comment character, defaulting to a hash ('#') character.

NB: The **argument** program attribute (see Section 7.5.1 [program attributes], page 90) must begin with the [character, to indicate that there are command operands, but that they are optional.

For an example of the produced main procedure, in the **autoopts/test** build directory, type the following command and look at **main.c**:

```
    make verbose TESTS=main.test
```

procedure to handle each argument

The `handler-proc` attribute is required. It is used to name the procedure to call. That procedure is presumed to be external, but if you provide the code for it, then the procedure is emitted as a static procedure in the generated code.

This procedure should return 0 on success, a cumulative error code on warning and exit without returning on an unrecoverable error. As the cumulative warning codes are or-ed together, the codes should be some sort of bit mask in order to be ultimately decipherable (if you need to do that).

If the called procedure needs to cause a fail-exit, it is expected to call `exit(3)` directly. If you want to cause a warning exit code, then this handler function should return a non-zero status. That value will be **OR**-ed into a result integer for computing the final exit code. E.g., here is part of the emitted code:

```
int res = 0;
if (argc > 0) {
    do  {
        res |= my_handler( *(argv++) );
    } while (--argc > 0);
} else { ...
```

handler procedure type

If you do not supply the `handler-type` attribute, your handler procedure must be the default type. The profile of the procedure must be:

```
int my_handler(char const * pz_entry);
```

However, if you do supply this attribute, you may set the value to any of four alternate flavors:

'`name-of-file`'
> This is essentially the same as the default handler type, except that before your procedure is invoked, the generated code has verified that the string names an existing file. The profile is unchanged.

'`file-X`' Before calling your procedure, the file is f-opened according to the X, where X may be any of the legal modes for `fopen(3C)`. In this case, the profile for your procedure must be:

```
int my_handler(char const * pz_fname, FILE * entry_fp);
```

> When processing inputs as file pointer stream files, there are several ways of treating standard input. It may be an ordinary input file, or it may contain a list of files to operate on.

> If the file handler type is more specifically set to '`file-r`' and a command line operand consists of a single hyphen, then *my_handler* will be called with `entry_fp` set to `stdin` and the `pz_fname` set to the translatable string, `"standard input"`. Consequently, in this case, if the input list is being read from `stdin`, a line containing a hyphen by itself will be ignored.

'`stdin-input`'
> This attribute specifies that standard input is a data input file. By default, `for-each` main procedures will read standard input for operands if no operands

appear on the command line. If there are operands after the command line options, then standard input is typically ignored. It can always be processed as an input data file, however, if a single bare hyphen is put on the command line.

'text-of-file'
'some-text-of-file'

> Before calling your procedure, the contents of the file are read or mapped into memory. (Excessively large files may cause problems.) The 'some-text-of-file' disallows empty files. Both require regular files. In this case, the profile for your procedure must be:

```
program_exit_code_t
my_handler(char const * fname, char * file_text,
          size_t text_size);
```

> Note that though the `file_text` is not `const`, any changes made to it are not written back to the original file. It is merely a memory image of the file contents. Also, the memory allocated to hold the text is `text_size + 1` bytes long and the final byte is always `NUL`. The file contents need not be text, as the data are read with the `read(2)` system call.

> `file_text` is automatically freed, unless you specify a `handler-frees` attribute. Then your code must `free(3)` the text.

If you select one of these file type handlers, then on access or usage errors the `PROGRAM_EXIT_FAILURE` exit code will, by default, be or-ed into the final exit code. This can be changed by specifying the global `file-fail-code` attribute and naming a different value. That is, something other than `failure`. You may choose `success`, in which case file access issues will not affect the exit code and the error message will not be printed.

code for handler procedure

With the `MYHANDLER-code` attribute, you provide the code for your handler procedure in the option definition file. Note that the spelling of this attribute depends on the name provided with the `handler-proc` attribute, so we represent it here with `MYHANDLER` as a place holder. As an example, your `main()` procedure specification might look something like this:

```
main = {
  main-type     = for-each;
  handler-proc = MYHANDLER;
  MYHANDLER-code = <<- EndOfMyCode
/* whatever you want to do */
EndOfMyCode;
};
```

and instead of an emitted external reference, a procedure will be emitted that looks like this:

```
static int
MYHANDLER( char const* pz_entry )
{
```

```
        int res = 0;
        <<MYHANDLER-code goes here>>
        return res;
}
```

for-each main procedure options

These attributes affect the main procedure and how it processes each argument or input line.

'`interleaved`'

> If this attribute is specified, then options and operands may be interleaved. Arguments or input lines beginning with a hyphen will cause it to be passed through to an option processing function and will take effect for the remainder of the operands (or input lines) processed.

'`main-init`'

> This is code that gets inserted after the options have been processed, but before the handler procs get invoked.

'`main-fini`'

> This is code that gets inserted after all the entries have been processed, just before returning from `main()`.

'`comment-char`'

> When reading operands from standard input, if you wish comment lines to start with a character other than a hash (#) character, then specify one character with this attribute. If string value is empty, then only blank lines will be considered comments.

7.5.5 Option Attributes

For each option you wish to specify, you must have a block macro named **flag** defined. There are two required attributes: **name** and **descrip**. If any options do not have a **value** (traditional flag character) attribute, then the **long-opts** program attribute must also be defined. As a special exception, if no options have a **value and long-opts** is not defined **and argument** is not defined, then all arguments to the program are named options. In this case, the - and -- command line option markers are optional.

7.5.5.1 Required Attributes

Every option must have exactly one copy of both of these attributes.

'`name`'   Long name for the option. Even if you are not accepting long options and are only accepting flags, it must be provided. AutoOpts generates private, named storage that requires this name. This name also causes a `#define`-d name to be emitted. It must not conflict with any other names you may be using in your program.

> For example, if your option name is, **debug** or **munged-up**, you must not use the `#define` names DEBUG (or MUNGED_UP) in your program for non-AutoOpts related purposes. They are now used by AutoOpts.

Sometimes (most especially under Windows), you may get a surprise. For example, `INTERFACE` is apparently a user space name that one should be free to use. Windows usurps this name. To solve this, you must do one of the following:

1. Change the name of your option
2. add the program attribute (see Section 7.5.1 [program attributes], page 90):

   ```
   export = '#undef INTERFACE';
   ```
3. add the program attribute:

   ```
   guard-option-names;
   ```

'descrip'   Except for documentation options, a **very** brief description of the option. About 40 characters on one line, maximum, not counting any texinfo markups. Texinfo markups are stripped before printing in the usage text. It appears on the `usage()` output next to the option name.

If, however, the option is a documentation option, it will appear on one or more lines by itself. It is thus used to visually separate and comment upon groups of options in the usage text.

7.5.5.2 Common Option Attributes

These option attributes are optional. Any that do appear in the definition of a flag, may appear only once.

'value'   The flag character to specify for traditional option flags, e.g., -L.

'max'   Maximum occurrence count (invalid if *disable* present). The default maximum is 1. `NOLIMIT` can be used for the value, otherwise it must be a number or a `#define` that evaluates to a number.

'min'   Minimum occurrence count. If present, then the option **must** appear on the command line. Do not define it with the value zero (0).

'must-set'

   If an option must be specified, but it need not be specified on the command line, then specify this attribute for the option.

'deprecated'

   There are two effects to this attribute: the usage text will not show the option, and the generated documentation will mark it with: *NOTE: THIS OPTION IS DEPRECATED.*

'disable'   Prefix for disabling (inverting sense of) the option. Only useful if long option names are being processed. When an option has this attribute, the test `ENABLED_OPT(OPTNAME)` is false when either of the following is true:

   - The option has not been specified and the `enable` attribute has not been specified.
   - The option has been specified with this disabling prefix.

   To detect that the option has been specified with the disabling prefix, you must use:

$$\texttt{HAVE\_OPT(OPTNAME) \&\& ! ENABLED\_OPT(OPTNAME)}$$

'enable'   Long-name prefix for enabling the option (invalid if *disable* **not** present). Only useful if long option names are being processed.

'enabled'   If default is for option being enabled. (Otherwise, the OPTST_DISABLED bit is set at compile time.) Only useful if the option can be disabled.

'ifdef'
'ifndef'
'omitted-usage'

If an option is relevant on certain platforms or when certain features are enabled or disabled, you can specify the compile time flag used to indicate when the option should be compiled in or out. For example, if you have a configurable feature, `mumble` that is indicated with the compile time define, WITH_MUMBLING, then add:

```
ifdef = WITH_MUMBLING;
```

Take care when using these. There are several caveats:

- The case and spelling must match whatever is specified.

- Do not confuse these attributes with the AutoGen directives of the same names, See Section 2.5 [Directives], page 12. These cause C preprocessing directives to be inserted into the generated C text.

- Only one of `ifdef` and `ifndef` may apply to any one option.

- The VALUE_OPT_ values are #define-d. If WITH_MUMBLING is not defined, then the associated VALUE_OPT_ value will not be #define-d either. So, if you have an option named, MUMBLING that is active only if WITH_MUMBLING is #define-d, then VALUE_OPT_MUMBLING will be #define-d iff WITH_MUMBLING is #define-d. Watch those switch statements.

- If you specify `omitted-usage`, then the option will be recognized as disabled when it is configured out of the build, but will yield the message, "This option has been disabled." You may specify an alternate message by giving `omitted-usage` a string value. e.g.:

```
omitted-usage = 'you cannot do this';
```

'no-command'

This option specifies that the option is not allowed on the command line. Such an option may not take a **value** (flag character) attribute. The program must have the `homerc` (see Section 7.5.1 [program attributes], page 90) option set.

7.5.5.3 Immediate Action Attributes

Certain options may need to be processed early. For example, in order to suppress the processing of configuration files, it is necessary to process the command line option `--no-load-cpts` **before** the config files are processed. To accommodate this, certain options may have their enabled or disabled forms marked for immediate processing. The consequence of this is that they are processed ahead of all other options in the reverse of normal order.

Normally, the first options processed are the options specified in the first `homerc` file, followed by then next `homerc` file through to the end of config file processing. Next, environment variables are processed and finally, the command line options. The later options override settings processed earlier. That actually gives them higher priority. Command line immediate action options actually have the lowest priority of all. They would be used only if they are to have an effect on the processing of subsequent options.

'`immediate`'
> Use this option attribute to specify that the enabled form of the option is to be processed immediately. The `help` and `more-help` options are so specified. They will also call `exit()` upon completion, so they **do** have an effect on the processing of the remaining options :-).

'`immed-disable`'
> Use this option attribute to specify that the disabled form of the option is to be processed immediately. The `load-opts` option is so specified. The `--no-load-opts` command line option will suppress the processing of config files and environment variables. Contrariwise, the `--load-opts` command line option is processed normally. That means that the options specified in that file will be processed after all the `homerc` files and, in fact, after options that precede it on the command line.

'`also`' If either the `immediate` or the `immed-disable` attributes are set to the string, `also`, then the option will actually be processed twice: first at the immediate processing phase and again at the normal time.

7.5.5.4 Option Conflict Attributes

These attributes may be used as many times as you need. They are used at the end of the option processing to verify that the context within which each option is found does not conflict with the presence or absence of other options.

This is not a complete cover of all possible conflicts and requirements, but it simple to implement and covers the more common situations.

'`flags-must`'
> one entry for every option that **must** be present when this option is present

'`flags-cant`'
> one entry for every option that **cannot** be present when this option is present

7.5.5.5 Program may set option

If the option can be set outside of option processing, specify `settable`. If this attribute is defined, special macros for setting this particular option will be inserted into the interface file. For example, `TEMPL_DIRS` is a settable option for AutoGen, so a macro named `SET_OPT_TEMPL_DIRS(a)` appears in the interface file. This attribute interacts with the *documentation* attribute.

7.5.5.6 Option cannot be pre-configured

If presetting this option is not allowed, specify `no-preset`. (Thus, environment variables and values set in configuration files will be ignored.)

7.5.5.7 Option Equivalence Class

Generally, when several options are mutually exclusive and basically serve the purpose of selecting one of several processing modes, specify the **equivalence** attribute. These options will be considered an equivalence class. Sometimes, it is just easier to deal with them as such. All members of the equivalence class must contain the same equivalenced-to option, including the equivalenced-to option itself. Thus, it must be a class member.

For an option equivalence class, there is a single occurrence counter for the class It can be referenced with the interface macro, `COUNT_OPT(BASE_OPTION)`, where *BASE_OPTION* is the equivalenced-to option name.

Also, please take careful note: since the options are mapped to the equivalenced-to option descriptor, any option argument values are mapped to that descriptor also. Be sure you know which "equivalent option" was selected before getting an option argument value!

During the presetting phase of option processing (see Section 7.10 [Presetting Options], page 146), equivalenced options may be specified. However, if different equivalenced members are specified, only the last instance will be recognized and the others will be discarded. A conflict error is indicated only when multiple different members appear on the command line itself.

As an example of where equivalenced options might be useful, `cpio(1)` has three options `-o`, `-i`, and `-p` that define the operational mode of the program (**create**, **extract** and **pass-through**, respectively). They form an equivalence class from which one and only one member must appear on the command line. If `cpio` were an AutoOpt-ed program, then each of these option definitions would contain:

```
equivalence = create;
```

and the program would be able to determine the operating mode with code that worked something like this:

```
switch (WHICH_IDX_CREATE) {
case INDEX_OPT_CREATE:        ...
case INDEX_OPT_EXTRACT:       ...
case INDEX_OPT_PASS_THROUGH: ...
default:    /* cannot happen */
}
```

7.5.5.8 Option Aliasing

Sometimes, for backwards compatibility or tradition or just plain convenience, it works better to define one option as a pure alias for another option. For such situations, provide the following pieces of information:

```
flag = {
   name  = aliasing-option-name;
   value = aliasing-flag-char; // optional !
   aliases = aliased-to-option;
};
```

Do not provide anything else. The usage text for such an option will be:

```
This is an alias for aliased-to-option
```

7.5.5.9 Default Option

If your program processes its arguments in named option mode (See `long-opts` in Section 7.5.1 [program attributes], page 90), then you may select **one** of your options to be the default option. Do so by using attribute `default` with one of the options. The option so specified must have an `arg-type` (see Section 7.5.6 [Option Arguments], page 110) specified, but not the `arg-optional` (see Section 7.5.6.11 [arg-optional], page 115) attribute. That is to say, the option argument must be required.

If you have done this, then any arguments that do not match an option name and do not contain an equal sign (=) will be interpreted as an option argument to the default option.

7.5.5.10 Option Sectioning Comment

This attribute means the option exists for the purpose of separating option description text in the usage output and texi documentation. Without this attribute, every option is a separate node in the texi docs. With this attribute, the documentation options become texi doc nodes and the options are collected under them. Choose the name attribute carefully because it will appear in the texi documentation.

Libraries may also choose to make it settable so that the library can determine which command line option is the first one that pertains to the library.

If the 'documentation' attribute is present, then all other attributes are disabled except `settable`, `call-proc` and `flag-code`. `settable` must be and is only specified if `call-proc`, `extract-code` or `flag-code` has been specified. When present, the `descrip` attribute will be displayed only when the `--help` option has been specified. It will be displayed flush to the left hand margin and may consist of one or more lines of text, filled to 72 columns.

The name of the option will not be printed in the help text. It *will*, however, be printed as section headers in the texi documentation. If the attribute is given a non-empty value, this text will be reproduced in the man page and texi doc immediately after the `descrip` text.

7.5.5.11 Translator Notes

If you need to give the translators a special note about a particular option, please use the `translators` attribute. The attribute text will be emitted into the generated `.c` text where the option related strings get defined. To make a general comment about all of the option code, add comments to an `include` attribute (see Section 7.5.1 [program attributes], page 90). Do **not** use this attribute globally, or it will get emitted into every option definition block.

7.5.6 Option Argument Specification

Command line options come in three flavors: options that do not take arguments, those that do and those that may. Without an "arg-type" attribute, AutoOpts will not process an argument to an option. If "arg-type" is specified and "arg-optional" is also specified, then the next command line token will be taken to be an argument, unless it looks like the name of another option.

If the argument type is specified to be anything other than "str[ing]", then AutoOpts will specify a callback procedure to handle the argument. Some of these procedures will be created and inserted into the generated `.c` file, and others are already built into the libopts library. Therefore, if you write your own callback procedure (see Section 7.5.7 [Option Argument Handling], page 115), then you must either not specify an "arg-type" attribute, or else specify it to be of type "str[ing]". Your callback function will be able to place its own restrictions on what that string may contain or represent.

Option argument handling attributes depend upon the value set for the **arg-type** attribute. It specifies the type of argument the option will take. If not present, the option cannot take an argument. If present, it must be an entry in the following table. The first three letters is sufficient.

7.5.6.1 Arg Type String

arg-type = string;

The argument may be any arbitrary string, though your program or option callback procedure may place additional constraints upon it.

7.5.6.2 Arg Type Number

arg-type = number;

The argument must be a correctly formed integer, without any trailing U's or L s. AutoOpts contains a library procedure to convert the string to a number. If you specify range checking with **arg-range** (see below), then AutoOpts produces a special purpose procedure for this option.

'scaled'   scaled marks the option so that suffixes of 'k', 'K', 'm', 'M', 'g', 'G', 't', and 'T' will multiply the given number by a power of 1000 or 1024. Lower case letters scale by a power of 1000 and upper case scale by a power of 1024.

'arg-range'
             arg-range is used to create a callback procedure for validating the range of the option argument. It must match one of the range entries. Each **arg-range** should consist of either an integer by itself or an integer range. The integer range is specified by one or two integers separated by the two character sequence, ->. Be sure to quote the entire range string. The definitions parser will not accept the range syntax as a single string token.

The generated procedure imposes the range constraints as follows:

* A number by itself will match that one value.
* The high end of the range may not be INT_MIN, both for obvious reasons and because that value is used to indicate a single-valued match.
* An omitted lower value implies a lower bound of INT_MIN.
* An omitted upper value implies a upper bound of INT_MAX.
* The argument value is required. It may not be optional.
* The value must match one of the entries. If it can match more than one, then you have redundancies, but no harm will come of it.

7.5.6.3 Arg Type Boolean

arg-type = boolean;

The argument will be interpreted and always yield either AG_TRUE or AG_FALSE. False values are the empty string, the number zero, or a string that starts with f, F, n or N (representing False or No). Anything else will be interpreted as True.

7.5.6.4 Arg Type Keyword

`arg-type = keyword;`

The argument must match a specified list of strings (see Section 7.5.6.10 [arg-keyword], page 115). Assuming you have named the option, optn-name, the strings will be converted into an enumeration of type **te_Optn_Name** with the values OPTN_NAME_KEYWORD.* If you have **not** specified a default value, the value OPTN_NAME_UNDEFINED will be inserted with the value zero. The option will be initialized to that value. You may now use this in your code as follows:

```
te_Optn_Name opt = OPT_VALUE_OPTN_NAME;
switch (opt) {
case OPTN_NAME_UNDEFINED:  /* undefined things */ break;
case OPTN_NAME_KEYWORD:    /* 'keyword' things */ break;
default: /* utterly impossible */ ;
}
```

AutoOpts produces a special purpose procedure for this option. You may not specify an alternate handling procedure.

If you have need for the string name of the selected keyword, you may obtain this with the macro, OPT_OPTN_NAME_VAL2STR(val). The value you pass would normally be OPT_VALUE_OPTN_NAME, but anything with numeric value that is legal for **te_Optn_Name** may be passed. Anything out of range will result in the string, '"*INVALID*"' being returned. The strings are read only. It may be used as in:

```
te_Optn_Name opt = OPT_VALUE_OPTN_NAME;
printf( "you selected the %s keyword\n",
        OPT_OPTN_NAME_VAL2STR(opt) );
```

* Note: you may replace the OPTN_NAME enumeration prefix with another prefix by specifying a **prefix-enum** attribute.

Finally, users may specify the argument either by name or by number. Since the numeric equivalents change by having new entries inserted into the keyword list, this would not be a recommended practice. However, either -1 or ~0 will always be equivalent to specifying the last keyword.

7.5.6.5 Arg Type Set Membership

`arg-type = set;`

The argument must be a list of names each of which must match the strings "all", "none" or one of the keywords (see Section 7.5.6.10 [arg-keyword], page 115) specified for this option. all will turn on all membership bits and none will turn them all off. Specifying one of the keywords will set the corresponding set membership bit on (or off, if negated) . Literal numbers may also be used and may, thereby, set or clear more than one bit.

The membership result starts with the previous (or initialized) result. To clear previous results, either start the membership string with 'none +' or with the equals character ('='). To invert (bit flip) the final result (regardless of whether the previous result is carried over or not), start the string with a carat character ('^'). If you wish to invert the result and start without a carried over value, use one of the following: =^ or ^none+. These are equivalent.

The list of names or numbers must be separated by one of the following characters: '+-|!,' or whitespace. The comma is equivalent to whitespace, except that only one may appear between two entries and it may not appear in conjunction with the *or* bar ('|'). The '+|' leading characters or unadorned name signify adding the next named bit to the mask, and the '-!' leading characters indicate removing it.

The number of keywords allowed is constrained by the number of bits in a pointer, as the bit set is kept in a void * pointer.

If, for example, you specified **first** in your list of keywords, then you can use the following code to test to see if either **first** or **all** was specified:

```
uintptr_t opt = OPT_VALUE_OPTN_NAME;
if (opt & OPTN_NAME_FIRST)
    /* OPTN_NAME_FIRST bit was set */ ;
```

AutoOpts produces a special purpose procedure for this option. To set multiple bits as the default (initial) value, you must specify an initial numeric value (which might become inaccurate over time), or else specify **arg-default** multiple times. Do not specify a series of names conjoined with + symbols as the value for any of the **arg-default** attributes. That works for option parsing, but not for the option code generation.

7.5.6.6 Arg Type Hierarchical

```
arg-type = hierarchy;
arg-type = nested;
```

This denotes an option with a structure-valued argument, a.k.a. **subopts** in **getopts** terminology. The argument is parsed and the values made available to the program via the find and find next calls (See Section 7.6.32.5 [libopts-optionFindValue], page 135, See Section 7.6.32.7 [libopts-optionGetValue], page 136, and see Section 7.6.32.4 [libopts-optionFindNextValue], page 135).

```
tOptionValue * val = optionGetValue(VALUE_OPT_OPTN_NAME, "name');
while (val != NULL) {
  process(val);
  val = optionNextValue(VALUE_OPT_OPTN_NAME, val);
  if (wrong_name(val, "name"))
    break;
}
```

7.5.6.7 Arg Type File Name

```
arg-type = file;
```

This argument type will have some validations on the argument and, optionally, actually open the file. You must specify several additonal attributes for the option:

'file-exists'

>   If not specified or empty, then the directory portion of the name is checked. The directory must exist or the argument is rejected and the usage procedure is invoked.

Otherwise, both the directory as above and the full name is tested for existence. If the value begins with the two letters **no**, then the file must not pre-exist. Otherwise, the file is expected to exist.

'open-file'

If not specified or empty, the file is left alone. If the value begins with the four letters **desc**[*riptor*], then **open(2)** is used and **optArg.argFd** is set. Otherwise, the file is opened with **fopen** and **optArg.argFp** is set.

'file-mode'

If **open-file** is set and not empty, then you must specify the open mode. Set the value to the flag bits or mode string as appropriate for the open type.

7.5.6.8 Arg Type Time Duration

arg-type = time-duration;

The argument will be converted into a number of seconds. It may be a multi-part number with different parts being multiplied into a seconds value and added into the final result. Valid forms are in the table below. Upper cased letters represent numbers that must be used in the expressions.

'[[HH:]MM:]SS'

HH is multiplied by 3600 and MM multiplied by 60 before they are added to SS. This time specification may not be followed by any other time specs. HH and MM are both optional, though HH cannot be specified without MM.

'DAYS d'   DAYS is multiplied by the number of seconds in a day. This value may be followed by (and added to) values specified by HH:MM:SS or the suffixed values below. If present, it must always be first.

'HRS h'   HRS is multiplied by the number of seconds in an hour. This value may be followed by (and added to) values specified by MM:SS or the suffixed values below.

'MINS m'   MINS is multiplied by the number of seconds in a minute. This value may be followed by (and added to) a count of seconds.

'SECS s'   This value can only be the last value in a time specification. The s suffix is optional.

```
5 d 1:10:05     ==> 5 days + 1 hour 10 minutes and 5 seconds
5 d 1 h 10 m 5 ==> yields: 436205 seconds
5d1h10m5s       ==> same result -- spaces are optional.
```

When saved into a config file, the value will be stored as a simple count of seconds. There are actually more (many) accepted time duration strings. The full documentation can be found with ISO-8601 documentation and the more extedded documentation when **parse_duration()** becomes more widely available.

7.5.6.9 Arg Type Time and Date

arg-type = time-date;

The argument will be converted into the number of seconds since the epoch. The conversion rules are very complicated, please see the **getdate_r(3GNU)** man page. There are some additional restrictions:

1. Your project must be compiled with **PKGDATADIR** defined and naming a valid directory.
2. The **DATEMSK** environment variable will be set to the **datemsk** file within that directory.

If that file is not accessible for any reason, the string will be parsed as a time duration (see Section 7.5.6.8 [arg-type time-duration], page 114) instead of a specific date and time.

7.5.6.10 Keyword list

If the **arg-type** is **keyword** (see Section 7.5.6.4 [arg-type keyword], page 112) or **set-membership** (see Section 7.5.6.5 [arg-type set membership], page 112), then you must specify the list of keywords by a series of **keyword** entries. The interface file will contain values for **<OPTN_NAME>_<KEYWORD>** for each keyword entry. **keyword** option types will have an enumeration and **set-membership** option types will have a set of unsigned bits **#define**-d.

If the **arg-type** is specifically **keyword**, you may also add special handling code with a **extra-code** attribute. After **optionEnumerationVal** has converted the input string into an enumeration, you may insert code to process this enumeration value (**pOptDesc->optArg.argEnum**).

7.5.6.11 Option Argument Optional

The **arg-optional** attribute indicates that the argument to the option is optional (need not be specified on the command line). This is only valid if the *arg-type* is **string** (see Section 7.5.6.1 [arg-type string], page 111) or **keyword** (see Section 7.5.6.4 [arg-type keyword], page 112). If it is **keyword**, then this attribute may also specify the default keyword to assume when the argument is not supplied. If left empty, *arg-default* (see Section 7.5.6.12 [arg-default], page 115) or the zero-valued keyword will be used.

The syntax rules for identifying the option argument are:

- If the option is specified with a flag character and there is a character following the flag character, then string following that flag character is the option argument.
- If the flag character is the last character in an argument, then the first character of the next argument is examined. If it is a hyphen, then the option is presumed to not have an argument. Otherwise, the entire next argument is the argument for the option.
- If the option is specified with a long option name and that name is ended with an equal sign character (=), then everything after that character is the option argument.
- If the long name is ended by the end of the argument, then the first character of the next argument is examined, just as with the flag character ending an argument string.

This is overridden and the options are required if the libopts library gets configured with **--disable-optional-args**.

7.5.6.12 Default Option Argument Value

This specifies the default option argument value to be used when the option is not specified or preset. You may specify multiple **arg-default** values if the argument type is **set membership**.

7.5.7 Option Argument Handling

AutoOpts will either specify or automatically generate callback procedures for options that take specialized arguments. The only option argument types that are not specialized are plain string arguments and no argument at all. For options that fall into one of those two categories, you may specify your own callback function, as specified below. If you do this and if you specify that options are resettable (see Section 7.5.10 [automatic options], page 121), then your option handling code **must** look for the 'OPTST_RESET' bit in the `fOptState` field of the option descriptor.

If the option takes a string argument, then the `stack-arg` attribute can be used to specify that the option is to be handled by the `libopts` `stackOptArg()` and `unstackOptArg()` library procedures (see below). In this case, you may not provide option handling code.

Finally, '`documentation`' options (see Section 7.5.5.10 [opt-attr documentation], page 110) may also be marked as `settable` (see Section 7.5.5.5 [opt-attr settable], page 108) and have special callback functions (either '`flag-code`', '`extract-code`', or '`call-proc`').

'`flag-code`'
　　　　statements to execute when the option is encountered. This may be used in conjunction with option argument types that cause AutoOpts to emit handler code. If you do this, the '`flag-code`' with index zero (0) is emitted into the handler code *before* the argument is handled, and the entry with index one (1) is handled afterward.

The generated procedure will be laid out something like this:

```
static void
doOpt<name>(tOptions* pOptions, tOptDesc* pOptDesc)
{
<flag-code[0]>
<AutoOpts defined handler code>
<flag-code[1]>
}
```

Only certain fields within the `tOptions` and `tOptDesc` structures may be accessed. See Section 7.6.1 [Option Processing Data], page 125. When writing this code, you must be very careful with the `pOptions` pointer. The handler code is called with this pointer set to special values for handling special situations. Your code must handle them. As an example, look at `optionEnumerationVal` in `enum.c`.

'`extract-code`'
　　　　This is effectively identical to `flag-code`, except that the source is kept in the output file instead of the definitions file and you cannot use this in conjunction with options with arguments, other than string arguments.

A long comment is used to demarcate the code. You must not modify that marker. *Before* regenerating the option code file, the old file is renamed from MUMBLE.c to MUMBLE.c.save. The template will be looking there for the text to copy into the new output file.

'`call-proc`'
　　　　external procedure to call when option is encountered. The calling sequence must conform to the sequence defined above for the generated procedure, `doOpt<name>`. It has the same restrictions regarding the fields within the

structures passed in as arguments. See Section 7.6.1 [Option Processing Data], page 125.

'flag-proc'

> Name of another option whose **flag-code** can be executed when this option is encountered.

'stack-arg'

> Call a special library routine to stack the option's arguments. Special macros in the interface file are provided for determining how many of the options were found (STACKCT_OPT(NAME)) and to obtain a pointer to a list of pointers to the argument values (STACKLST_OPT(NAME)). Obviously, for a stackable argument, the **max** attribute (see Section 7.5.5.2 [Common Attributes], page 106) needs to be set higher than **1**.
>
> If this stacked argument option has a disablement prefix, then the entire stack of arguments will be cleared by specifying the option with that disablement prefix.

'unstack-arg'

> Call a special library routine to remove (**unstack**) strings from a **stack-arg** option stack. This attribute must name the option that is to be **unstacked**. Neither this option nor the stacked argument option it references may be equivalenced to another option.

7.5.8 Internationalizing Options

Normally, AutoOpts produces usage text that is difficult to translate. It is pieced together on the fly using words and phrases scattered around here and there, piecing together toe document. This does not translate well.

Incorporated into this package are some ways around the problem. First, you should specify the **full-usage** and **short-usage** program attributes (see Section 7.5.1 [program attributes], page 90). This will enable your translators to translate the usage text as a whole.

Your translators will also be able to translate long option names. The option name translations will then become the names searched for both on the command line and in configuration files. However, it will not affect the names of environment variable names used to configure your program.

If it is considered desireable to keep configuration files in the C locale, then several macros are available to suppress or delay the translations of option names at run time. These are all disabled if ENABLE_NLS is not defined at compile time or if no-xlate has been set to the value *anything*. These macros **must** be invoked before the first invocation of optionProcess.

'OPT_NO_XLAT_CFG_NAMES;'
'OPT_XLAT_CFG_NAMES;'

> Disable (or enable) the translations of option names for configuration files. If you enable translation for config files, then they will be translated for command line options.

'`OPT_NO_XLAT_OPT_NAMES;`'
'`OPT_XLAT_OPT_NAMES;`'

> Disable (or enable) the translations of option names for command line processing. If you disable the translation for command line processing, you will also disable it for configuration file processing. Once translated, the option names will remain translated.

7.5.9 Man and Info doc Attributes

AutoOpts includes AutoGen templates for producing abbreviated man pages and for producing the invoking section of an info document. To take advantage of these templates, you must add several attributes to your option definitions.

7.5.9.1 Per option documentation attributes

These attributes are sub-attributes (*sub-stanzas*) of the `flag` stanzas.

'`arg-name`'

> If an option has an argument, the argument should have a name for documentation purposes. It will default to `arg-type`, but it will likely be clearer with something else like, `file-name` instead of `string` (the type).

'`doc`'

> First, every `flag` definition *other than* `documentation` definitions, must have a `doc` attribute defined. If the option takes an argument, then it will need an `arg-name` attribute as well. The `doc` text should be in plain sentences with minimal formatting. The Texinfo commands @code, and @var will have its enclosed text made into **\fB** entries in the man page, and the @file text will be made into **\fI** entries. The `arg-name` attribute is used to display the option's argument in the man page.

> Options marked with the `documentation` attribute are for documenting the usage text. All other options should have the `doc` attribute in order to document the usage of the option in the generated man pages.

> Since these blocks of text are inserted into all output forms, any markup text included in these blocks must be massaged for each output format. By default, it is presumed to be `texi` format.

7.5.9.2 Global documentation attributes

'`cmd-section`'

> If your command is a game or a system management command, specify this attribute with the value 5 or 8, respectively. The default is a user command (section 1).

'`detail`'

> This attribute is used to add a very short explanation about what a program is used for when the `title` attribute is insufficient. If there is no `doc-section` stanza of type DESCRIPTION, then this text is used for the man page DESCRIPTION section, too.

'`addtogroup`'

> This attribute tells the template that the generated code should be surrounded with the following doxygen comments:

```
/** @file <header-or-code-file-name>
 *  @addtogroup <value-of-addtogroup>
 *  @{
 */
```

and

```
/** @} */
```

`'option-format'`

> Specify the default markup style for the doc stanzas. By default, it is `texi`, but
> `man` and `mdoc` may also be selected. There are nine converter programs that
> do a partial job of converting one form of markup into another. `texi2texi`,
> `man2man` and `mdoc2mdoc` work pretty well.
>
> You may also post process the document by using doc-sub stanzas, see below.

`'option-info'`

> This text will be inserted as a lead-in paragraph in the OPTIONS section of the
> generated man page.

`'doc-section'`

> This is a compound attribute that requires three *sub*attributes:
>
> *ds-format*   This describes the format of the associated `ds-text` section. `man`,
> `mdoc` and `texi` formats are supported. Regardless of the chosen
> format, the formatting tags in the output text will be converted to
> `man` macros for `man` pages, `mdoc` macros for `mdoc` pages, and `texi`
> macros for `texinfo` pages.
>
> *ds-text*   This is the descriptive text, written according to the rules for `ds-format` documents.
>
> *ds-type*   This describes the section type. Basically, the title of the section
> that will be added to all output documentation. There may be only
> one `doc-section` for any given `ds-type`. If there are duplicates,
> the results are undefined (it might work, it might not).
>
> There are five categories of `ds-type` sections. They are those that
> the documentation templates would otherwise:
>
> 1. always create itself, ignoring any `ds-types` by this name.
>   These are marked, below, as `ao-only`.
>
> 2. create if none was provided. These are marked, **alternate**.
>
> 3. create but augment if the `doc-section` was provided. These
>   are marked, **augments**.
>
> 4. do nothing, but inserts them into the output in a prescribed
>   order. These are marked, **known**
>
> 5. knows nothing about them. They will be alphabetized and
>   inserted after the list of leading sections and before the list of
>   trailing sections. These are not marked because I don't know
>   their names.

Some of these are emitted by the documentation templates only
if certain conditions are met. If there are conditions, they are ex-
plained below. If there are no conditions, then you will always see
the named section in the output.

The output sections will appear in this order:

'NAME'   `ao-only`.

'SYNOPSIS'
       `alternate`.

'DESCRIPTION'
       `augments`.

'OPTIONS'   `ao-only`.

'OPTION PRESETS'
       `ao-only`, if environment presets or configuration file
       processing has been specified.

'unknown'   At this point, the unknown, alphabetized sections are
       inserted.

'IMPLEMENTATION NOTES'
       `known`

'ENVIRONMENT'
       `augments`, if environment presets have been specified.

'FILES'   `augments`, if configuration file processing has been
       specified.

'EXAMPLES'
       `known`

'EXIT STATUS'
       `augments`.

'ERRORS'   `known`

'COMPATIBILITY'
       `known`

'SEE ALSO'   `known`

'CONFORMING TO'
       `known`

'HISTORY'   `known`

'AUTHORS'   `alternate`, if the `copyright` stanza has either an
       `author` or an `owner` attribute.

'COPYRIGHT'
       `alternate`, if there is a `copyright` stanza.

'BUGS'   `augments`, if the `copyright` stanza has an `eaddr` at-
       tribute.

```
                  'NOTES'    augments.
```

Here is an example of a doc-section for a SEE ALSO type.

```
    doc-section = {
      ds-type   = 'SEE ALSO'; // or anything else
      ds-format = 'man';      // or texi or mdoc format
      ds-text   = <<-_EOText_
    text relevant to this section type,
    in the chosen format
    _EOText_;
    };
```

'doc-sub'   This attribute will cause the resulting documentation to be post-processed.
             This is normally with sed, see doc-sub-cmd below. This attribute has several
             sub-attributes:

'sub-name'
             This is the name of an autogen text definition value, like prog-
             name or version. In the sub-text field, occurrences of this name
             preceded by two less than characters and followed by two greater
             than characters will be replaced by the text value of the definition,
             e.g. '<<prog-name>>'.

'sub-text'
             The text that gets added to the command file for the post processing
             program.

'sub-type'
             If this command only applies to certain types of output, specify this
             with a regular expression that will match one of the valid output
             format types, e.g. 'man|mdoc' will match those two kinds, but not
             texi output. If omitted, it will always apply.

For example, if you want to reference the program name in the doc text for an
option common to two programs, put '#PROG#' into the text. The following will
replace all occurrences of '#PROG#' with the current value for prog:

```
    doc-sub = {
      sub-name = prog-name;
      sub-text = 's/#PROG#/<<prog-name>>/g';
    };
```

'doc-sub-cmd'
             A formatting string for constructing the post-processing command. The first
             parameter is the name of the file with editing commands in it, and the second
             is the file containing the unprocessed document. The default value is:

```
    sed -f %s %s
```

7.5.10 Automatically Supported Options

AutoOpts provides automated support for several options. help and more-help are always
provided. The others are conditional upon various global program attributes being defined
See Section 7.5.1 [program attributes], page 90.

Below are the option names and default flag values. The flags are activated if and only if at least one user-defined option also uses a flag value. The long names are supported as option names if `long-opts` has been specified. These option flags may be deleted or changed to characters of your choosing by specifying `xxx-value = "y";`, where `xxx` is one of the option names below and `y` is either empty or the character of your choice. For example, to change the help flag from `?` to `h`, specify `help-value = "h";`; and to require that `save-opts` be specified only with its long option name, specify `save-opts-value = "";`.

Additionally, the procedure that prints out the program version may be replaced by specifying `version-proc`. This procedure must be defined to be of external scope (non-static). By default, the AutoOpts library provides `optionPrintVersion` and it will be the specified callback function in the option definition structure.

With the exception of the `load-opts` option, none of these automatically supported options will be recognized in configuration files or environment variables.

'help -?'   This option will immediately invoke the `USAGE()` procedure and display the usage line, a description of each option with its description and option usage information. This is followed by the contents of the definition of the `detail` text macro.

'more-help -!'
             This option is identical to the `help` option, except that the output is passed through a pager program. (`more` by default, or the program identified by the `PAGER` environment variable.)

'usage -u'   This option must be requested by specifying, `usage-opt` in the option definition file. It will produce abbreviated help text to `stdout` and exit with zero status (`EXIT_SUCCESS`).

'version -v'
             This will print the program name, title and version. If it is followed by the letter `c` and a value for `copyright` and `owner` have been provided, then the copyright will be printed, too. If it is followed by the letter `n`, then the full copyright notice (if available) will be printed. The `version` attribute must be specified in the option definition file.

'load-opts -<'
             This option will load options from the named file. They will be treated exactly as if they were loaded from the normally found configuration files, but will not be loaded until the option is actually processed. This can also be used within another configuration file, causing them to nest. This is the **only** automatically supported option that can be activated inside of config files or with environment variables.

             Specifying the negated form of the option (`--no-load-opts`) will suppress the processing of configuration files and environment variables.

             This option is activated by specifying one or more `homerc` attributes.

'save-opts ->'
             This option will cause the option state to be printed in the configuration file format when option processing is done but not yet verified for consistency. The

program will terminate successfully without running when this has completed. Note that for most shells you will have to quote or escape the flag character to restrict special meanings to the shell.

The output file will be the configuration file name (default or provided by `rcfile`) in the last directory named in a `homerc` definition.

This option may be set from within your program by invoking the `"SET_OPT_SAVE_OPTS(filename)"` macro (see Section 7.6.20 [SET_OPT_name], page 129). Invoking this macro will set the file name for saving the option processing state, but the state will **not** actually be saved. You must call `optionSaveFile` to do that (see Section 7.6.32.16 [libopts-optionSaveFile], page 140). **CAVEAT**: if, after invoking this macro, you call `optionProcess`, the option processing state will be saved to this file and `optionProcess` will not return. You may wish to invoke `CLEAR_OPT( SAVE_OPTS )` (see Section 7.6.2 [CLEAR_OPT], page 126) beforehand if you do need to reinvoke `optionProcess`.

This option is activated by specifying one or more `homerc` attributes.

‘reset-option -R’

This option takes the name of an option for the current program and resets its state such that it is set back to its original, compile-time initialized value. If the option state is subsequently stored (via `--save-opts`), the named option will not appear in that file.

This option is activated by specifying the `resettable` attribute.

BEWARE: If the `resettable` attribute is specified, all option callbacks **must** look for the `OPTST_RESET` bit in the `fOptState` field of the option descriptor. If set, the `optCookie` and `optArg` fields will be unchanged from their last setting. When the callback returns, these fields will be set to their original values. If you use this feature and you have allocated data hanging off of the cookie, you need to deallocate it.

7.5.11 Library of Standard Options

AutoOpts has developed a set of standardized options. You may incorporate these options in your program simply by *first* adding a `#define` for the options you want, and then the line,

```
#include stdoptions.def
```

in your option definitions. The supported options are specified thus:

```
#define DEBUG
#define DIRECTORY
#define DRY_RUN
#define INPUT
#define INTERACTIVE
#define OUTPUT
#define WARN

#define SILENT
#define QUIET
```

```
#define BRIEF
#define VERBOSE
```

By default, only the long form of the option will be available. To specify the short (flag) form, suffix these names with _FLAG. e.g.,

```
#define DEBUG_FLAG
```

--silent, --quiet, --brief and --verbose are related in that they all indicate some level of diagnostic output. These options are all designed to conflict with each other. Instead of four different options, however, several levels can be incorporated by #define-ing VERBOSE_ENUM. In conjunction with VERBOSE, it incorporates the notion of 5 levels in an enumeration: silent, quiet, brief, informative and verbose; with the default being brief.

Here is an example program that uses the following set of definitions:

```
AutoGen Definitions options;

prog-name  = default-test;
prog-title = 'Default Option Example';
homerc     = '$$/../share/default-test', '$HOME', '.';
environrc;
long-opts;
gnu-usage;
usage-opt;
version    = '1.0';
main = {
  main-type = shell-process;
};
#define DEBUG_FLAG
#define WARN_FLAG
#define WARN_LEVEL
#define VERBOSE_FLAG
#define VERBOSE_ENUM
#define DRY_RUN_FLAG
#define OUTPUT_FLAG
#define INPUT_FLAG
#define DIRECTORY_FLAG
#define INTERACTIVE_FLAG
#include stdoptions.def
```

Running a few simple commands on that definition file:

```
autogen default-test.def
copts="-DTEST_DEFAULT_TEST_OPTS `autoopts-config cflags`"
lopts="`autoopts-config ldflags`"
cc -o default-test ${copts} default-test.c ${lopts}
```

Yields a program which, when run with --help, prints out:

```
exit 0
```

7.6 Programmatic Interface

The user interface for access to the argument information is completely defined in the generated header file and in the portions of the distributed file "options.h" that are marked "public".

In the following macros, text marked *<NAME>* or *name* is the name of the option **in upper case** and **segmented with underscores** _. The macros and enumerations defined in the options header (interface) file are used as follows:

To see how these **#define** macros are used in a program, the reader is referred to the several **opts.h** files included with the AutoGen sources.

7.6.1 Data for Option Processing

This section describes the data that may be accessed from within the option processing callback routines. The following fields may be used in the following ways and may be used for read only. The first set is addressed from the **tOptDesc*** pointer:

'optIndex'
'optValue'

> These may be used by option procedures to determine which option they are working on (in case they handle several options).

'optActualIndex'
'optActualValue'

> These may be used by option procedures to determine which option was used to set the current option. This may be different from the above if the options are members of an equivalence class.

'optOccCt'

> If AutoOpts is processing command line arguments, then this value will contain the current occurrence count. During the option preset phase (reading configuration files and examining environment variables), the value is zero.

'fOptState'

> The field may be tested for the following bit values (prefix each name with OPTST_, e.g. OPTST_INIT):

> 'INIT'   Initial compiled value. As a bit test, it will always yield FALSE.

> 'SET'   The option was set via the SET_OPT() macro.

> 'PRESET'   The option was set via a configuration file.

> 'DEFINED'   The option was set via a command line option.

> 'SET_MASK'

> > This is a mask of flags that show the set state, one of the above four values.

> 'EQUIVALENCE'

> > This bit is set when the option was selected by an equivalenced option.

'DISABLED'

> This bit is set if the option is to be disabled. (Meaning it was a long option prefixed by the disablement prefix, or the option has not been specified yet and initializes as `disabled`.)

As an example of how this might be used, in AutoGen I want to allow template writers to specify that the template output can be left in a writable or read-only state. To support this, there is a Guile function named `set-writable` (see Section 3.4.50 [SCM set-writable], page 36). Also, I provide for command options `--writable` and `--not-writable`. I give precedence to command line and RC file options, thus:

```
switch (STATE_OPT( WRITABLE )) {
case OPTST_DEFINED:
case OPTST_PRESET:
    fprintf(stderr, zOverrideWarn, pCurTemplate->pzFileName,
            pCurMacro->lineNo);
    break;

default:
    if (gh_boolean_p( set ) && (set == SCM_BOOL_F))
        CLEAR_OPT( WRITABLE );
    else
        SET_OPT_WRITABLE;
}
```

'pzLastArg'

> Pointer to the latest argument string. BEWARE If the argument type is numeric, an enumeration or a bit mask, then this will be the argument **value** and not a pointer to a string.

The following two fields are addressed from the `tOptions*` pointer:

'pzProgName'

> Points to a NUL-terminated string containing the current program name, as retrieved from the argument vector.

'pzProgPath'

> Points to a NUL-terminated string containing the full path of the current program, as retrieved from the argument vector. (If available on your system.)

Note these fields get filled in during the first call to `optionProcess()`. All other fields are private, for the exclusive use of AutoOpts code and are subject to change.

7.6.2 CLEAR_OPT(<NAME>) - Clear Option Markings

Make as if the option had never been specified. `HAVE_OPT(<NAME>)` will yield `FALSE` after invoking this macro.

7.6.3 COUNT_OPT(<NAME>) - Definition Count

This macro will tell you how many times the option was specified on the command line. It does not include counts of preset options.

```
if (COUNT_OPT( NAME ) != desired-count) {
    make-an-undesirable-message.
}
```

7.6.4 DESC(<NAME>) - Option Descriptor

This macro is used internally by other AutoOpt macros. It is not for general use. It is used to obtain the option description corresponding to its **UPPER CASED** option name argument. This is primarily used in other macro definitions.

7.6.5 DISABLE_OPT_name - Disable an option

This macro is emitted if it is both settable and it can be disabled. If it cannot be disabled, it may always be CLEAR-ed (see above).

The form of the macro will actually depend on whether the option is equivalenced to another, and/or has an assigned handler procedure. Unlike the SET_OPT macro, this macro does not allow an option argument.

```
DISABLE_OPT_NAME;
```

7.6.6 ENABLED_OPT(<NAME>) - Is Option Enabled?

Yields true if the option defaults to disabled and ISUNUSED_OPT() would yield true. It also yields true if the option has been specified with a disablement prefix, disablement value or the DISABLE_OPT_NAME macro was invoked.

7.6.7 ERRSKIP_OPTERR - Ignore Option Errors

When it is necessary to continue (return to caller) on option errors, invoke this option. It is reversible. See Section 7.6.8 [ERRSTOP_OPTERR], page 127.

7.6.8 ERRSTOP_OPTERR - Stop on Errors

After invoking this macro, if optionProcess() encounters an error, it will call exit(1) rather than return. This is the default processing mode. It can be overridden by specifying allow-errors in the definitions file, or invoking the macro See Section 7.6.7 [ERRSKIP_OPTERR], page 127.

7.6.9 HAVE_OPT(<NAME>) - Have this option?

This macro yields true if the option has been specified in any fashion at all. It is used thus:

```
if (HAVE_OPT( NAME )) {
    <do-things-associated-with-opt-name>;
}
```

7.6.10 ISSEL_OPT(<NAME>) - Is Option Selected?

This macro yields true if the option has been specified either on the command line or via a SET/DISABLE macro.

7.6.11 ISUNUSED_OPT(<NAME>) - Never Specified?

This macro yields true if the option has never been specified, or has been cleared via the CLEAR_OPT() macro.

7.6.12 OPTION_CT - Full Count of Options

The full count of all options, both those defined and those generated automatically by AutoOpts. This is primarily used to initialize the program option descriptor structure.

7.6.13 OPT_ARG(<NAME>) - Option Argument String

The option argument value as a pointer to string. Note that argument values that have been specified as numbers are stored as numbers or keywords. For such options, use instead the OPT_VALUE_name define. It is used thus:

```
if (HAVE_OPT( NAME )) {
    char* p = OPT_ARG( NAME );
    <do-things-with-opt-name-argument-string>;
}
```

7.6.14 OPT_NO_XLAT_CFG_NAMES - option name xlation

Invoking this macro will disable the translation of option names only while processing configuration files and environment variables. This must be invoked before the first call to optionProcess.. You need not invoke this if your option definition file contains the attribute assignment, no-xlate = opt-cfg;.

7.6.15 OPT_NO_XLAT_OPT_NAMES - option name xlation

Invoking this macro will completely disable the translation of option names. This must be invoked before the first call to optionProcess. You need not invoke this if your option definition file contains the attribute assignment, no-xlate = opt;.

7.6.16 OPT_VALUE_name - Option Argument Value

This macro gets emitted only for options that take numeric, keyword or set membership arguments. The macro yields a word-sized integer containing the enumeration, bit set or numeric value for the option argument.

```
int opt_val = OPT_VALUE_name;
```

7.6.17 OPT_XLAT_CFG_NAMES - option name xlation

If ENABLE_NLS is defined and no-xlate has been not set to the value *anything*, this macro will cause the translation of option names to happen before starting the processing of configuration files and environment variables. This will change the recognition of options within the $PROGRAMNAME environment variable, but will not alter the names used for setting options via $PROGRAMNAME_name environment variables.

This must be invoked before the first call to optionProcess. You might need to use this macro if your option definition file contains the attribute assignment, no-xlate = opt; or no-xlate = opt-cfg;, and you have determined in some way that you wish to override that.

7.6.18 OPT_XLAT_OPT_NAMES - option name xlation

If ENABLE_NLS is defined and no-xlate has been not set to the value *anything*, translate the option names before processing the command line options. Long option names may thus be localized. (If the names were translated before configuration processing, they will not be re-translated.)

This must be invoked before the first call to option_Process. You might need to use this macro if your option definition file contains the attribute assignment, no-xlate = opt; and you have determined in some way that you wish to override that.

7.6.19 RESTART_OPT(n) - Resume Option Processing

If option processing has stopped (either because of an error or something was encountered that looked like a program argument), it can be resumed by providing this macro with the index n of the next option to process and calling optionProcess() again.

```
int main(int argc, char ** argv) {
  for (int ai = 0; ai < argc ;) {
  restart:
    ai = optionProcess(&progOptions, argc, argv);
    for (; ai < argc; ai++) {
      char * arg = arg[ai];
      if (*arg == '-') {
        RESTART_OPT(ai);
        goto restart;
      }
      process(arg);
    }
  }
}
```

If you want a program to operate this way, you might consider specifying a for-each main function (see Section 7.5.4.7 [main for-each], page 102) with the interleaved attribute. It will allow you to process interleaved operands and options from either the command line or when reading them from standard input.

7.6.20 SET_OPT_name - Force an option to be set

This macro gets emitted only when the given option has the settable attribute specified.

The form of the macro will actually depend on whether the option is equivalenced to another, has an option argument and/or has an assigned handler procedure. If the option has an argument, then this macro will too. Beware that the argument is not reallocated, so the value must not be on the stack or deallocated in any other way for as long as the value might get referenced.

If you have supplied at least one homerc file (see Section 7.5.1 [program attributes], page 90), this macro will be emitted for the --save-opts option.

```
SET_OPT_SAVE_OPTS( "filename" );
```

See Section 7.5.10 [automatic options], page 121, for a discussion of the implications of using this particular example.

7.6.21 STACKCT_OPT(<NAME>) - Stacked Arg Count

When the option handling attribute is specified as stack_arg, this macro may be used to determine how many of them actually got stacked.

Do not use this on options that have not been stacked or has not been specified (the
`stack_arg` attribute must have been specified, and HAVE_OPT(<NAME>) must yield TRUE).
Otherwise, you will likely seg fault.

```
if (HAVE_OPT( NAME )) {
    int    ct = STACKCT_OPT(  NAME );
    char** pp = STACKLST_OPT( NAME );

    do  {
        char* p = *pp++;
        do-things-with-p;
    } while (--ct > 0);
}
```

7.6.22 STACKLST_OPT(<NAME>) - Argument Stack

The address of the list of pointers to the option arguments. The pointers are ordered by the
order in which they were encountered in the option presets and command line processing.

Do not use this on options that have not been stacked or has not been specified (the
`stack_arg` attribute must have been specified, and HAVE_OPT(<OPTION>) must yield
TRUE). Otherwise, you will likely seg fault.

```
if (HAVE_OPT( NAME )) {
    int    ct = STACKCT_OPT(  NAME );
    char** pp = STACKLST_OPT( NAME );

    do  {
        char* p = *pp++;
        do-things-with-p;
    } while (--ct > 0);
}
```

7.6.23 START_OPT - Restart Option Processing

This is just a shortcut for RESTART_OPT(1) (See Section 7.6.19 [RESTART_OPT],
page 129.)

7.6.24 STATE_OPT(<NAME>) - Option State

If you need to know if an option was set because of presetting actions (configuration
file processing or environment variables), versus a command line entry versus one of the
SET/DISABLE macros, then use this macro. It will yield one of four values: OPTST_INIT,
OPTST_SET, OPTST_PRESET or OPTST_DEFINED. It is used thus:

```
switch (STATE_OPT( NAME )) {
    case OPTST_INIT:
        not-preset, set or on the command line.  (unless CLEAR-ed)

    case OPTST_SET:
        option set via the SET_OPT_NAME() macro.

    case OPTST_PRESET:
```

```
                    option set via an configuration file or environment variable

              case OPTST_DEFINED:
                  option set via a command line option.

              default:
                  cannot happen :)
        }
```

7.6.25 USAGE(exit-code) - Usage invocation macro

This macro invokes the procedure registered to display the usage text. Normally, this will be `optionUsage` from the AutoOpts library, but you may select another procedure by specifying `usage = "proc_name"` program attribute. This procedure must take two arguments first, a pointer to the option descriptor, and second the exit code. The macro supplies the option descriptor automatically. This routine is expected to call `exit(3)` with the provided exit code.

The `optionUsage` routine also behaves differently depending on the exit code:

EXIT_SUCCESS (the value zero)

It is assumed that full usage help has been requested. Consequently, more information is provided than when displaying usage and exiting with a non-zero exit code. Output will be sent to **stdout** and the program will exit with a zero status code.

EX_USAGE (64)

The abbreviated usage will be printed to **stdout** and the program will exit with a zero status code. **EX_USAGE** may or may not be 64. If your system provides `/usr/include/sysexits.h` that has a different value, then that value will be used.

any other value

The abbreviated usage will be printed to stderr and the program will exit with the provided status code.

7.6.26 VALUE_OPT_name - Option Flag Value

This is a #define for the flag character used to specify an option on the command line. If `value` was not specified for the option, then it is a unique number associated with the option. `option value` refers to this value, `option argument` refers to the (optional) argument to the option.

```
        switch (WHICH_OPT_OTHER_OPT) {
        case VALUE_OPT_NAME:
            this-option-was-really-opt-name;
        case VALUE_OPT_OTHER_OPT:
            this-option-was-really-other-opt;
        }
```

7.6.27 VERSION - Version and Full Version

If the version attribute is defined for the program, then a stringified version will be #defined as PROGRAM_VERSION and PROGRAM_FULL_VERSION. PROGRAM_FULL_VERSION is used for printing the program version in response to the version option. The version option is automatically supplied in response to this attribute, too.

You may access PROGRAM_VERSION via programOptions.pzFullVersion.

7.6.28 WHICH_IDX_name - Which Equivalenced Index

This macro gets emitted only for equivalenced-to options. It is used to obtain the index for the one of the several equivalence class members set the equivalenced-to option.

```
switch (WHICH_IDX_OTHER_OPT) {
case INDEX_OPT_NAME:
    this-option-was-really-opt-name;
case INDEX_OPT_OTHER_OPT:
    this-option-was-really-other-opt;
}
```

7.6.29 WHICH_OPT_name - Which Equivalenced Option

This macro gets emitted only for equivalenced-to options. It is used to obtain the value code for the one of the several equivalence class members set the equivalenced-to option.

```
switch (WHICH_OPT_OTHER_OPT) {
case VALUE_OPT_NAME:
    this-option-was-really-opt-name;
case VALUE_OPT_OTHER_OPT:
    this-option-was-really-other-opt;
}
```

7.6.30 teOptIndex - Option Index and Enumeration

This enum defines the complete set of options, both user specified and automatically provided. This can be used, for example, to distinguish which of the equivalenced options was actually used.

```
switch (pOptDesc->optActualIndex) {
case INDEX_OPT_FIRST:
    stuff;
case INDEX_OPT_DIFFERENT:
    different-stuff;
default:
    unknown-things;
}
```

7.6.31 OPTIONS_STRUCT_VERSION - active version

You will not actually need to reference this value, but you need to be aware that it is there. It is the first value in the option descriptor that you pass to optionProcess. It contains a magic number and version information. Normally, you should be able to work with a more recent option library than the one you compiled with. However, if the library is changed incompatibly, then the library will detect the out of date magic marker, explain the difficulty and exit. You will then need to rebuild and recompile your option definitions. This has rarely been necessary.

7.6.32 libopts External Procedures

These are the routines that libopts users may call directly from their code. There are several other routines that can be called by code generated by the libopts option templates, but they are not to be called from any other user code. The `options.h` header is fairly clear about this, too.

This subsection was automatically generated by AutoGen using extracted information and the aginfo3.tpl template.

7.6.32.1 ao_string_tokenize

tokenize an input string

Usage:

```
token_list_t * res = ao_string_tokenize( string );
```

Where the arguments are:

Name	Type	Description
string	char const *	string to be tokenized
returns	token_list_t *	pointer to a structure that lists each token

This function will convert one input string into a list of strings. The list of strings is derived by separating the input based on white space separation. However, if the input contains either single or double quote characters, then the text after that character up to a matching quote will become the string in the list.

The returned pointer should be deallocated with `free(3C)` when are done using the data. The data are placed in a single block of allocated memory. Do not deallocate individual token/strings.

The structure pointed to will contain at least these two fields:

'tkn_ct'   The number of tokens found in the input string.

'tok_list'

An array of `tkn_ct + 1` pointers to substring tokens, with the last pointer set to NULL.

There are two types of quoted strings: single quoted (') and double quoted ("). Singly quoted strings are fairly raw in that escape characters (\\) are simply another character, except when preceding the following characters:

```
\\   double backslashes reduce to one
'    incorporates the single quote into the string
\n   suppresses both the backslash and newline character
```

Double quote strings are formed according to the rules of string constants in ANSI-C programs.

NULL is returned and `errno` will be set to indicate the problem:

- **EINVAL** - There was an unterminated quoted string.
- **ENOENT** - The input string was empty.
- **ENOMEM** - There is not enough memory.

7.6.32.2 configFileLoad

parse a configuration file

Usage:

```
const tOptionValue * res = configFileLoad( fname );
```

Where the arguments are:

Name	Type	Description
fname	char const *	the file to load
returns	const tOption-Value *	An allocated, compound value structure

This routine will load a named configuration file and parse the text as a hierarchically valued option. The option descriptor created from an option definition file is not used via this interface. The returned value is "named" with the input file name and is of type "OPARG_TYPE_HIERARCHY". It may be used in calls to optionGetValue(), optionNextValue() and optionUnloadNested().

If the file cannot be loaded or processed, NULL is returned and *errno* is set. It may be set by a call to either open(2) mmap(2) or other file system calls, or it may be:

- **ENOENT** - the file was not found.
- **ENOMSG** - the file was empty.
- **EINVAL** - the file contents are invalid – not properly formed.
- **ENOMEM** - not enough memory to allocate the needed structures.

7.6.32.3 optionFileLoad

Load the locatable config files, in order

Usage:

```
int res = optionFileLoad( opts, prog );
```

Where the arguments are:

Name	Type	Description
opts	tOptions *	program options descriptor
prog	char const *	program name
returns	int	0 -> SUCCESS, -1 -> FAILURE

This function looks in all the specified directories for a configuration file ("rc" file or "ini" file) and processes any found twice. The first time through, they are processed in reverse order (last file first). At that time, only "immediate action" configurables are processed. For example, if the last named file specifies not processing any more configuration files, then no more configuration files will be processed. Such an option in the **first** named directory will have no effect.

Once the immediate action configurables have been handled, then the directories are handled in normal, forward order. In that way, later config files can override the settings of earlier config files.

See the AutoOpts documentation for a thorough discussion of the config file format.

Configuration files not found or not decipherable are simply ignored.

Returns the value, "-1" if the program options descriptor is out of date or indecipherable. Otherwise, the value "0" will always be returned.

7.6.32.4 optionFindNextValue

find a hierarcicaly valued option instance

Usage:

```
const tOptionValue * res = optionFindNextValue( odesc, pPrevVal, name, value );
```

Where the arguments are:

Name	Type	Description
odesc	const tOptDesc *	an option with a nested arg type
pPrevVal	const tOptionValue *	the last entry
name	char const *	name of value to find
value	char const *	the matching value
returns	const tOption-Value *	a compound value structure

This routine will find the next entry in a nested value option or configurable. It will search through the list and return the next entry that matches the criteria.

The returned result is NULL and errno is set:

* EINVAL - the pOptValue does not point to a valid hierarchical option value.
* ENOENT - no entry matched the given name.

7.6.32.5 optionFindValue

find a hierarcicaly valued option instance

Usage:

```
const tOptionValue * res = optionFindValue( odesc, name, val );
```

Where the arguments are:

Name	Type	Description
odesc	const tOptDesc *	an option with a nested arg type
name	char const *	name of value to find
val	char const *	the matching value

| | returns | const tOption-Value * | a compound value structure |

This routine will find an entry in a nested value option or configurable. It will search through the list and return a matching entry.

The returned result is NULL and errno is set:

- EINVAL - the pOptValue does not point to a valid hierarchical option value.
- ENOENT - no entry matched the given name.

7.6.32.6 optionFree

free allocated option processing memory

Usage:

```
optionFree( pOpts );
```

Where the arguments are:

Name	Type	Description
pOpts	tOptions *	program options descriptor

AutoOpts sometimes allocates memory and puts pointers to it in the option state structures. This routine deallocates all such memory.

As long as memory has not been corrupted, this routine is always successful.

7.6.32.7 optionGetValue

get a specific value from a hierarcical list

Usage:

```
const tOptionValue * res = optionGetValue( pOptValue, valueName );
```

Where the arguments are:

Name	Type	Description
pOptValue	const tOptionValue *	a hierarchcal value
valueName	char const *	name of value to get
returns	const tOption-Value *	a compound value structure

This routine will find an entry in a nested value option or configurable. If "valueName" is NULL, then the first entry is returned. Otherwise, the first entry with a name that exactly matches the argument will be returned. If there is no matching value, NULL is returned and errno is set to ENOENT. If the provided option value is not a hierarchical value, NULL is also returned and errno is set to EINVAL.

The returned result is NULL and errno is set:

- EINVAL - the pOptValue does not point to a valid hierarchical option value.
- ENOENT - no entry matched the given name.

7.6.32.8 optionLoadLine

process a string for an option name and value

Usage:

```
optionLoadLine( opts, line );
```

Where the arguments are:

Name	Type	Description
opts	tOptions *	program options descriptor
line	char const *	NUL-terminated text

This is a client program callable routine for setting options from, for example, the contents of a file that they read in. Only one option may appear in the text. It will be treated as a normal (non-preset) option.

When passed a pointer to the option struct and a string, it will find the option named by the first token on the string and set the option argument to the remainder of the string. The caller must NUL terminate the string. The caller need not skip over any introductory hyphens. Any embedded new lines will be included in the option argument. If the input looks like one or more quoted strings, then the input will be "cooked". The "cooking" is identical to the string formation used in AutoGen definition files (see Section 3.3.2 [basic expression], page 24), except that you may not use backquotes.

Invalid options are silently ignored. Invalid option arguments will cause a warning to print, but the function should return.

7.6.32.9 optionMemberList

Get the list of members of a bit mask set

Usage:

```
char * res = optionMemberList( od );
```

Where the arguments are:

Name	Type	Description
od	tOptDesc *	the set membership option description
returns	char *	the names of the set bits

This converts the OPT_VALUE_name mask value to a allocated string. It is the caller's responsibility to free the string.

7.6.32.10 optionNextValue

get the next value from a hierarchical list

Usage:

```
const tOptionValue * res = optionNextValue( pOptValue, pOldValue );
```

Where the arguments are:

Name	Type	Description

pOptValue	const tOptionValue *	a hierarchcal list value
pOldValue	const tOptionValue *	a value from this list
returns	const tOption-Value *	a compound value structure

This routine will return the next entry after the entry passed in. At the end of the list, NULL will be returned. If the entry is not found on the list, NULL will be returned and "*errno*" will be set to EINVAL. The "*pOldValue*" must have been gotten from a prior call to this routine or to "`opitonGetValue()`".

The returned result is NULL and errno is set:

- EINVAL - the `pOptValue` does not point to a valid hierarchical option value or `pOldValue` does not point to a member of that option value.

- ENOENT - the supplied `pOldValue` pointed to the last entry.

7.6.32.11 optionOnlyUsage

Print usage text for just the options

Usage:

        optionOnlyUsage(pOpts, ex_code);

Where the arguments are:

Name	Type	Description
pOpts	tOptions *	program options descriptor
ex_code	int	exit code for calling exit(3)

This routine will print only the usage for each option. This function may be used when the emitted usage must incorporate information not available to AutoOpts.

7.6.32.12 optionPrintVersion

Print the program version

Usage:

        optionPrintVersion(opts, od);

Where the arguments are:

Name	Type	Description
opts	tOptions *	program options descriptor
od	tOptDesc *	the descriptor for this arg

This routine will print the version to stdout.

7.6.32.13 optionPrintVersionAndReturn

Print the program version

Usage:

```
optionPrintVersionAndReturn( opts, od );
```

Where the arguments are:

Name	Type	Description
opts	tOptions *	program options descriptor
od	tOptDesc *	the descriptor for this arg

This routine will print the version to stdout and return instead of exiting. Please see the source for the `print_ver` funtion for details on selecting how verbose to be after this function returns.

7.6.32.14 optionProcess

this is the main option processing routine

Usage:

```
int res = optionProcess( opts, a_ct, a_v );
```

Where the arguments are:

Name	Type	Description
opts	tOptions *	program options descriptor
a_ct	int	program arg count
a_v	char **	program arg vector
returns	int	the count of the arguments processed

This is the main entry point for processing options. It is intended that this procedure be called once at the beginning of the execution of a program. Depending on options selected earlier, it is sometimes necessary to stop and restart option processing, or to select completely different sets of options. This can be done easily, but you generally do not want to do this.

The number of arguments processed always includes the program name. If one of the arguments is "−", then it is counted and the processing stops. If an error was encountered and errors are to be tolerated, then the returned value is the index of the argument causing the error. A hyphen by itself ("-") will also cause processing to stop and will *not* be counted among the processed arguments. A hyphen by itself is treated as an operand. Encountering an operand stops option processing.

Errors will cause diagnostics to be printed. `exit(3)` may or may not be called. It depends upon whether or not the options were generated with the "allow-errors" attribute, or if the ERRSKIP_OPTERR or ERRSTOP_OPTERR macros were invoked.

7.6.32.15 optionRestore

restore option state from memory copy

Usage:

        optionRestore(pOpts);

Where the arguments are:

Name	Type	Description
pOpts	tOptions *	program options descriptor

Copy back the option state from saved memory. The allocated memory is left intact, so this routine can be called repeatedly without having to call optionSaveState again. If you are restoring a state that was saved before the first call to optionProcess(3AO), then you may change the contents of the argc/argv parameters to optionProcess.

If you have not called `optionSaveState` before, a diagnostic is printed to `stderr` and exit is called.

7.6.32.16 optionSaveFile

saves the option state to a file

Usage:

        optionSaveFile(opts);

Where the arguments are:

Name	Type	Description
opts	tOptions *	program options descriptor

This routine will save the state of option processing to a file. The name of that file can be specified with the argument to the `--save-opts` option, or by appending the `rcfile` attribute to the last `homerc` attribute. If no `rcfile` attribute was specified, it will default to .*programnamerc*. If you wish to specify another file, you should invoke the `SET_OPT_SAVE_OPTS(filename)` macro.

The recommend usage is as follows:

        optionProcess(&progOptions, argc, argv);
        if (i_want_a_non_standard_place_for_this)
        SET_OPT_SAVE_OPTS("myfilename");
        optionSaveFile(&progOptions);

If no `homerc` file was specified, this routine will silently return and do nothing. If the output file cannot be created or updated, a message will be printed to `stderr` and the routine will return.

7.6.32.17 optionSaveState

saves the option state to memory

Usage:

        optionSaveState(pOpts);

Where the arguments are:

Name	Type	Description
pOpts	tOptions *	program options descriptor

This routine will allocate enough memory to save the current option processing state. If this routine has been called before, that memory will be reused. You may only save one copy of the option state. This routine may be called before optionProcess(3AO). If you do call it before the first call to optionProcess, then you may also change the contents of argc/argv after you call optionRestore(3AO)

In fact, more strongly put: it is safest to only use this function before having processed any options. In particular, the saving and restoring of stacked string arguments and hierarchical values is disabled. The values are not saved.

If it fails to allocate the memory, it will print a message to stderr and exit. Otherwise, it will always succeed.

7.6.32.18 optionUnloadNested

Deallocate the memory for a nested value

Usage:

        optionUnloadNested(pOptVal);

Where the arguments are:

Name	Type	Description
pOptVal	tOptionValue const *	the hierarchical value

A nested value needs to be deallocated. The pointer passed in should have been gotten from a call to configFileLoad() (See see Section 7.6.32.2 [libopts-configFileLoad], page 134).

7.6.32.19 optionVersion

return the compiled AutoOpts version number

Usage:

        char const * res = optionVersion();

Where the arguments are:

Name	Type	Description
returns	char const *	the version string in constant memory

Returns the full version string compiled into the library. The returned string cannot be modified.

7.6.32.20 strequate

map a list of characters to the same value

Usage:

        strequate(ch_list);

Where the arguments are:

Name	Type	Description
ch_list	char const *	characters to equivalence

Each character in the input string get mapped to the first character in the string. This function name is mapped to option_strequate so as to not conflict with the POSIX name space.

none.

7.6.32.21 streqvcmp

compare two strings with an equivalence mapping

Usage:

```
int res = streqvcmp( str1, str2 );
```

Where the arguments are:

Name	Type	Description
str1	char const *	first string
str2	char const *	second string
returns	int	the difference between two differing characters

Using a character mapping, two strings are compared for "equivalence". Each input character is mapped to a comparison character and the mapped-to characters are compared for the two NUL terminated input strings. This function name is mapped to option_streqvcmp so as to not conflict with the POSIX name space.

none checked. Caller responsible for seg faults.

7.6.32.22 streqvmap

Set the character mappings for the streqv functions

Usage:

```
streqvmap( from, to, ct );
```

Where the arguments are:

Name	Type	Description
from	char	Input character
to	char	Mapped-to character
ct	int	compare length

Set the character mapping. If the count (ct) is set to zero, then the map is cleared by setting all entries in the map to their index value. Otherwise, the "From" character is mapped to the "To" character. If ct is greater than 1, then From and To are incremented and the process repeated until ct entries have been set. For example,

```
streqvmap('a', 'A', 26);
```

will alter the mapping so that all English lower case letters will map to upper case.

This function name is mapped to option_streqvmap so as to not conflict with the POSIX name space.

none.

7.6.32.23 strneqvcmp

compare two strings with an equivalence mapping

Usage:

```
int res = strneqvcmp( str1, str2, ct );
```

Where the arguments are:

Name	Type	Description
str1	char const *	first string
str2	char const *	second string
ct	int	compare length
returns	int	the difference between two differing characters

Using a character mapping, two strings are compared for "equivalence". Each input character is mapped to a comparison character and the mapped-to characters are compared for the two NUL terminated input strings. The comparison is limited to ct bytes. This function name is mapped to option_strneqvcmp so as to not conflict with the POSIX name space.

none checked. Caller responsible for seg faults.

7.6.32.24 strtransform

convert a string into its mapped-to value

Usage:

```
strtransform( dest, src );
```

Where the arguments are:

Name	Type	Description
dest	char *	output string
src	char const *	input string

Each character in the input string is mapped and the mapped-to character is put into the output. This function name is mapped to option_strtransform so as to not conflict with the POSIX name space.

The source and destination may be the same.

none.

7.7 Multi-Threading

AutoOpts was designed to configure a program for running. This generally happens before much real work has been started. Consequently, it is expected to be run before multi-threaded applications have started multiple threads. However, this is not always the case. Some applications may need to reset and reload their running configuration, and some may use `SET_OPT_xxx()` macros during processing. If you need to dynamically change your option configuration in your multi-threaded application, it is your responsibility to prevent all threads from accessing the option configuration state, except the one altering the configuration.

The various accessor macros (`HAVE_OPT()`, etc.) do not modify state and are safe to use in a multi-threaded application. It is safe as long as no other thread is concurrently modifying state, of course.

7.8 Option Descriptor File

This is the module that is to be compiled and linked with your program. It contains internal data and procedures subject to change. Basically, it contains a single global data structure containing all the information provided in the option definitions, plus a number of static strings and any callout procedures that are specified or required. You should never have need for looking at this, except, perhaps, to examine the code generated for implementing the `flag-code` construct.

7.9 Using AutoOpts

There are actually several levels of **using** autoopts. Which you choose depends upon how you plan to distribute (or not) your application.

7.9.1 local-only use

To use AutoOpts in your application where you do not have to worry about distribution issues, your issues are simple and few.

- Create a file 'myopts.def', according to the documentation above. It is probably easiest to start with the example in Section 7.4 [Quick Start], page 88 and edit it into the form you need.

- Run AutoGen to create the option interface file (`myopts.h`) and the option descriptor code (`myopts.c`):

      autogen myopts.def

- In all your source files where you need to refer to option state, `#include "myopts.h"`.

- In your main routine, code something along the lines of:

```
#define ARGC_MIN some-lower-limit
#define ARGC_MAX some-upper-limit
main( int argc, char** argv )
{
    {
        int arg_ct = optionProcess( &myprogOptions, argc, argv );
        argc -= arg_ct;
        if ((argc < ARGC_MIN) || (argc > ARGC_MAX)) {
```

```
                     fprintf( stderr, "%s ERROR:  remaining args (%d) "
                              "out of range\n", myprogOptions.pzProgName,
                              argc );

                     USAGE( EXIT_FAILURE );
                 }
                 argv += arg_ct;
             }
             if (HAVE_OPT(OPTN_NAME))
                 respond_to_optn_name();
             ...
         }
```

- Compile 'myopts.c' and link your program with the following additional arguments:

      `autoopts-config cflags ldflags` myopts.c

7.9.2 binary distro, AutoOpts not installed

If you will be distributing (or copying) your project to a system that does not have AutoOpts installed, you will need to statically link the AutoOpts library, libopts into your program. Get the link information with static-libs instead of ldflags:

      `autoopts-config static-libs`

7.9.3 binary distro, AutoOpts pre-installed

If you will be distributing (or copying) your project to a system that does have AutoOpts (or only libopts) installed, you will still need to ensure that the library is findable at program load time, or you will still have to statically link. The former can be accomplished by linking your project with --rpath or by setting the LD_LIBRARY_PATH appropriately. Otherwise, See Section 7.9.2 [binary not installed], page 145.

7.9.4 source distro, AutoOpts pre-installed

If you will be distributing your project to a system that will build your product but it may not be pre-installed with AutoOpts, you will need to do some configuration checking before you start the build. Assuming you are willing to fail the build if AutoOpts has not been installed, you will still need to do a little work.

AutoOpts is distributed with a configuration check M4 script, autoopts.m4. It will add an autoconf macro named, AG_PATH_AUTOOPTS. Add this to your configure.ac script and use the following substitution values:

AUTOGEN   the name of the autogen executable

AUTOGEN_TPLIB
            the directory where AutoGen template library is stored

AUTOOPTS_CFLAGS
            the compile time options needed to find the AutoOpts headers

AUTOOPTS_LIBS
            the link options required to access the libopts library

7.9.5 source distro, AutoOpts not installed

If you will be distributing your project to a system that will build your product but it may not be pre-installed with AutoOpts, you may wish to incorporate the sources for `libopts` in your project. To do this, I recommend reading the tear-off libopts library **README** that you can find in the `pkg/libopts` directory. You can also examine an example package (blocksort) that incorporates this tear off library in the autogen distribution directory. There is also a web page that describes what you need to do:

```
http://autogen.sourceforge.net/blocksort.html
```

Alternatively, you can pull the `libopts` library sources into a build directory and build it for installation along with your package. This can be done approximately as follows:

```
tar -xzvf `autoopts-config libsrc`
cd libopts-*
./bootstrap
configure
make
make install
```

That will install the library, but not the headers or anything else.

7.10 Configuring your program

AutoOpts supports the notion of **presetting** the value or state of an option. The values may be obtained either from environment variables or from configuration files (`rc` or `ini` files). In order to take advantage of this, the AutoOpts client program must specify these features in the option descriptor file (see Section 7.5.1 [program attributes], page 90) with the `rcfile` or `environrc` attributes.

It is also possible to configure your program *without* using the command line option parsing code. This is done by using only the following four functions from the `libopts` library:

'configFileLoad'
> (see Section 7.6.32.2 [libopts-configFileLoad], page 134) will parse the contents of a config file and return a pointer to a structure representing the hierarchical value. The values are sorted alphabetically by the value name and all entries with the same name will retain their original order. Insertion sort is used.

'optionGetValue'
> (see Section 7.6.32.7 [libopts-optionGetValue], page 136) will find the first value within the hierarchy with a name that matches the name passed in.

'optionNextValue'
> (see Section 7.6.32.10 [libopts-optionNextValue], page 137) will return the next value that follows the value passed in as an argument. If you wish to get all the values for a particular name, you must take note when the name changes.

'optionUnloadNested'
> (see Section 7.6.32.18 [libopts-optionUnloadNested], page 141). The pointer passed in must be of type, **OPARG_TYPE_HIERARCHY** (see the autoopts/options.h header file). `configFileLoad` will return a **tOptionValue** pointer of that type.

This function will release all the associated memory. `AutoOpts` generated code uses this function for its own needs. Client code should only call this function with pointers gotten from `configFileLoad`.

7.10.1 configuration file presets

Configuration files are enabled by specifying the program attribute `homerc` (see Section 7.5.1 [program attributes], page 90). Any option not marked with the `no-preset` attribute may appear in a configuration file. The files loaded are selected both by the `homerc` entries and, optionally, via a command line option. The first component of the `homerc` entry may be an environment variable such as `$HOME`, or it may also be '`$$`' (**two** dollar sign characters) to specify the directory of the executable. For example:

```
homerc = "$$/../share/autogen";
```

will cause the AutoOpts library to look in the normal autogen datadir relative to the current installation directory for autogen.

The configuration files are processed in the order they are specified by the `homerc` attribute, so that each new file will normally override the settings of the previous files. This may be overridden by marking some options for `immediate action` (see Section 7.5.5.3 [Immediate Action], page 107). Any such options are acted upon in **reverse** order. The disabled `load-opts` (`--no-load-opts`) option, for example, is an immediate action option. Its presence in the last `homerc` file will prevent the processing of any prior `homerc` files because its effect is immediate.

Configuration file processing can be completely suppressed by specifying `--no-load-opts` on the command line, or `PROGRAM_LOAD_OPTS=no` in the environment (if `environrc` has been specified).

See the `Configuration File Format` section (see Section 7.11 [Config File Format], page 155) for details on the format of the file.

7.10.2 Saving the presets into a configuration file

When configuration files are enabled for an application, the user is also provided with an automatically supplied `--save-opts` option. All of the known option state will be written to either the specified output file or, if it is not specified, then to the last specified `homerc` file.

7.10.3 Creating a sample configuration file

AutoOpts is shipped with a template named, `rc-sample.tpl`. If your option definition file specifies the `homerc` attribute, then you may invoke `autogen` thus:

```
autogen -Trc-sample <your-option-def-file>
```

This will, by default, produce a sample file named, `sample-<prog-name>rc`. It will be named differently if you specify your configuration (rc) file name with the `rcfile` attribute. In that case, the output file will be named, `sample-<rcfile-name>`. It will contain all of the program options not marked as `no-preset`. It will also include the text from the `doc` attribute.

Doing so with getdefs' option definitions yields this sample-getdefsrc file. I tend to be wordy in my `doc` attributes:

```
# getdefs sample configuration file
## This source file is copyrighted and licensed under the following terms:
#
#  Copyright (C) 1999-2014 Bruce Korb, all rights reserved.
#  This is free software. It is licensed for use, modification and
#  redistribution under the terms of the GNU General Public License,
#  version 3 or later <http://gnu.org/licenses/gpl.html>
#
#  getdefs is free software: you can redistribute it and/or modify it
#  under the terms of the GNU General Public License as published by the
#  Free Software Foundation, either version 3 of the License, or
#  (at your option) any later version.
#
#  getdefs is distributed in the hope that it will be useful, but
#  WITHOUT ANY WARRANTY; without even the implied warranty of
#  MERCHANTABILITY or FITNESS FOR A PARTICULAR PURPOSE.
#  See the GNU General Public License for more details.
#
#  You should have received a copy of the GNU General Public License along
#  with this program.  If not, see <http://www.gnu.org/licenses/>.

# defs_to_get -- Regexp to look for after the "/*="
#
#
#
#
# If you want definitions only from a particular category, or even
# with names matching particular patterns, then specify this regular
# expression for the text that must follow the @code{/*=}.
# Example:
#
#defs_to_get reg-ex

# subblock -- subblock definition names
#
#
#
#
# This option is used to create shorthand entries for nested definitions.
# For example, with:
# @table @r
# @item using subblock thus
# @code{--subblock=arg=argname,type,null}
# @item and defining an @code{arg} thus
# @code{arg: this, char *}
# @item will then expand to:
# @code{arg = @{ argname = this; type = "char *"; @};}
```

```
# @end table
# The "this, char *" string is separated at the commas, with the
# white space removed.  You may use characters other than commas by
# starting the value string with a punctuation character other than
# a single or double quote character.  You may also omit intermediate
# values by placing the commas next to each other with no intervening
# white space.  For example, "+mumble++yes+" will expand to:
# @*
# @code{arg = @{ argname = mumble; null = "yes"; @};}.
# Example:
#
#subblock sub-def

# listattr -- attribute with list of values
#
#
#
#
# This option is used to create shorthand entries for definitions
# that generally appear several times.  That is, they tend to be
# a list of values.  For example, with:
# @*
# @code{listattr=foo} defined, the text:
# @*
# @code{foo: this, is, a, multi-list} will then expand to:
# @*
# @code{foo = 'this', 'is', 'a', 'multi-list';}
# @*
# The texts are separated by the commas, with the
# white space removed.  You may use characters other than commas by
# starting the value string with a punctuation character other than
# a single or double quote character.
# Example:
#
#listattr def

# ordering -- Alphabetize or use named file
#
#
#
#
# By default, ordering is alphabetical by the entry name.  Use,
# @code{no-ordering} if order is unimportant.  Use @code{ordering}
# with no argument to order without case sensitivity.  Use
# @code{ordering=<file-name>} if chronological order is important.
# getdefs will maintain the text content of @code{file-name}.
# @code{file-name} need not exist.
```

```
# Example:
#
#ordering file-name

# first_index -- The first index to apply to groups
#
# This configuration value takes an integer number as its argument.
#
#
# By default, the first occurrence of a named definition will have an
# index of zero.  Sometimes, that needs to be a reserved value.  Provide
# this option to specify a different starting point.
# Example:
#
#first_index 0

# filelist -- Insert source file names into defs
#
#
#
#
# Inserts the name of each input file into the output definitions.
# If no argument is supplied, the format will be:
# @example
# infile = '%s';
# @end example
# If an argument is supplied, that string will be used for the entry
# name instead of @var{infile}.
# Example:
#
#filelist file

# assign -- Global assignments
#
#
#
#
# The argument to each copy of this option will be inserted into
# the output definitions, with only a semicolon attached.
# Example:
#
#assign ag-def

# common_assign -- Assignments common to all blocks
#
#
#
```

```
#
# The argument to each copy of this option will be inserted into
# each output definition, with only a semicolon attached.
# Example:
#
#common_assign ag-def

# copy -- File(s) to copy into definitions
#
#
#
#
# The content of each file named by these options will be inserted into
# the output definitions.
# Example:
#
#copy file

# srcfile -- Insert source file name into each def
#
#
#
#
# Inserts the name of the input file where a definition was found
# into the output definition.
# If no argument is supplied, the format will be:
# @example
# srcfile = '%s';
# @end example
# If an argument is supplied, that string will be used for the entry
# name instead of @var{srcfile}.
# Example:
#
#srcfile file

# linenum -- Insert source line number into each def
#
#
#
#
# Inserts the line number in the input file where a definition
# was found into the output definition.
# If no argument is supplied, the format will be:
# @example
# linenum = '%s';
# @end example
# If an argument is supplied, that string will be used for the entry
```

```
# name instead of @var{linenum}.
# Example:
#
#linenum def-name

# input -- Input file to search for defs
#
#
#
#
# All files that are to be searched for definitions must be named on
# the command line or read from @code{stdin}.  If there is only one
# @code{input} option and it is the string, "-", then the input file
# list is read from @code{stdin}.  If a command line argument is not
# an option name and does not contain an assignment operator
# (@code{=}), then it defaults to being an input file name.
# At least one input file must be specified.
# Example:
#
#input src-file

# output -- Output file to open
#
#
#
#
# If you are not sending the output to an AutoGen process,
# you may name an output file instead.
# Example:
#
#output file

# autogen -- Invoke AutoGen with defs
#
#
#
#
# This is the default output mode.  Specifying @code{no-autogen} is
# equivalent to @code{output=-}.  If you supply an argument to this
# option, that program will be started as if it were AutoGen and
# its standard in will be set to the output definitions of this program.
# Example:
#
#autogen ag-cmd

# template -- Template Name
#
```

```
#
#
#
# Specifies the template name to be used for generating the final output.
# Example:
#
#template file

# agarg -- AutoGen Argument
#
#
#
#
# This is a pass-through argument.  It allows you to specify any
# arbitrary argument to be passed to AutoGen.
# Example:
#
#agarg ag-opt

# base_name -- Base name for output file(s)
#
#
#
#
# When output is going to AutoGen, a base name must either be supplied
# or derived.  If this option is not supplied, then it is taken from
# the @code{template} option.  If that is not provided either, then
# it is set to the base name of the current directory.
# Example:
#
#base_name name
```

7.10.4 environment variable presets

If the AutoOpts client program specifies `environrc` in its option descriptor file, then environment variables will be used for presetting option state. Variables will be looked for that are named, `PROGRAM_OPTNAME` and `PROGRAM`. `PROGRAM` is the upper cased `C-name` of the program, and *OPTNAME* is the upper cased `C-name` of a specific option. (The C-names are the regular names with all special characters converted to underscores (_).)

Option specific environment variables are processed after (and thus take precedence over) the contents of the `PROGRAM` environment variable. The option argument string for these options takes on the string value gotten from the environment. Consequently, you can only have one instance of the *OPTNAME*.

If a particular option may be disabled, then its disabled state is indicated by setting the `PROGRAM_OPTNAME` value to the disablement prefix. So, for example, if the disablement prefix were `dont`, then you can disable the `optname` option by setting the `PROGRAM_OPTNAME'` environment variable to *dont*. See Section 7.5.5.2 [Common Attributes], page 106.

The `PROGRAM` environment string is tokenized and parsed much like a command line. Doubly quoted strings have backslash escapes processed the same way they are processed in C program constant strings. Singly quoted strings are pretty raw in that backslashes are honored before other backslashes, apostrophes, newlines and cr/newline pairs. The options must be introduced with hyphens in the same way as the command line.

Note that not all options may be preset. Options that are specified with the `no-preset` attribute and the `--help`, `--more-help`, and `--save-opts` auto-supported options may not be preset.

7.10.5 Config file only example

If for some reason it is difficult or unworkable to integrate configuration file processing with command line option parsing, the `libopts` (see Section 7.6.32 [libopts procedures], page 133) library can still be used to process configuration files. Below is a `Hello, World!` greeting program that tries to load a configuration file `hello.conf` to see if it should use an alternate greeting or to personalize the salutation.

```
#include <config.h>
#include <sys/types.h>
#include <stdio.h>
#include <pwd.h>
#include <string.h>
#ifdef   HAVE_UNISTD_H
#include <unistd.h>
#endif
#include <autoopts/options.h>
int main(int argc, char ** argv) {
  char const * greeting = "Hello";
  char const * greeted  = "World";
  tOptionValue const * pOV = configFileLoad("hello.conf");

  if (pOV != NULL) {
    const tOptionValue* pGetV = optionGetValue(pOV, "greeting");

    if (  (pGetV != NULL)
       && (pGetV->valType == OPARG_TYPE_STRING))
      greeting = strdup(pGetV->v.strVal);

    pGetV = optionGetValue(pOV, "personalize");
    if (pGetV != NULL) {
      struct passwd * pwe = getpwuid(getuid());
      if (pwe != NULL)
        greeted = strdup(pwe->pw_gecos);
    }

    optionUnloadNested(pOV); /* deallocate config data */
  }
  printf("%s, %s!\n", greeting, greeted);
```

```
    return 0;
}
```

With that text in a file named "hello.c", this short script:

```
cc -o hello hello.c `autoopts-config cflags ldflags`
./hello
echo 'greeting Buzz off' > hello.conf
./hello
echo personalize > hello.conf
./hello
```

will produce the following output:

```
Hello, World!
Buzz off, World!
Hello, Bruce Korb!
```

7.11 Configuration File Format

The configuration file is designed to associate names and values, much like an AutoGen Definition File (see Chapter 2 [Definitions File], page 7). Unfortunately, the file formats are different. Specifically, AutoGen Definitions provide for simpler methods for the precise control of a value string and provides for dynamically computed content. Configuration files have some established traditions in their layout. So, they are different, even though they do both allow for a single name to be associated with multiple values and they both allow for hierarchical values.

7.11.1 assigning a string value to a configurable

The basic syntax is a name followed by a value on a single line. They are separated from each other by either white space, a colon (:) or an equal sign (=). The colon or equal sign may optionally be surrounded by additional white space. If more than one value line is needed, a backslash (\) may be used to continue the value. The backslash (but not the newline) will be erased. Leading and trailing white space is always stripped from the value.

Fundamentally, it looks like this:

```
name  value for that name
name = another \
    multi-line value \
    for that name.
name: a *third* value for name
```

If you need more control over the content of the value, you may enclose the value in XML style brackets:

```
<name>value </name>
```

Within these brackets you need not (must not) continue the value data with backslashes. You may also select the string formation rules to use, just add the attribute after the name, thus: `<name keep>`.

`keep`   This mode will keep all text between the brackets and not strip any white space.

'uncooked'
> This mode strips leading and trailing white space, but not do any quote processing. This is the default and need not be specified.

'cooked' The text is trimmed of leading and trailing white space and XML encodings are processed. These encodings are slightly expanded over the XML specification. They are specified with an ampersand followed by a value name or numeric value and then a semicolon:

'amp'
'lt'
'gt'
'quot'
'apos'
'#dd'
'#xHH'

> These are all per fairly standad HTML and/or XML encodings. Additionally:

'bs' The ASCII back space character.

'ff' The ASCII form feed character.

'ht' The ASCII horizontal (normal) tab character.

'cr' The ASCII carriage return character.

'vt' The ASCII vertical tab character.

'bel' The ASCII alarm bell character.

'nl' The ASCII new line character.

'space' The ASCII space character. Normally not necessary, but if you want to preserve leading or trailing space characters, then use this.

And here is an example of an XML-styled value:

```
<name cooked>
    This is&nl;&ht;another multi-line
&ht;string example.
</name>
```

The string value associated with **name** will be exactly the text enclosed in quotes with the encoded characters **cooked** as you would expect (three text lines with the last line not ending with a newline, but ending with a period).

7.11.2 integer values

A name can be specified as having an integer value. To do this, you must use the XML-ish format and specify a **type** attribute for the name:

```
<name type=integer> 1234 </name>
```

Boolean, enumeration and set membership types will be added as time allows. **type=string** is also supported, but also is the default.

7.11.3 hierarchical values

In order to specify a hierarchical value, you *must* use XML-styled formatting, specifying a type that is shorter and easier to spell:

```
<structured-name type=nested>
    [[....]]
</structured-name>
```

The ellipsis may be filled with any legal configuration file name/value assignments.

7.11.4 configuration file directives

The `<?` marker indicates an XML directive. There is only one directive supported: program sectioning, though two syntaxes are supported.

If, for example, you have a collection of programs that work closely together and, likely, have a common set of options, these programs may use a single, sectioned, configuration file. The file may be sectioned in either of two ways. The two ways may not be intermixed in a single configuration file. All text before the first segmentation line is processed, then only the segment that applies:

`'<?auto-options ...>'`

> The ... ellipsis may contain AutoOpts option processing options. Currently, that consists of one or both of:
>
> gnu
> autoopts   to indicate GNU-standard or AutoOpts-standard layout of usage and version information, and/or
>
> misuse-usage
> no-misuse-usage
> > to indicate whether the available options should be listed when an invalid option appears on the command line.
>
> Anything else will be silently ignored.

`'<?program prog-name>'`

> The `<?` marker indicates an XML directive. The file is partitioned by these lines and the options are processed for the **prog-name** program only before the first `<?program` directive and the program section with a matching program name.

`'[PROG_NAME]'`

> This is basically an alias for `<?program prog-name>`, except that the program name must be upper cased and segmented only with underscores.

Segmentation does not apply if the config file is being parsed with the `configFileLoad(3AutoOpts)` function.

7.11.5 comments in the configuration file

Comments are lines beginning with a hash mark (#), XML-style comments (`<!-- arbitrary text -->`), and unrecognized XML directives.

```
# this is a comment
<!-- this is also
```

```
         a comment -->
      <?this is
       a bad comment ;->
```

7.12 AutoOpts for Shell Scripts

AutoOpts may be used with shell scripts either by automatically creating a complete program that will process command line options and pass back the results to the invoking shell by issuing shell variable assignment commands, or it may be used to generate portable shell code that can be inserted into your script.

The functionality of these features, of course, is somewhat constrained compared with the normal program facilities. Specifically, you cannot invoke callout procedures with either of these methods. Additionally, if you generate a shell script to do the parsing:

1. You cannot obtain options from configuration files.
2. You cannot obtain options from environment variables.
3. You cannot save the option state to an option file.
4. Option conflict/requirement verification is disabled.

Both of these methods are enabled by running AutoGen on the definitions file with the additional main procedure attribute:

```
      main = { main-type = shell-process; };
```

or:

```
      main = { main-type = shell-parser; };
```

If you do not supply a `proc-to-call`, it will default to `optionPutShell`. That will produce a program that will process the options and generate shell text for the invoking shell to interpret (see Section 7.12.1 [binary-parser], page 158). If you supply the name, `optionParseShell`, then you will have a program that will generate a shell script that can parse the options (see Section 7.12.2 [script-parser], page 159). If you supply a different procedure name, you will have to provide that routine and it may do whatever you like.

7.12.1 Parsing with an Executable

The following commands are approximately all that is needed to build a shell script command line option parser from an option definition file:

```
      autogen -L <opt-template-dir> test-errors.def
      cc -o test-errors -L <opt-lib-dir> -I <opt-include-dir> \
            -DTEST_PROGRAM_OPTS test-errors.c -lopts
```

The resulting program can then be used within your shell script as follows:

```
      eval `./test-errors "$@"`
      if [ -z "${OPTION_CT}" ] ; then exit 1 ; fi
      test ${OPTION_CT} -gt 0 && shift ${OPTION_CT}
```

Here is the usage output example from AutoOpts error handling tests. The option definition has argument reordering enabled:

```
      test_errors - Test AutoOpts for errors
      Usage:  errors [ -<flag> [<val>] | --<name>[{=| }<val>] ]... arg ...
        Flg Arg Option-Name    Description
```

```
-o no  option         The option option descrip
-s Str second         The second option descrip
                          - may appear up to 10 times
-i --- ignored        we have dumped this
-X no  another        Another option descrip
                          - may appear up to 5 times
-? no  help           display extended usage information and exit
-! no  more-help      extended usage information passed thru pager
-> opt save-opts      save the option state to a config file
-< Str load-opts      load options from a config file
                              - disabled as '--no-load-opts'
                              - may appear multiple times
```

Options are specified by doubled hyphens and their name or by a single
hyphen and the flag character.
Operands and options may be intermixed. They will be reordered.

The following option preset mechanisms are supported:
 - reading file errorsRC
Packaged by Bruce (2015-08-21)
Report test_errors bugs to bkorb@gnu.org

Using the invocation,

```
test-errors operand1 -s first operand2 -X -- -s operand3
```

you get the following output for your shell script to evaluate:

```
OPTION_CT=4
export OPTION_CT
TEST_ERRORS_SECOND='first'
export TEST_ERRORS_SECOND
TEST_ERRORS_ANOTHER=1 # 0x1
export TEST_ERRORS_ANOTHER
set -- 'operand1' 'operand2' '-s' 'operand3'
OPTION_CT=0
```

7.12.2 Parsing with a Portable Script

If you had used test-main = optionParseShell instead, then you can, at this point, merely
run the program and it will write the parsing script to standard out. You may also provide
this program with command line options to specify the shell script file to create or edit,
and you may specify the shell program to use on the first shell script line. That program's
usage text would look something like the following and the script parser itself would be very
verbose:

```
genshellopt - Generate Shell Option Processing Script - Ver. 1
Usage:  genshellopt [ -<flag> [<val>] | --<name>[{=| }<val>] ]...
  Flg Arg Option-Name    Description
   -o Str script         Output Script File
   -s Str shell          Shell name (follows "#!" magic)
                             - disabled as '--no-shell'
```

```
                                       - enabled by default
   -v opt version         output version information and exit
   -? no  help            display extended usage information and exit
   -! no  more-help       extended usage information passed thru pager
```

Options are specified by doubled hyphens and their name or by a single
hyphen and the flag character.
Note that 'shell' is only useful if the output file does not already exist.
If it does, then the shell name and optional first argument will be
extracted from the script file.
If the script file already exists and contains Automated Option Processing
text, the second line of the file through the ending tag will be replaced
by the newly generated text. The first '#!' line will be regenerated.
Packaged by Bruce (2015-08-21)
Report genshellopt bugs to bkorb@gnu.org

= = = = = = = =

This incarnation of genshell will produce
a shell script to parse the options for getdefs:

getdefs (GNU AutoGen) - AutoGen Definition Extraction Tool - Ver. 1.5
Usage: getdefs [<option-name>[{=| }<val>]]...
```

```
   Arg Option-Name   Description
   Str defs-to-get   Regexp to look for after the "/*="
   Str subblock   subblock definition names
   Str listattr   attribute with list of values
   opt ordering   Alphabetize or use named file
   Num first-index   The first index to apply to groups
   opt filelist   Insert source file names into defs
   Str assign   Global assignments
   Str common-assign   Assignments common to all blocks
   Str copy   File(s) to copy into definitions
   opt srcfile   Insert source file name into each def
   opt linenum   Insert source line number into each def
   Str input   Input file to search for defs
   Str output   Output file to open
   opt autogen   Invoke AutoGen with defs
   Str template   Template Name
   Str agarg   AutoGen Argument
   Str base-name   Base name for output file(s)
   opt version   output version information and exit
   no help   display extended usage information and exit
   no more-help   extended usage information passed thru pager
   opt save-opts   save the option state to a config file
   Str load-opts   load options from a config file
```
```

```
      All arguments are named options.
      If no 'input' argument is provided or is set to simply "-", and if 'stdin'
      is not a 'tty', then the list of input files will be read from 'stdin'.
      Packaged by Bruce (2015-08-21)
      Report getdefs bugs to bkorb@gnu.org
```

Resulting in the following script:

```
      #! /bin/sh
      # # # # # # # # # -- do not modify this marker --
      #
      #  DO NOT EDIT THIS SECTION
       OF /u/bkorb/ag/ag/doc/ag-texi-17516.d/.ag-Zq75tt/genshellopt.sh
      #
      #  From here to the next '-- do not modify this marker --',
      #  the text has been generated Friday August 21, 2015 at 01:11:48 PM PDT
      #  From the GETDEFS option definitions
      #
      GETDEFS_LONGUSAGE_TEXT='getdefs (GNU AutoGen) - AutoGen Definition Extraction Tool
      Usage:  getdefs [ <option-name>[{=| }<val>] ]...

      Specify which definitions are of interest and what to say about them:

          Arg Option-Name     Description
          Str defs-to-get     Regexp to look for after the "/*="
          Str subblock        subblock definition names
                                      - may appear multiple times
          Str listattr        attribute with list of values
                                      - may appear multiple times


      specify how to number the definitions:

          Arg Option-Name     Description
          opt ordering        Alphabetize or use named file
                                      - disabled as '\''--no-ordering'\''
                                      - enabled by default
          Num first-index     The first index to apply to groups


      Definition insertion options:

          Arg Option-Name     Description
          opt filelist        Insert source file names into defs
          Str assign          Global assignments
                                      - may appear multiple times
          Str common-assign   Assignments common to all blocks
                                      - may appear multiple times
          Str copy            File(s) to copy into definitions
                                      - may appear multiple times
```

```
    opt srcfile          Insert source file name into each def
    opt linenum          Insert source line number into each def

specify which files to search for markers:

    Arg Option-Name      Description
    Str input            Input file to search for defs
                                   - may appear multiple times
                                   - default option for unnamed options

Definition output disposition options::

    Arg Option-Name      Description
    Str output           Output file to open
                                   - an alternate for '\''autogen'\''
    opt autogen          Invoke AutoGen with defs
                                   - disabled as '\''--no-autogen'\''
                                   - enabled by default
    Str template         Template Name
    Str agarg            AutoGen Argument
                                   - prohibits the option '\''output'\''
                                   - may appear multiple times
    Str base-name        Base name for output file(s)
                                   - prohibits the option '\''output'\''

Version, usage and configuration options:

    Arg Option-Name      Description
    opt version          output version information and exit
    no  help             display extended usage information and exit
    no  more-help        extended usage information passed thru pager
    opt save-opts        save the option state to a config file
    Str load-opts        load options from a config file
                                   - disabled as '\''--no-load-opts'\''
                                   - may appear multiple times

All arguments are named options.
If no '\''input'\'' argument is provided or is set to simply "-", and if '\''s
is not a '\''tty'\'', then the list of input files will be read from '\''stdin

The following option preset mechanisms are supported:
 - reading file /dev/null
This program extracts AutoGen definitions from a list of source files.
Definitions are delimited by '\''/*=<entry-type> <entry-name>\n'\'' and '\''=*
Packaged by Bruce (2015-08-21)
Report getdefs bugs to bkorb@gnu.org'
```

```
GETDEFS_USAGE_TEXT='getdefs (GNU AutoGen) - AutoGen Definition Extraction Tool - Ve:
Usage:  getdefs [ <option-name>[{=| }<val>] ]...
   Arg Option-Name      Description
   Str defs-to-get      Regexp to look for after the "/*="
   Str subblock         subblock definition names
   Str listattr         attribute with list of values
   opt ordering         Alphabetize or use named file
   Num first-index      The first index to apply to groups
   opt filelist         Insert source file names into defs
   Str assign           Global assignments
   Str common-assign    Assignments common to all blocks
   Str copy             File(s) to copy into definitions
   opt srcfile          Insert source file name into each def
   opt linenum          Insert source line number into each def
   Str input            Input file to search for defs
   Str output           Output file to open
   opt autogen          Invoke AutoGen with defs
   Str template         Template Name
   Str agarg            AutoGen Argument
   Str base-name        Base name for output file(s)
   opt version          output version information and exit
   no  help             display extended usage information and exit
   no  more-help        extended usage information passed thru pager
   opt save-opts        save the option state to a config file
   Str load-opts        load options from a config file

All arguments are named options.
If no '\''input'\'' argument is provided or is set to simply "-", and if '\''stdin'"
is not a '\''tty'\'', then the list of input files will be read from '\''stdin'\''.
Packaged by Bruce (2015-08-21)
Report getdefs bugs to bkorb@gnu.org'


GETDEFS_DEFS_TO_GET=${GETDEFS_DEFS_TO_GET}
GETDEFS_DEFS_TO_GET_set=false
export GETDEFS_DEFS_TO_GET

if test -z "${GETDEFS_SUBBLOCK}"
then
  GETDEFS_SUBBLOCK_CT=0
  export GETDEFS_SUBBLOCK_CT
else
  GETDEFS_SUBBLOCK_CT=1
  GETDEFS_SUBBLOCK_1=${GETDEFS_SUBBLOCK}
  export GETDEFS_SUBBLOCK_CT GETDEFS_SUBBLOCK_1
fi
```

```
if test -z "${GETDEFS_LISTATTR}"
then
  GETDEFS_LISTATTR_CT=0
  export GETDEFS_LISTATTR_CT
else
  GETDEFS_LISTATTR_CT=1
  GETDEFS_LISTATTR_1=${GETDEFS_LISTATTR}
  export GETDEFS_LISTATTR_CT GETDEFS_LISTATTR_1
fi

GETDEFS_ORDERING=${GETDEFS_ORDERING}
GETDEFS_ORDERING_set=false
export GETDEFS_ORDERING

GETDEFS_FIRST_INDEX=${GETDEFS_FIRST_INDEX-'0'}
GETDEFS_FIRST_INDEX_set=false
export GETDEFS_FIRST_INDEX

GETDEFS_FILELIST=${GETDEFS_FILELIST}
GETDEFS_FILELIST_set=false
export GETDEFS_FILELIST

if test -z "${GETDEFS_ASSIGN}"
then
  GETDEFS_ASSIGN_CT=0
  export GETDEFS_ASSIGN_CT
else
  GETDEFS_ASSIGN_CT=1
  GETDEFS_ASSIGN_1=${GETDEFS_ASSIGN}
  export GETDEFS_ASSIGN_CT GETDEFS_ASSIGN_1
fi

if test -z "${GETDEFS_COMMON_ASSIGN}"
then
  GETDEFS_COMMON_ASSIGN_CT=0
  export GETDEFS_COMMON_ASSIGN_CT
else
  GETDEFS_COMMON_ASSIGN_CT=1
  GETDEFS_COMMON_ASSIGN_1=${GETDEFS_COMMON_ASSIGN}
  export GETDEFS_COMMON_ASSIGN_CT GETDEFS_COMMON_ASSIGN_1
fi

if test -z "${GETDEFS_COPY}"
then
  GETDEFS_COPY_CT=0
  export GETDEFS_COPY_CT
else
```

```
  GETDEFS_COPY_CT=1
  GETDEFS_COPY_1=${GETDEFS_COPY}
  export GETDEFS_COPY_CT GETDEFS_COPY_1
fi

GETDEFS_SRCFILE=${GETDEFS_SRCFILE}
GETDEFS_SRCFILE_set=false
export GETDEFS_SRCFILE

GETDEFS_LINENUM=${GETDEFS_LINENUM}
GETDEFS_LINENUM_set=false
export GETDEFS_LINENUM

if test -z "${GETDEFS_INPUT}"
then
  GETDEFS_INPUT_CT=0
  export GETDEFS_INPUT_CT
else
  GETDEFS_INPUT_CT=1
  GETDEFS_INPUT_1=${GETDEFS_INPUT}
  export GETDEFS_INPUT_CT GETDEFS_INPUT_1
fi

GETDEFS_OUTPUT=${GETDEFS_OUTPUT}
GETDEFS_OUTPUT_set=false
export GETDEFS_OUTPUT

GETDEFS_AUTOGEN=${GETDEFS_AUTOGEN}
GETDEFS_AUTOGEN_set=false
export GETDEFS_AUTOGEN

GETDEFS_TEMPLATE=${GETDEFS_TEMPLATE}
GETDEFS_TEMPLATE_set=false
export GETDEFS_TEMPLATE

if test -z "${GETDEFS_AGARG}"
then
  GETDEFS_AGARG_CT=0
  export GETDEFS_AGARG_CT
else
  GETDEFS_AGARG_CT=1
  GETDEFS_AGARG_1=${GETDEFS_AGARG}
  export GETDEFS_AGARG_CT GETDEFS_AGARG_1
fi

GETDEFS_BASE_NAME=${GETDEFS_BASE_NAME}
GETDEFS_BASE_NAME_set=false
```

```
      export GETDEFS_BASE_NAME

ARG_COUNT=$#
OPT_ARG=$1
while [ $# -gt 0 ]
do
    OPT_ELEMENT=''
    OPT_ARG_VAL=''
    OPT_ARG=${1}
        OPT_CODE=`echo "X${OPT_ARG}"|sed 's/^X-*//'`
        shift
        OPT_ARG=$1
        case "${OPT_CODE}" in *=* )
            OPT_ARG_VAL=`echo "${OPT_CODE}"|sed 's/^[^=]*=//'`
            OPT_CODE=`echo "${OPT_CODE}"|sed 's/=.*$//'` ;; esac
        case "${OPT_CODE}" in
        'de' | \
        'def' | \
        'defs' | \
        'defs-' | \
        'defs-t' | \
        'defs-to' | \
        'defs-to-' | \
        'defs-to-g' | \
        'defs-to-ge' | \
        'defs-to-get' )
            if [ -n "${GETDEFS_DEFS_TO_GET}" ] && ${GETDEFS_DEFS_TO_GET_set} ;
                echo 'Error:  duplicate DEFS_TO_GET option'
                echo "$GETDEFS_USAGE_TEXT"
                exit 1
            fi >&2
            GETDEFS_DEFS_TO_GET_set=true
            OPT_NAME='DEFS_TO_GET'
            OPT_ARG_NEEDED=YES
            ;;

        'su' | \
        'sub' | \
        'subb' | \
        'subbl' | \
        'subblo' | \
        'subbloc' | \
        'subblock' )
            GETDEFS_SUBBLOCK_CT=`expr ${GETDEFS_SUBBLOCK_CT} + 1`
            OPT_ELEMENT="_${GETDEFS_SUBBLOCK_CT}"
            OPT_NAME='SUBBLOCK'
            OPT_ARG_NEEDED=YES
```

```
            ;;

'li' | \
'lis' | \
'list' | \
'lista' | \
'listat' | \
'listatt' | \
'listattr' )
    GETDEFS_LISTATTR_CT=`expr ${GETDEFS_LISTATTR_CT} + 1`
    OPT_ELEMENT="_${GETDEFS_LISTATTR_CT}"
    OPT_NAME='LISTATTR'
    OPT_ARG_NEEDED=YES
    ;;

'or' | \
'ord' | \
'orde' | \
'order' | \
'orderi' | \
'orderin' | \
'ordering' )
    if [ -n '${GETDEFS_ORDERING}" ] && ${GETDEFS_ORDERING_set} ; then
        echo 'Error:  duplicate ORDERING option'
        echo "$GETDEFS_USAGE_TEXT"
        exit 1
    fi >&2
    GETDEFS_ORDERING_set=true
    OPT_NAME='ORDERING'
    eval GETDEFS_ORDERING${OPT_ELEMENT}=true
    export GETDEFS_ORDERING${OPT_ELEMENT}
    OPT_ARG_NEEDED=OK
    ;;

'no-' | \
'no-o' | \
'no-or' | \
'no-ord' | \
'no-orde' | \
'no-order' | \
'no-orderi' | \
'no-orderin' | \
'no-ordering' )
    if [ -n "S{GETDEFS_ORDERING}" ] && ${GETDEFS_ORDERING_set} ; then
        echo 'Error:  duplicate ORDERING option'
        echo "$GETDEFS_USAGE_TEXT"
        exit 1
```

```
        fi >&2
        GETDEFS_ORDERING_set=true
        GETDEFS_ORDERING='no'
        export GETDEFS_ORDERING
        OPT_NAME='ORDERING'
        OPT_ARG_NEEDED=NO
        ;;

'fi' | \
'fir' | \
'firs' | \
'first' | \
'first-' | \
'first-i' | \
'first-in' | \
'first-ind' | \
'first-inde' | \
'first-index' )
    if [ -n "${GETDEFS_FIRST_INDEX}" ] && ${GETDEFS_FIRST_INDEX_set} ;
        echo 'Error:  duplicate FIRST_INDEX option'
        echo "$GETDEFS_USAGE_TEXT"
        exit 1
    fi >&2
    GETDEFS_FIRST_INDEX_set=true
    OPT_NAME='FIRST_INDEX'
    OPT_ARG_NEEDED=YES
        ;;

'fi' | \
'fil' | \
'file' | \
'filel' | \
'fileli' | \
'filelis' | \
'filelist' )
    if [ -n "${GETDEFS_FILELIST}" ] && ${GETDEFS_FILELIST_set} ; then
        echo 'Error:  duplicate FILELIST option'
        echo "$GETDEFS_USAGE_TEXT"
        exit 1
    fi >&2
    GETDEFS_FILELIST_set=true
    OPT_NAME='FILELIST'
    eval GETDEFS_FILELIST${OPT_ELEMENT}=true
    export GETDEFS_FILELIST${OPT_ELEMENT}
    OPT_ARG_NEEDED=OK
        ;;
```

```
'as' | \
'ass' | \
'assi' | \
'assig' | \
'assign' )
    GETDEFS_ASSIGN_CT=`expr ${GETDEFS_ASSIGN_CT} + 1`
    OPT_ELEMENT="_${GETDEFS_ASSIGN_CT}"
    OPT_NAME='ASSIGN'
    OPT_ARG_NEEDED=YES
    ;;

'co' | \
'com' | \
'comm' | \
'commo' | \
'common' | \
'common-' | \
'common-a' | \
'common-as' | \
'common-ass' | \
'common-assi' | \
'common-assig' | \
'common-assign' )
    GETDEFS_COMMON_ASSIGN_CT=`expr ${GETDEFS_COMMON_ASSIGN_CT} + 1`
    OPT_ELEMENT="_${GETDEFS_COMMON_ASSIGN_CT}"
    OPT_NAME='COMMON_ASSIGN'
    OPT_ARG_NEEDED=YES
    ;;

'co' | \
'cop' | \
'copy' )
    GETDEFS_COPY_CT=`expr ${GETDEFS_COPY_CT} + 1`
    OPT_ELEMENT="_${GETDEFS_COPY_CT}"
    OPT_NAME='COPY'
    OPT_ARG_NEEDED=YES
    ;;

'sr' | \
'src' | \
'srcf' | \
'srcfi' | \
'srcfil' | \
'srcfile' )
    if [ -n "${GETDEFS_SRCFILE}" ] && ${GETDEFS_SRCFILE_set} ; then
        echo 'Error:  duplicate SRCFILE option'
        echo "$GETDEFS_USAGE_TEXT"
```

```
            exit 1
        fi >&2
        GETDEFS_SRCFILE_set=true
        OPT_NAME='SRCFILE'
        eval GETDEFS_SRCFILE${OPT_ELEMENT}=true
        export GETDEFS_SRCFILE${OPT_ELEMENT}
        OPT_ARG_NEEDED=OK
        ;;

'li' | \
'lin' | \
'line' | \
'linen' | \
'linenu' | \
'linenum' )
        if [ -n "${GETDEFS_LINENUM}" ] && ${GETDEFS_LINENUM_set} ; then
            echo 'Error:  duplicate LINENUM option'
            echo "$GETDEFS_USAGE_TEXT"
            exit 1
        fi >&2
        GETDEFS_LINENUM_set=true
        OPT_NAME='LINENUM'
        eval GETDEFS_LINENUM${OPT_ELEMENT}=true
        export GETDEFS_LINENUM${OPT_ELEMENT}
        OPT_ARG_NEEDED=OK
        ;;

'in' | \
'inp' | \
'inpu' | \
'input' )
        GETDEFS_INPUT_CT=`expr ${GETDEFS_INPUT_CT} + 1`
        OPT_ELEMENT="_${GETDEFS_INPUT_CT}"
        OPT_NAME='INPUT'
        OPT_ARG_NEEDED=YES
        ;;

'ou' | \
'out' | \
'outp' | \
'outpu' | \
'output' )
        if [ -n "${GETDEFS_OUTPUT}" ] && ${GETDEFS_OUTPUT_set} ; then
            echo 'Error:  duplicate OUTPUT option'
            echo "$GETDEFS_USAGE_TEXT"
            exit 1
        fi >&2
```

```
        GETDEFS_OUTPUT_set=true
        OPT_NAME='OUTPUT'
        OPT_ARG_NEEDED=YES
        ;;

'au' | \
'aut' | \
'auto' | \
'autog' | \
'autoge' | \
'autogen' )
    if [ -n "${GETDEFS_AUTOGEN}' ] && ${GETDEFS_AUTOGEN_set} ; then
        echo 'Error:  duplicate AUTOGEN option'
        echo "$GETDEFS_USAGE_TEXT"
        exit 1
    fi >&2
    GETDEFS_AUTOGEN_set=true
    OPT_NAME='AUTOGEN'
    eval GETDEFS_AUTOGEN${OPT_ELEMENT}=true
    export GETDEFS_AUTOGEN${OPT_ELEMENT}
    OPT_ARG_NEEDED=OK
    ;;

'no-' | \
'no-a' | \
'no-au' | \
'no-aut' | \
'no-auto' | \
'no-autog' | \
'no-autoge' | \
'no-autogen' )
    if [ -n "${GETDEFS_AUTOGEN}" ] && ${GETDEFS_AUTOGEN_set} ; then
        echo 'Error:  duplicate AUTOGEN option'
        echo "$GETDEFS_USAGE_TEXT"
        exit 1
    fi >&2
    GETDEFS_AUTOGEN_set=true
    GETDEFS_AUTOGEN='no'
    export GETDEFS_AUTOGEN
    OPT_NAME='AUTOGEN'
    OPT_ARG_NEEDED=NO
    ;;

'te' | \
'tem' | \
'temp' | \
'templ' | \
```

```
'templa' | \
'templat' | \
'template' )
    if [ -n "${GETDEFS_TEMPLATE}" ] && ${GETDEFS_TEMPLATE_set} ; then
        echo 'Error:  duplicate TEMPLATE option'
        echo "$GETDEFS_USAGE_TEXT"
        exit 1
    fi >&2
    GETDEFS_TEMPLATE_set=true
    OPT_NAME='TEMPLATE'
    OPT_ARG_NEEDED=YES
    ;;

'ag' | \
'aga' | \
'agar' | \
'agarg' )
    GETDEFS_AGARG_CT=`expr ${GETDEFS_AGARG_CT} + 1`
    OPT_ELEMENT="_${GETDEFS_AGARG_CT}"
    OPT_NAME='AGARG'
    OPT_ARG_NEEDED=YES
    ;;

'ba' | \
'bas' | \
'base' | \
'base-' | \
'base-n' | \
'base-na' | \
'base-nam' | \
'base-name' )
    if [ -n "${GETDEFS_BASE_NAME}" ] && ${GETDEFS_BASE_NAME_set} ; then
        echo 'Error:  duplicate BASE_NAME option'
        echo "$GETDEFS_USAGE_TEXT"
        exit 1
    fi >&2
    GETDEFS_BASE_NAME_set=true
    OPT_NAME='BASE_NAME'
    OPT_ARG_NEEDED=YES
    ;;

've' | \
'ver' | \
'vers' | \
'versi' | \
'versio' | \
'version' )
```

```
        echo "$GETDEFS_LONGUSAGE_TEXT"
        exit 0
        ;;

'he' | \
'hel' | \
'help' )
    echo "$GETDEFS_LONGUSAGE_TEXT"
    exit 0
    ;;

'mo' | \
'mor' | \
'more' | \
'more-' | \
'more-h' | \
'more-he' | \
'more-hel' | \
'more-help' )
    echo "$GETDEFS_LONGUSAGE_TEXT" | ${PAGER-more}
    exit 0
    ;;

'sa' | \
'sav' | \
'save' | \
'save-' | \
'save-o' | \
'save-op' | \
'save-opt' | \
'save-opts' )
    echo 'Warning:  Cannot save options files' >&2
    OPT_ARG_NEEDED=OK
    ;;

'lo' | \
'loa' | \
'load' | \
'load-' | \
'load-o' | \
'load-op' | \
'load-opt' | \
'load-opts' )
    echo 'Warning:  Cannot load options files' >&2
    OPT_ARG_NEEDED=YES
    ;;
```

```
'no-' | \
'no-l' | \
'no-lo' | \
'no-loa' | \
'no-load' | \
'no-load-' | \
'no-load-o' | \
'no-load-op' | \
'no-load-opt' | \
'no-load-opts' )
    echo 'Warning:  Cannot suppress the loading of options files' >&2
    OPT_ARG_NEEDED=NO
    ;;

* )
    echo Unknown option: "${OPT_CODE}" >&2
    echo "$GETDEFS_USAGE_TEXT" >&2
    exit 1
    ;;
esac
case "${OPT_ARG_NEEDED}" in
NO )
    OPT_ARG_VAL=''
    ;;
YES )
    if [ -z "${OPT_ARG_VAL}" ]
    then
        if [ $# -eq 0 ]
        then
            echo No argument provided for ${OPT_NAME} option
            echo "$GETDEFS_USAGE_TEXT"
            exit 1
        fi >&2
        OPT_ARG_VAL=${OPT_ARG}
        shift
        OPT_ARG=$1
    fi
    ;;
OK )
    if [ -z "${OPT_ARG_VAL}" ] && [ $# -gt 0 ]
    then
        case "${OPT_ARG}" in -* ) ;; * )
            OPT_ARG_VAL=${OPT_ARG}
            shift
            OPT_ARG=$1 ;; esac
    fi
    ;;
```

```
            esac
        if [ -n "S{OPT_ARG_VAL}" ]
        then
            eval GETDEFS_${OPT_NAME}${OPT_ELEMENT}="'${OPT_ARG_VAL}'"
            export GETDEFS_${OPT_NAME}${OPT_ELEMENT}
        fi
    done
    OPTION_COUNT=`expr $ARG_COUNT - $#`
    OPERAND_COUNT=$#
    unset OPT_PROCESS || :
    unset OPT_ELEMENT || :
    unset OPT_ARG      || :
    unset OPT_ARG_NEEDED || :
    unset OPT_NAME      || :
    unset OPT_CODE      || :
    unset OPT_ARG_VAL  || :

    # # # # # # # # #
    #
    #   END OF AUTOMATED OPTION PROCESSING
    #
    # # # # # # # # # # -- do not modify this marker --

    env | grep '^GETDEFS_'
```

7.13 Automated Info Docs

AutoOpts provides two templates for producing .texi documentation. agtexi-cmd.tpl for the invoking section, and aginfo3.tpl for describing exported library functions and macros.

For both types of documents, the documentation level is selected by passing a '-DLEVEL=<level-name>' argument to AutoGen when you build the document. (See the example invocation below.)

Two files will be produced, a .texi file and a .menu file. You should include the text in the .menu file in a @menu list, either with @include-ing it or just copying text. The .texi file should be @include-ed where the invoking section belongs in your document.

The .texi file will contain an introductory paragraph, a menu and a subordinate section for the invocation usage and for each documented option. The introductory paragraph is normally the boiler plate text, along the lines of:

```
This chapter documents the @file{AutoOpts} generated usage text
and option meanings for the @file{your-program} program.
```

or:

```
These are the publicly exported procedures from the libname library.
Any other functions mentioned in the header file are for the private use
of the library.
```

7.13.1 invoking **info docs**

Using the option definitions for an AutoOpt client program, the `agtexi-cmd.tpl` template will produce texinfo text that documents the invocation of your program. The text emitted is designed to be included in the full texinfo document for your product. It is not a stand-alone document. The usage text for the Section 5.1 [autogen usage], page 67, Section 8.6.1 [getdefs usage], page 199 and Section 8.5.1 [columns usage], page 191 programs, are included in this document and are all generated using this template.

If your program's option definitions include a 'prog-info-descrip' section, then that text will replace the boilerplate introductory paragraph.

These files are produced by invoking the following command:

```
autogen -L ${prefix}/share/autogen -Tagtexi-cmd.tpl \
        -DLEVEL=section your-opts.def
```

Where `${prefix}` is the AutoGen installation prefix and `your-opts.def` is the name of your product's option definition file.

7.13.2 library info docs

The `texinfo` doc for libraries is derived from mostly the same information as is used for producing man pages See Section 7.14.2 [man3], page 177. The main difference is that there is only one output file and the individual functions are referenced from a `texi` menu. There is also a small difference in the global attributes used:

lib_description
: A description of the library. This text appears before the menu. If not provided, the standard boilerplate version will be inserted.

see_also
: The **SEE ALSO** functionality is not supported for the `texinfo` documentation, so any `see_also` attribute will be ignored.

These files are produced by invoking the following commands:

```
getdefs linenum srcfile template=aginfo3.tpl output=libexport.def \
        <source-file-list>


autogen -L ${prefix}/share/autogen -DLEVEL=section libexport.def
```

Where `${prefix}` is the AutoGen installation prefix and `libexport.def` is some name that suits you.

An example of this can be seen in this document, See Section 7.6.32 [libopts procedures], page 133.

7.14 Automated Man Pages

AutoOpts provides two templates for producing man pages. The command (`man1`) pages are derived from the options definition file, and the library (`man3`) pages are derived from stylized comments (see Section 8.6 [getdefs Invocation], page 198).

Man pages include a date in the footer. By default, this is derived from the current date. However, this may be overridden with the `MAN_PAGE_DATE` environment variable. If set and not empty, its contents will be copied into where the output of `date '+%d %b %Y'` would otherwise go.

Man pages may be formatted as either traditional man pages or using `mdoc` formatting. The format is selected by selecting the appropriate template.

7.14.1 command line man pages

Man pages for commands are documented using the `agman-cmd.tpl` and `agmdoc-cmd.tpl` templates. If the options specify pulling information from `RC/ini/cfg` files, then you may use the `rc-sample.tpl` template to produce an example config file for your program.

Using the option definitions for an AutoOpts client program, the '`agman-cmd.tpl`' template will produce an nroff document suitable for use as a '`man(1)`' page document for a command line command. The description section of the document is either the '`prog-man-descrip`' text, if present, or the '`detail`' text.

Each option in the option definitions file is fully documented in its usage. This includes all the information documented above for each option (see Section 7.5.5 [option attributes], page 105), plus the '`doc`' attribute is appended. Since the '`doc`' text is presumed to be designed for `texinfo` documentation, `sed` is used to convert some constructs from `texi` to nroff-for-man-pages. Specifically.

```
convert @code, @var and @samp into \fB...\fP phrases
convert @file into \fI...\fP phrases
Remove the '@' prefix from curly braces
Indent example regions
Delete the example commands
Replace 'end example' command with ".br"
Replace the '@*' command with ".br"
```

This document is produced by invoking the following command:

```
autogen -L ${prefix}/share/autogen -Tagman-cmd.tpl options.def
```

Where `${prefix}` is the AutoGen installation prefix and `options.def` is the name of your product's option definition file. I do not use this very much, so any feedback or improvements would be greatly appreciated.

7.14.2 library man pages

Man pages for libraries are documented using the `agman-3.tpl` template.

Two global definitions are required, and then one library man page is produced for each `export_func` definition that is found. It is generally convenient to place these definitions as `getdefs` comments (see Section 8.6 [getdefs Invocation], page 198) near the procedure definition, but they may also be a separate AutoGen definitions file (see Chapter 2 [Definitions File], page 7). Each function will be cross referenced with their sister functions in a **SEE ALSO** section. A global `see_also` definition will be appended to this cross referencing text.

The two global definitions required are:

library   This is the name of your library, without the `lib` prefix. The AutoOpts library is named `libopts.so...`, so the `library` attribute would have the value `opts`.

header   Generally, using a library with a compiled program entails
                #include-ing a header file. Name that header with this attribute.
                In the case of AutoOpts, it is generated and will vary based on the
                name of the option definition file. Consequently, your-opts.h is
                specified.

The export_func definition should contain the following attributes:

name   The name of the procedure the library user may call.
what   A brief sentence describing what the procedure does.
doc   A detailed description of what the procedure does. It may ramble
                on for as long as necessary to properly describe it.
err   A short description of how errors are handled.
ret_type   The data type returned by the procedure. Omit this for **void**
                procedures.
ret_desc   Describe what the returned value is, if needed.
private   If specified, the function will **not** be documented. This is used, for
                example, to produce external declarations for functions that are not
                available for public use, but are used in the generated text.
arg   This is a compound attribute that contains:

                arg_type   The data type of the argument.
                arg_name   A short name for it.
                arg_desc   A brief description.

As a getdefs comment, this would appear something like this:

```
/*=--subblock=arg=arg_type,arg_name,arg_desc =*/
/*=*
 * library: opts
 * header:  your-opts.h
=*/
/*=export_func optionProcess
 *
 * what: this is the main option processing routine
 * arg:  + tOptions* + pOpts + program options descriptor +
 * arg:  + int       + argc  + program arg count  +
 * arg:  + char**    + argv  + program arg vector +
 * ret_type:  int
 * ret_desc:  the count of the arguments processed
 *
 * doc:  This is what it does.
 * err:  When it can't, it does this.
=*/
```

Note the **subblock** and **library** comments. **subblock** is an embedded getdefs option (see
[getdefs subblock], page 201) that tells it how to parse the **arg** attribute. The **library** and
header entries are global definitions that apply to all the documented functions.

7.15 Using getopt(3C)

There is a template named, `getopt.tpl` that is distributed with AutoOpts. Using that template instead of `options.tpl` will produce completely independent source code that will parse command line options. It will utilize either the standard `getopt(3C)` or the GNU `getopt_long(3GNU)` function to drive the parsing. Which is used is selected by the presence or absence of the `long-opts` program attribute. It will save you from being dependent upon the `libopts` library *and* it produces code ready for internationalization. However, it also carries with it some limitations on the use of AutoOpts features and some requirements on the build environment.

PLEASE NOTE: in processing the option definitions to produce the usage text, it is necessary to compile some generated code in a temporary directory. That means that all the include directories needed to compile the code must be full path names and not relative directory names. "." is a relative directory name. To specify "-I." in the `CFLAGS` environment variable, you must expand it. For example, use:

```
CFLAGS=-I`pwd`
```

7.15.1 getopt feature limitations

This list of limitations is relative to the full list of AutoOpts supported features, See Section 7.1 [Features], page 83.

1. You cannot automatically take advantage of environment variable options or automated parsing of configuration files (`rc` or `ini` files). Consequently, the resulting code does not support `--load-opts` or `--save-opts` options automatically.

2. You cannot use set membership, enumerated, range checked or stacked argument type options. In fact, you cannot use anything that depends upon the `libopts` library. You are constrained to options that take **string** arguments, though you may handle the option argument with a callback procedure.

3. Special disablement and/or enablement prefixes are not recognized.

4. Option coordination with external libraries will not work.

5. Every option must be **settable** because the emitted code depends upon the `SET_OPT_XXX` macros having been defined. Specify this as a global (program) attribute.

6. You must specify a main procedure attribute (see Section 7.5.4 [Generated main], page 100). The `getopt.tpl` template depends upon being able to compile the traditional .c file into a program and get it to emit the usage text.

7. For the same reason, the traditional option parsing table code must be emitted **before** the `getopt.tpl` template gets expanded.

8. The usage text is, therefore, statically defined.

7.15.2 getopt build requirements

You must supply some compile and link options via environment variables.

'`srcdir`'   In case the option definition file lives in a different directory.

'`CFLAGS`'   Any special flags required to compile. The flags from `autoopts-config cflags` will be included automatically. Since the creation of the option parsing code includes creating a program that prints out help text, if it is necessary to include files from various directories to compile that program, you will need to specify those directories with `-Idirpath` text in the `CFLAGS`. Some experimentation may be necessary in that case.

NOTE: the `-Idirpath` text is only needed if your option callback functions include code that require additional `#include` directives.

'LDFLAGS'   Any special flags required to link. The flags from `autoopts-config ldflags` will be included automatically. This is required only if additional link flags for the help text emission program might be needed.

'CC'   This is needed only if `cc` cannot be found in `$PATH` (or it is not the one you want).

To use this, set the exported environment variables and specify `getopt` as the default template in your option definitions file (see Section 2.1 [Identification], page 7). You will have *four* new files. Assuming your definitions were in a file named `myprog-opts.def` and your program name was specified as `progname`, the resulting files would be created: `myprog-opts.h`, `myprog-opts.c`, `getopt-progname.h` and `getopt-progname.c`. You must compile and link both `.c` files into your program. If there are link failures, then you are using AutoOpts features that require the `libopts` library. You must remove these features, See Section 7.15.1 [getopt limitations], page 179.

These generated files depend upon configure defines to work correctly. Therefore, you must specify a `config-header` attribute (see Section 7.5.1.3 [programming attributes], page 93) and ensure it has `#defines` for either `HAVE_STDINT_H` or `HAVE_INTTYPES_H`; either `HAVE_SYS_LIMITS_H` or `HAVE_LIMITS_H`; and `HAVE_SYSEXITS_H`, if the `sysexits.h` header is available. The required header files for these defines are, respectively, the `/usr/include` files named:

- stdint.h
- inttypes.h
- sys/limits.h
- limits.h
- sysexits.h

The following header files must also exist on the build platform:

- sys/types.h
- stdio.h
- string.h
- unistd.h – or, for getopt_long:
- getopt.h

7.16 Internationalizing AutoOpts

The generated code for AutoOpts will enable and disable the translation of AutoOpts run time messages. If `ENABLE_NLS` is defined at compile time and `no-xlate` has been not set to the value *anything*, then the `_()` macro may be used to specify a translation function. If undefined, it will default to `gettext(3GNU)`. This define will also enable a callback function that `optionProcess` invokes at the beginning of option processing. The AutoOpts `libopts` library will always check for this *compiled with NLS* flag, so `libopts` does not need to be specially compiled. The strings returned by the translation function will be `strdup(3)-ed` and kept. They will not be re-translated, even if the locale changes, but they will also not be dependent upon reused or unmappable memory.

You should also ensure that the `ATTRIBUTE_FORMAT_ARG()` gets `#define-ed` to something useful. There is an autoconf macro named `AG_COMPILE_FORMAT_ARG` in `ag_macros.m4` that will set it appropriately for you. If you do not do this, then translated formatting strings may trigger GCC compiler warnings.

To internationalize option processing, you should first internationalize your program. Then, the option processing strings can be added to your translation text by processing the AutoOpts-generated `my-opts.c` file and adding the distributed `po/usage-txt.pot` file. (Also by extracting the strings yourself from the `usage-txt.h` file.) When you call `optionProcess`, all of the user visible AutoOpts strings will be passed through the localization procedure established with the `_()` preprocessing macro.

All of this is *dis*-abled if you specify the global attribute `no-xlate` to *anything*.

7.17 Naming Conflicts

AutoOpts generates a header file that contains many C preprocessing macros and several external names. For the most part, they begin with either `opt_` or `option`, or else they end with `_opt`. If this happens to conflict with other macros you are using, or if you are compiling multiple option sets in the same compilation unit, the conflicts can be avoided. You may specify an external name **prefix** (see Section 7.5.1 [program attributes], page 90) for all of the names generated for each set of option definitions.

Among these macros, several take an option name as a macro argument. Sometimes, this will inconveniently conflict. For example, if you specify an option named, `debug`, the emitted code will presume that `DEBUG` is not a preprocessing name. Or also, if you are building on a Windows platform, you may find that MicroSoft has usurped a number of user space names in its header files. Consequently, you will get a preprocessing error if you use, for example, `HAVE_OPT(DEBUG)` or `HAVE_OPT(INTERNAL)` (see Section 7.6.9 [HAVE_OPT], page 127) in your code. You may trigger an obvious warning for such conflicts by specifying the **guard-option-names** attribute (see Section 7.5.1 [program attributes], page 90). That emitted code will also `#undef-ine` the conflicting name.

7.18 All Attribute Names

This is the list of all the option attributes used in the various option processing templates. There are several flavors of attributes, and these are not distinguished here.

- Valid, current attributes that you are encouraged to use.
- Internally generated attributes that you cannot use at all. I need to prefix these with a distinguished prefix. e.g. `ao-`
- Valid attributes, but are deprecated. Alternates should be documented.

This list is derived by running many example option definitions through the option generation and man page templates and noting which attributes are actually used. There may be a few that are used but not exercised in my testing. If so, I need to ferret those out and test them, too.

addtogroup	aliases	allow_errors	arg_default
arg_name	arg_optional	arg_range	arg_type
argument	author	call_proc	cmd_section
comment_char	concept	config_header	copyright
date	default	deprecated	descrip
detail	die_code	disable	disable_load
disable_save	doc	doc_section	doc_sub
doc_sub_cmd	documentation	ds_format	ds_text
ds_type	eaddr	enable	enabled
environrc	equivalence	exit_desc	exit_name
explain	export	extract_code	field
file_fail_code	flag	flag_code	flag_proc
flags_cant	flags_must	full_usage	gnu_usage
guard_option_names	handler_proc	handler_type	help_type
help_value	home_rc	homerc	ifdef
ifndef	immed_disable	immediate	include
interleaved	keyword	lib_name	library
load_opts_value	long_opts	main_fini	main_init
main_type	max	min	more_help_value
must_set	name	no_command	no_libopts
no_misuse_usage	no_preset	no_xlate	omit_texi
omitted_usage	open_file	opt_state	option_format
option_info	owner	package	prefix
prefix_enum	preserve_case	prog_descrip	prog_info_descrip
prog_man_descrip	prog_name	prog_title	rcfile
reorder_args	reset_value	resettable	save_opts_value
scaled	set_desc	set_index	settable
short_usage	stack_arg	stdin_input	sub_name
sub_text	sub_type	test_main	translators
type	unshar_file_code	unstack_arg	usage
usage_message	usage_opt	usage_value	value
vendor_opt	version	version_proc	version_value

7.19 Option Definition Name Index

A

B

C

8 Add-on packages for AutoGen

This chapter includes several programs that either work closely with AutoGen (extracting definitions or providing special formatting functions), or leverage off of AutoGen technology. There is also a formatting library that helps make AutoGen possible.

AutoOpts ought to appear in this list as well, but since it is the primary reason why many people would even look into AutoGen at all, I decided to leave it in the list of chapters.

8.1 Automated Finite State Machine

The templates to generate a finite state machine in C or C++ is included with AutoGen. The documentation is not. The documentation is in HTML format for viewing, or you can download FSM.

8.2 Combined RPC Marshalling

The templates and NFSv4 definitions are not included with AutoGen in any way. The folks that designed NFSv4 noticed that much time and bandwidth was wasted sending queries and responses when many of them could be bundled. The protocol bundles the data, but there is no support for it in rpcgen. That means you have to write your own code to do that. Until now. Download this and you will have a large, complex example of how to use AutoXDR for generating the marshaling and unmarshaling of combined RPC calls. There is a brief example on the web, but you should download AutoXDR.

8.3 Automated Event Management

Large software development projects invariably have a need to manage the distribution and display of state information and state changes. In other words, they need to manage their software events. Generally, each such project invents its own way of accomplishing this and then struggles to get all of its components to play the same way. It is a difficult process and not always completely successful. This project helps with that.

AutoEvents completely separates the tasks of supplying the data needed for a particular event from the methods used to manage the distribution and display of that event. Consequently, the programmer writing the code no longer has to worry about that part of the problem. Likewise the persons responsible for designing the event management and distribution no longer have to worry about getting programmers to write conforming code.

This is a work in progress. See my web page on the subject, if you are interested. I have some useful things put together, but it is not ready to call a product.

8.4 Bit Maps and Enumerations

AutoGen provides two templates for managing enumerations and bit maps (flag words). They produce an enumeration of the enum or `#defines` for the bit maps, plus conversion functions for converting a string into one of these values or converting one of these values into a human readable string. Finally, for enumerations, you may specify one or more sets of dispatching functions that will be selected by identifying a keyword prefix of a string (see Section 8.4.2 [enum-code], page 187).

There is a separate project that produces a GDB add-on that will add these capabilities into GDB for bit masks. (GDB does just fine with enumerations.)

8.4.1 Enumerations

`str2enum.tpl`

Produce an enumeration for a list of input "cmd"s (names). Optionally, produce functions to:

- convert a string to an enumeration
- convert an enumeration value into a string
- invoke a function based on the first token name found in a string

The header file produced will contain the enumeration and declarations for the optional procedures. The code (`.c`) file will contain these optional procedures, but can be omitted if the `no-code` attribute is specified.

The following attributes are recognized with the `str2enum` template:

'cmd'
: You must provide a series of these attributes: they specify the list of names used in the enumeration. Specific values for the names may be specified by specifying a numeric index for these attributes. e.g. `cmd[5] = mumble;` will cause

```
FOO_CMD_MUMBLE = 5
```

to be inserted into the enumeration. Do not specify a value of "invalid", unless you specify the `invalid-name` attribute. (In that case, do not specify a `cmd` value that matches the `invalid-name` value.)

'prefix'
: This specifies the first segment of each enumeration name. If not specified, the first segment of the enumeration definition file name will be used. e.g. `foo-bar.def` will default to a `FOO` prefix.

'type'
: Normally, there is a second constant segment following the prefix. If not specified, it will be `CMD`, so if both `prefix` and `type` were to default from `foo-bar.def`, you will have enumeration values prefixed with `FOO_CMD_`. If specified as the empty string, there will be no "type" component to the name and the default constant prefix will thus be `FOO_`.

'base-name'
: This specifies the base name of the output files, enumeration type and the translation functions. The default is to use the `basename(3)` of the definition file. e.g. `foo-bar.def` results in a `base-name` of `foo-bar`.

'invalid-val'
>   The default invalid value is zero. Sometimes, it is useful for zero to be valid. If
>   so, you can specify ~0 or the empty string to be invalid. The empty string will
>   cause the enumeration count (maximum value plus 1) to be the invalid value.

'invalid-name'
>   By default, the invalid value is emitted into the enumeration as FOO_INVALID_
>   CMD. Specifying this attribute will replace INVALID with whatever you place in
>   this attribute.

'add-on-text'
>   Additional text to insert into the code or header file.

>   'ao-file'   Which file to insert the text into. There are four choices, only two
>   of which are relevant for the str2enum template: "enum-header",
>   "enum-code", "mask-header" or "mask-code".

>   'ao-text'   The text to insert.

8.4.2 Strings to Enums and Back

A continuation of the attributes for the **str2enum.tpl** template.

'no-code'   Do not emit any string to enumeration or enumeration to string code at all. If
             this is specified, the remainder of the attributes have no effect.

'no-name'   Do not emit the enumeration to name function.

'no-case'   When looking up a string, the case of the input string is ignored.

'alias'   A single punctuation character can be interpreted as a command. The first
             character of this attribute is the aliased character and the remainder the aliased-
             to command. e.g. "#comment" makes '#' an alias for the comment command.
             "#comment" must still be listed in the cmd attributes.

'length'   Specify how lengths are to be handled. Under the covers, gperf(1) is used to
             map a string to an enumeration value. The code it produces requires the string
             length to be passed in. You may pass in the length yourself, or the generated
             code may figure it out, or you may ask for that length to be returned back after
             being figured out.

             You have four choices with the length attribute:

             • Do not specify it. You will need to provide the length.
             • Specify "provided". You will need to provide the length.
             • Specify "returned". You must pass a pointer to a size_t object. If the
               name is found, the length will be put there.
             • Specify an empty string. The generated code will compute the length and
               that computed length will not be returned. The length parameter may be
               omitted. If the input strings contain only enumeration names, then this
               would be sufficient.
             • Specifying anything else is undefined.

'partial'   Normally, a name must fully match to be found successfully. This attribute causes the generated code to look for partial matches if the full match `gperf` function fails. Partial matches must be at least two characters long.

'undef-str'
               by default, the display string for an undefined value is "* UNDEFINED *". Use this to change that.

'equate'   A series of punctuation characters considered equivalent. Typically, "-_" but sometimes (Tandem) "-_^". Do not use '#' in the list of characters.

'dispatch'
               A lookup procedure will call a dispatch function for the procedure named after the keyword identified at the start of a string. Other than as specially noted below, for every named "cmd", must have a handling function, plus another function to handle errors, with "invalid" (or the `invalid-name` value) as the `cmd` name. Multiple `dispatch` definitions will produce multiple dispatching functions, each with (potentially) unique argument lists and return types.

               You may also use `add-on-text` to "#define" one function to another, thus allowing one function to handle multiple keywords or commands. The `d-nam` and `d-ret` attributes are required. The `d-arg`, `d-omit` and `d-only` attributes are optional:

               'd-nam'   This must be a printf format string with one formatting element: `%s`. The `%s` will be replaced by each `cmd` name. The `%s` will be stripped and the result will be combined with the base name to construct the dispatch procedure name.

               'd-ret'   The return type of the dispatched function, even if "void".

               'd-arg'   If there are additional arguments that are to be passed through to the dispatched function, specify this as though it were part of the procedure header. (It will be glued into the dispatching function as is and sedded into what is needed for the dispatched function.)

               'd-omit'   Instead of providing handling functions for all of the `cmd` names, the invalid function will be called for omitted command codes.

               'd-only'   You need only provide functions for the names listed by `d-only`, plus the "invalid" name. All other command values will trigger calls to the invalid handling function. Note that the invalid call can distinguish from a command that could not be found by examining the value of its first (`id`) argument.

               The handler functions will have the command enumeration as its first first argument, a pointer to a constant string that will be the character *after* the parsed command (keyword) name, plus any `d-arg` arguments that follow that.

               As an example, a file `samp-chk.def` containing this:

```
AutoGen Definitions str2enum;
cmd = one, two; invalid-name = oops;
dispatch = { d-nam = 'hdl_%s_cmd'; d-ret = void; };
```
               will produce a header containing:

```
typedef enum {
    SAMP_OOPS_CMD = 0,
    SAMP_CMD_ONE     = 1,
    SAMP_CMD_TWO     = 2,
    SAMP_COUNT_CMD
} samp_chk_enum_t;

extern samp_chk_enum_t
find_samp_chk_cmd(char const * str, size_t len);

typedef void(samp_chk_handler_t)(
    samp_chk_enum_t id, char const * str);

samp_chk_handler_t
        hdl_oops_cmd, hdl_one_cmd,  hdl_two_cmd;

extern void
disp_samp_chk(char * str, size_t len);

extern char const *
samp_chk_name(samp_chk_enum_t id);
```

- `find_samp_chk_cmd` will look up a `len` byte `str` and return the corresponding `samp_chk_enum_t` value. That value is `SAMP_OOPS_CMD` if the string is not "one" or "two".

- `samp_chk_handler_t` is the type of the callback procedures. Three must be provided for the dispatching function to call: `hdl_oops_cmd`, `hdl_one_cmd` and `hdl_two_cmd`. `hdl_oops_cmd` will receive calls when the string does not match.

- `disp_samp_chk` this function will call the handler function and return whatever the handler returns. In this case, it is void.

- `samp_chk_name` will return a string corresponding to the enumeration value argument. If the value is not valid, "* UNDEFINED *" (or the value of `undef-str`) is used.

8.4.3 Bit Maps and Masks

`str2mask.tpl`

This template leverages highly off of enumerations (see Section 8.4.1 [enums], page 186). It will produce a header file with bit masks defined for each bit specified with a `cmd` attribute. 63 is the highest legal bit number because this template has not been extended to cope with multiple word masks. (Patches would be welcome.)

There are a few constraints on the names allowed:

- names are constrained to alphanumerics and the underscore
- aliases are not allowed
- dispatch procedures are not allowed

no-code and no-name are honored. dispatch is not. The lookup function will examine each token in an input string, determine which bit is specified and add it into a result. The names may be prefixed with a hyphen (-) or tilde (~) to remove the bit(s) from the cumulative result. If the string begins with a plus (+), hyphen or tilde, a "base value" parameter is used for the starting mask, otherwise the conversion starts with zero.

Beyond the enumeration attributes that are used (or ignored), the str2mask template accepts a mask attribute. It takes a few "subattributes":

'm-name'   a special name for a sub-collection of the mask bits

'm-bit'   The name of each previously defined bit(s). If the desired previously defined value is a mask, that m-name must be suffixed with "-mask".

'm-invert'

When all done collecting the bits, x-or the value with the mask of all the bits in the collection.

A mask of all bits in the collection is always generated.

8.5 Invoking columns

This program was designed for the purpose of generating compact, columnized tables. It will read a list of text items from standard in or a specified input file and produce a columnized listing of all the non-blank lines. Leading white space on each line is preserved, but trailing white space is stripped. Methods of applying per-entry and per-line embellishments are provided. See the formatting and separation arguments below.

This program is used by AutoGen to help clean up and organize its output.

See `autogen/agen5/fsm.tpl` and the generated output `pseudo-fsm.h`.

This function was not implemented as an expression function because either it would have to be many expression functions, or a provision would have to be added to provide options to expression functions. Maybe not a bad idea, but it is not being implemented at the moment.

A side benefit is that you can use it outside of `autogen` to columnize input, a la the `ls` command.

This section was generated by **AutoGen**, using the `agtexi-cmd` template and the option descriptions for the `columns` program. This software is released under the GNU General Public License, version 3 or later.

8.5.1 columns help/usage (`--help`)

This is the automatically generated usage text for columns.

The text printed is the same whether selected with the `help` option (`--help`) or the `more-help` option (`--more-help`). `more-help` will print the usage text by passing it through a pager program. `more-help` is disabled on platforms without a working `fork(2)` function. The `PAGER` environment variable is used to select the program, defaulting to `more`. Both will exit with a status code of 0.

```
columns (GNU AutoGen) - Columnize Input Text - Ver. 1.2
Usage:  columns [ -<flag> [<val>] | --<name>[{=| }<val>] ]...

Specify the output dimensions:

   Flg Arg Option-Name    Description
    -W Num width          Maximum Line Width
                                - it must be in the range:
                                  16 to 4095
    -c Num columns        Desired number of columns
                                - it must be in the range:
                                  1 to 2048
    -w Num col-width      Set width of each column
                                - it must be in the range:
                                  1 to 2048
       Num tab-width      tab width

Specify how to lay out the text:

   Flg Arg Option-Name    Description
```

```
        Num spread              maximum spread added to column width
                                        - it must be in the range:
                                          1 to 1024
        no   fill               Fill lines with input
                                        - prohibits these options:
                                          spread
                                          col-width
                                          by-columns
     -I Str indent              Line prefix or indentation
        Str first-indent        First line prefix
                                        - requires the option 'indent'
     -f Str format              Formatting string for each input
     -S Str separation          Separation string - follows all but last
        Str line-separation     string at end of all lines but last
        Str ending              string at end of last line
```

Specify the ordering of the entries:

```
  Flg Arg Option-Name       Description
     no   by-columns         Print entries in column order
  -s opt  sort               Sort input text
```

Redirecting stdin to an alternate file:

```
  Flg Arg Option-Name       Description
  -i Str  input              Input file (if not stdin)
```

Version, usage and configuration options:

```
  Flg Arg Option-Name       Description
  -v opt  version            output version information and exit
  -? no   help               display extended usage information and exit
  -! no   more-help          extended usage information passed thru pager
  -> opt  save-opts          save the option state to a config file
  -< Str  load-opts          load options from a config file
                                     - disabled as '--no-load-opts'
                                     - may appear multiple times
```

Options are specified by doubled hyphens and their name or by a single
hyphen and the flag character.

The following option preset mechanisms are supported:
 - reading file ./.columnsrc
 - reading file $HOME/.columnsrc
 - examining environment variables named COLUMNS_*
Packaged by Bruce (2015-08-21)
Report columns bugs to bkorb@gnu.org

8.5.2 dimensions options

Specify the output dimensions.

width option (-W).

This is the "maximum line width" option. This option takes a number argument **num**. This option specifies the full width of the output line, including any start-of-line indentation. The output will fill each line as completely as possible, unless the column width has been explicitly specified. If the maximum width is less than the length of the widest input, you will get a single column of output.

columns option (-c).

This is the "desired number of columns" option. This option takes a number argument **count**. Use this option to specify exactly how many columns to produce. If that many columns will not fit within *line_width*, then the count will be reduced to the number that fit.

col-width option (-w).

This is the "set width of each column" option. This option takes a number argument **num**. Use this option to specify exactly how many characters are to be allocated for each column. If it is narrower than the widest entry, it will be over-ridden with the required width.

tab-width option.

This is the "tab width" option. This option takes a number argument **num**. If an indentation string contains tabs, then this value is used to compute the ending column of the prefix string.

8.5.3 treatment options

Specify how to lay out the text.

spread option.

This is the "maximum spread added to column width" option. This option takes a number argument **num**. Use this option to specify exactly how many characters may be added to each column. It allows you to prevent columns from becoming too far apart. Without this option, **columns** will attempt to widen columns to fill the full width.

fill option.

This is the "fill lines with input" option.

This option has some usage constraints. It:

- must not appear in combination with any of the following options: spread, col_width, by_columns.

Instead of columnizing the input text, fill the output lines with the input lines. Blank lines on input will cause a blank line in the output, unless the output is sorted. With sorted output, blank lines are ignored.

indent option (-I).

This is the "line prefix or indentation" option. This option takes a string argument `l-pfx`. If a number, then this many spaces will be inserted at the start of every line. Otherwise, it is a line prefix that will be inserted at the start of every line.

first-indent option.

This is the "first line prefix" option. This option takes a string argument `l-pfx`.

This option has some usage constraints. It:

* must appear in combination with the following options: indent.

If a number, then this many spaces will be inserted at the start of the first line. Otherwise, it is a line prefix that will be inserted at the start of that line. If its length exceeds "indent", then it will be emitted on a line by itself, suffixed by any line separation string. For example:

```
$ columns --first='#define TABLE' -c 2 -I4 --line=' \' <<_EOF_
one
two
three
four
_EOF_
#define TABLE \
    one   two \
    three four
```

format option (-f).

This is the "formatting string for each input" option. This option takes a string argument `fmt-str`. If you need to reformat each input text, the argument to this option is interpreted as an `sprintf(3)` format that is used to produce each output entry.

separation option (-S).

This is the "separation string - follows all but last" option. This option takes a string argument `sep-str`. Use this option if, for example, you wish a comma to appear after each entry except the last.

line-separation option.

This is the "string at end of all lines but last" option. This option takes a string argument `sep-str`. Use this option if, for example, you wish a backslash to appear at the end of every line, except the last.

ending option.

This is the "string at end of last line" option. This option takes a string argument **end-str**. This option puts the specified string at the end of the output.

8.5.4 ordering options

Specify the ordering of the entries.

by-columns option.

This is the "print entries in column order" option. Normally, the entries are printed out in order by rows and then columns. This option will cause the entries to be ordered within columns. The final column, instead of the final row, may be shorter than the others.

sort option (-s).

This is the "sort input text" option. This option takes an optional string argument **key-pat**. Causes the input text to be sorted. If an argument is supplied, it is presumed to be a pattern and the sort is based upon the matched text. If the pattern starts with or consists of an asterisk (*), then the sort is case insensitive.

8.5.5 input-text options

Redirecting stdin to an alternate file.

input option (-i).

This is the "input file (if not stdin)" option. This option takes a string argument **file**. This program normally runs as a **filter**, reading from standard input, columnizing and writing to standard out. This option redirects input to a file.

8.5.6 presetting/configuring columns

Any option that is not marked as *not presettable* may be preset by loading values from configuration ("rc" or "ini") files, and values from environment variables named `COLUMNS` and `COLUMNS_<OPTION_NAME>`. `<OPTION_NAME>` must be one of the options listed above in upper case and segmented with underscores. The `COLUMNS` variable will be tokenized and parsed like the command line. The remaining variables are tested for existence and their values are treated like option arguments.

`libopts` will search in 2 places for configuration files:

* $PWD
* $HOME

The environment variables `PWD`, and `HOME` are expanded and replaced when `columns` runs. For any of these that are plain files, they are simply processed. For any that are directories, then a file named `.columnsrc` is searched for within that directory and processed.

Configuration files may be in a wide variety of formats. The basic format is an option name followed by a value (argument) on the same line. Values may be separated from the option name with a colon, equal sign or simply white space. Values may be continued across multiple lines by escaping the newline with a backslash.

Multiple programs may also share the same initialization file. Common options are collected at the top, followed by program specific segments. The segments are separated by lines like:

```
[COLUMNS]
```

or by

```
<?program columns>
```

Do not mix these styles within one configuration file.

Compound values and carefully constructed string values may also be specified using XML syntax:

```
<option-name>
    <sub-opt>...&lt;...&gt;...</sub-opt>
</option-name>
```

yielding an `option-name.sub-opt` string value of

```
"...<...>..."
```

`AutoOpts` does not track suboptions. You simply note that it is a hierarchicly valued option. `AutoOpts` does provide a means for searching the associated name/value pair list (see: optionFindValue).

The command line options relating to configuration and/or usage help are:

version (-v)

Print the program version to standard out, optionally with licensing information, then exit 0. The optional argument specifies how much licensing detail to provide. The default is to print just the version. The licensing infomation may be selected with an option argument. Only the first letter of the argument is examined:

'version'   Only print the version. This is the default.

'copyright'
            Name the copyright usage licensing terms.

'verbose'   Print the full copyright usage licensing terms.

8.5.7 columns exit status

One of the following exit values will be returned:

'0 (EXIT_SUCCESS)'
            Successful program execution.

'1 (EXIT_FAILURE)'
            The operation failed or the command syntax was not valid.

'66 (EX_NOINPUT)'
            A specified configuration file could not be loaded.

'70 (EX_SOFTWARE)'
            libopts had an internal operational error. Please report it to autogen-users@lists.sourceforge.net. Thank you.

8.5.8 columns See Also

This program is documented more fully in the Columns section of the Add-On chapter in the AutoGen Info system documentation.

8.6 Invoking getdefs

If no `input` argument is provided or is set to simply "-", and if `stdin` is not a `tty`, then the list of input files will be read from `stdin`. This program extracts AutoGen definitions from a list of source files. Definitions are delimited by `/*=<entry-type> <entry-name>\n` and `=*/\n`. From that, this program creates a definition of the following form:

```
#line nnn "source-file-name"
entry_type = {
    name = entry_name;
    ...
};
```

1. The ellipsis ... is filled in by text found between the two delimiters. Each line of text is stripped of anything before the first asterisk, then leading asterisks, then any leading or trailing white space.

2. If what is left starts with what looks like a name followed by a colon, then it is interpreted as a name followed by a value.

3. If the first character of the value is either a single or double quote, then you are responsible for quoting the text as it gets inserted into the output definitions. So, if you want whitespace at the beginnings of the lines of text, you must do something like this:

```
* mumble:
* "  this is some\n"
* "  indented text."
```

4. If the `<entry-name>` is followed by a comma, the word `ifdef` (or `ifndef`) and a name `if_name`, then the above entry will be under `ifdef` control.

```
/*=group entry_name, ifdef FOO
 * attr: attribute value
=*/
```

Will produce the following:

```
#ifdef FOO
#line nnn "source-file-name"
group = {
    name = entry_name;
    attr = 'attribute value';
};
#endif
```

5. If you use of the `subblock` option, you can specify a nested value, See [getdefs subblock], page 201. That is, this text:

```
* arg:  int, this, what-it-is
```

with the `--subblock=arg=type,name,doc` option would yield:

```
arg = { type = int; name = this; doc = what-it-is; };
```

This section was generated by **AutoGen**, using the `agtexi-cmd` template and the option descriptions for the `getdefs` program. This software is released under the GNU General Public License, version 3 or later.

8.6.1 getdefs help/usage (help)

This is the automatically generated usage text for getdefs.

The text printed is the same whether selected with the help option (help) or the more-help option (more-help). more-help will print the usage text by passing it through a pager program. more-help is disabled on platforms without a working fork(2) function. The PAGER environment variable is used to select the program, defaulting to more. Both will exit with a status code of 0.

```
getdefs (GNU AutoGen) - AutoGen Definition Extraction Tool - Ver. 1.5
Usage:  getdefs [ <option-name>[{=| }<val>] ]...

Specify which definitions are of interest and what to say about them:

    Arg Option-Name      Description
    Str defs-to-get      Regex to look for after the "/*="
    Str subblock         subblock definition names
                                - may appear multiple times
    Str listattr         attribute with list of values
                                - may appear multiple times


specify how to number the definitions:

    Arg Option-Name      Description
    opt ordering         Alphabetize or use named file
                                - disabled as '--no-ordering'
                                - enabled by default
    Num first-index      The first index to apply to groups


Definition insertion options:

    Arg Option-Name      Description
    opt filelist         Insert source file names into defs
    Str assign           Global assignments
                                - may appear multiple times
    Str common-assign    Assignments common to all blocks
                                - may appear multiple times
    Str copy             File(s) to copy into definitions
                                - may appear multiple times
    opt srcfile          Insert source file name into each def
    opt linenum          Insert source line number into each def


specify which files to search for markers:

    Arg Option-Name      Description
    Str input            Input file to search for defs
                                - may appear multiple times
                                - default option for unnamed options
```

```
Definition output disposition options::

    Arg Option-Name     Description
    Str output          Output file to open
                                    - an alternate for 'autogen'
    opt autogen         Invoke AutoGen with defs
                                    - disabled as '--no-autogen'
                                    - enabled by default
    Str template        Template Name
    Str agarg           AutoGen Argument
                                    - prohibits the option 'output'
                                    - may appear multiple times
    Str base-name       Base name for output file(s)
                                    - prohibits the option 'output'

Version, usage and configuration options:

    Arg Option-Name     Description
    opt version         output version information and exit
    no  help            display extended usage information and exit
    no  more-help       extended usage information passed thru pager
    opt save-opts       save the option state to a config file
    Str load-opts       load options from a config file
                                    - disabled as '--no-load-opts'
                                    - may appear multiple times

All arguments are named options.
If no 'input' argument is provided or is set to simply "-", and if 'stdin'
is not a 'tty', then the list of input files will be read from 'stdin'.

The following option preset mechanisms are supported:
 - reading file /dev/null
This program extracts AutoGen definitions from a list of source files.
Definitions are delimited by '/*=<entry-type> <entry-name>\n' and '=*/\n'.
Packaged by Bruce (2015-08-21)
Report getdefs bugs to bkorb@gnu.org
```

8.6.2 def-selection options

Specify which definitions are of interest and what to say about them.

defs-to-get option.

This is the "regexp to look for after the "/*="" option. This option takes a string argument reg-ex. If you want definitions only from a particular category, or even with names matching particular patterns, then specify this regular expression for the text that must follow the /*=.

subblock option.

This is the "subblock definition names" option. This option takes a string argument sub-def.

This option has some usage constraints. It:

- may appear an unlimited number of times.

This option is used to create shorthand entries for nested definitions. For example, with:
using subblock thus

        --subblock=arg=argname,type,null

and defining an **arg** thus

        arg: this, char *

will then expand to:

        arg = { argname = this; type = "char *"; };

The "this, char *" string is separated at the commas, with the white space removed. You may use characters other than commas by starting the value string with a punctuation character other than a single or double quote character. You may also omit intermediate values by placing the commas next to each other with no intervening white space. For example, "+mumble++yes+" will expand to:

arg = { argname = mumble; null = "yes"; };.

listattr option.

This is the "attribute with list of values" option. This option takes a string argument def.

This option has some usage constraints. It:

- may appear an unlimited number of times.

This option is used to create shorthand entries for definitions that generally appear several times. That is, they tend to be a list of values. For example, with:
listattr=foo defined, the text:

foo: this, is, a, multi-list will then expand to:

foo = 'this', 'is', 'a', 'multi-list';

The texts are separated by the commas, with the white space removed. You may use characters other than commas by starting the value string with a punctuation character other than a single or double quote character.

8.6.3 enumerating options

specify how to number the definitions.

ordering option.

This is the "alphabetize or use named file" option. This option takes an optional string argument file-name.

This option has some usage constraints. It:

- can be disabled with –no-ordering.

- It is enabled by default.

By default, ordering is alphabetical by the entry name. Use, `no-ordering` if order is unimportant. Use `ordering` with no argument to order without case sensitivity. Use `ordering=<file-name>` if chronological order is important. getdefs will maintain the text content of `file-name`. `file-name` need not exist.

first-index option.

This is the "the first index to apply to groups" option. This option takes a number argument `first-index`. By default, the first occurrence of a named definition will have an index of zero. Sometimes, that needs to be a reserved value. Provide this option to specify a different starting point.

8.6.4 doc-insert options

Definition insertion options.

filelist option.

This is the "insert source file names into defs" option. This option takes an optional string argument `file`. Inserts the name of each input file into the output definitions. If no argument is supplied, the format will be:

```
infile = '%s';
```

If an argument is supplied, that string will be used for the entry name instead of *infile*.

assign option.

This is the "global assignments" option. This option takes a string argument `ag-def`.
This option has some usage constraints. It:

- may appear an unlimited number of times.

The argument to each copy of this option will be inserted into the output definitions, with only a semicolon attached.

common-assign option.

This is the "assignments common to all blocks" option. This option takes a string argument `ag-def`.
This option has some usage constraints. It:

- may appear an unlimited number of times.

The argument to each copy of this option will be inserted into each output definition, with only a semicolon attached.

copy option.

This is the "file(s) to copy into definitions" option. This option takes a string argument `file`.
This option has some usage constraints. It:

- may appear an unlimited number of times.

The content of each file named by these options will be inserted into the output definitions.

srcfile option.

This is the "insert source file name into each def" option. This option takes an optional string argument `file`. Inserts the name of the input file where a definition was found into the output definition. If no argument is supplied, the format will be:

```
srcfile = '%s';
```

If an argument is supplied, that string will be used for the entry name instead of *srcfile*.

linenum option.

This is the "insert source line number into each def" option. This option takes an optional string argument `def-name`. Inserts the line number in the input file where a definition was found into the output definition. If no argument is supplied, the format will be:

```
linenum = '%s';
```

If an argument is supplied, that string will be used for the entry name instead of *linenum*.

8.6.5 input-files options

specify which files to search for markers.

input option.

This is the "input file to search for defs" option. This option takes a string argument `src-file`.

This option has some usage constraints. It:

- may appear an unlimited number of times.

All files that are to be searched for definitions must be named on the command line or read from `stdin`. If there is only one `input` option and it is the string, "-", then the input file list is read from `stdin`. If a command line argument is not an option name and does not contain an assignment operator (=), then it defaults to being an input file name. At least one input file must be specified.

8.6.6 doc-output options

Definition output disposition options:.

output option.

This is the "output file to open" option. This option takes a string argument `file`.

This option has some usage constraints. It:

- is a member of the autogen class of options.

If you are not sending the output to an AutoGen process, you may name an output file instead.

autogen option.

This is the "invoke autogen with defs" option. This option takes an optional string argument `ag-cmd`.

This option has some usage constraints. It:

- can be disabled with –no-autogen.
- It is enabled by default.
- is a member of the autogen class of options.

This is the default output mode. Specifying `no-autogen` is equivalent to `output=-`. If you supply an argument to this option, that program will be started as if it were AutoGen and its standard in will be set to the output definitions of this program.

template option.

This is the "template name" option. This option takes a string argument `file`. Specifies the template name to be used for generating the final output.

agarg option.

This is the "autogen argument" option. This option takes a string argument `ag-opt`.

This option has some usage constraints. It:

- may appear an unlimited number of times.
- must not appear in combination with any of the following options: output.

This is a pass-through argument. It allows you to specify any arbitrary argument to be passed to AutoGen.

base-name option.

This is the "base name for output file(s)" option. This option takes a string argument `name`.

This option has some usage constraints. It:

- must not appear in combination with any of the following options: output.

When output is going to AutoGen, a base name must either be supplied or derived. If this option is not supplied, then it is taken from the `template` option. If that is not provided either, then it is set to the base name of the current directory.

8.6.7 presetting/configuring getdefs

Any option that is not marked as *not presettable* may be preset by loading values from configuration ("rc" or "ini") files.

`libopts` will search in `/dev/null` for configuration (option) data. If this is a plain file, it is simply processed. If it is a directory, then a file named `.getdefsrc` is searched for within that directory.

Configuration files may be in a wide variety of formats. The basic format is an option name followed by a value (argument) on the same line. Values may be separated from the option name with a colon, equal sign or simply white space. Values may be continued across multiple lines by escaping the newline with a backslash.

Multiple programs may also share the same initialization file. Common options are collected at the top, followed by program specific segments. The segments are separated by lines like:

```
[GETDEFS]
```

or by

```
<?program getdefs>
```

Do not mix these styles within one configuration file.

Compound values and carefully constructed string values may also be specified using XML syntax:

```
<option-name>
   <sub-opt>...&lt;...&gt;...</sub-opt>
</option-name>
```

yielding an `option-name.sub-opt` string value of

```
"...<...>..."
```

AutoOpts does not track suboptions. You simply note that it is a hierarchicly valued option. AutoOpts does provide a means for searching the associated name/value pair list (see: optionFindValue).

The command line options relating to configuration and/or usage help are:

version

Print the program version to standard out, optionally with licensing information, then exit 0. The optional argument specifies how much licensing detail to provide. The default is to print just the version. The licensing infomation may be selected with an option argument. Only the first letter of the argument is examined:

'version'   Only print the version. This is the default.

'copyright'
          Name the copyright usage licensing terms.

'verbose'   Print the full copyright usage licensing terms.

8.6.8 getdefs exit status

One of the following exit values will be returned:

'0 (EXIT_SUCCESS)'
          Successful program execution.

'1 (EXIT_FAILURE)'
          The operation failed or the command syntax was not valid.

'66 (EX_NOINPUT)'
          A specified configuration file could not be loaded.

'70 (EX_SOFTWARE)'
          libopts had an internal operational error. Please report it to autogen-users@lists.sourceforge.net. Thank you.

8.6.9 getdefs See Also

This program is documented more fully in the Getdefs section of the Add-On chapter in the `AutoGen` Info system documentation.

8.7 Invoking xml2ag

This program will convert any arbitrary XML file into equivalent AutoGen definitions, and invoke AutoGen. The template used will be derived from either:

- The **–override-tpl** command line option
- A top level XML attribute named, `"template"`

One or the other **must** be provided, or the program will exit with a failure message.

The *base-name* for the output will similarly be either:

- The **–base-name** command line option.
- The base name of the `.xml` file.

The definitions derived from XML generally have an extra layer of definition. Specifically, this XML input:

```
<mumble attr="foo">
  mumble-1
  <grumble>
  grumble, grumble, grumble.
  </grumble>mumble, mumble
</mumble>
```

Will get converted into this:

```
mumble = {
  grumble = {
    text = 'grumble, grumble, grumble';
  };
  text = 'mumble-1';
  text = 'mumble, mumble';
};
```

Please notice that some information is lost. AutoGen cannot tell that "grumble" used to lie between the mumble texts. Also please note that you cannot assign:

```
grumble = 'grumble, grumble, grumble.';
```

because if another "grumble" has an attribute or multiple texts, it becomes impossible to have the definitions be the same type (compound or text values).

This section was generated by **AutoGen**, using the `agtexi-cmd` template and the option descriptions for the `xml2ag` program. This software is released under the GNU General Public License, version 3 or later.

8.7.1 xml2ag help/usage (`--help`)

This is the automatically generated usage text for xml2ag.

The text printed is the same whether selected with the `help` option (`--help`) or the more-help option (`--more-help`). `more-help` will print the usage text by passing it through a pager program. `more-help` is disabled on platforms without a working `fork(2)` function. The `PAGER` environment variable is used to select the program, defaulting to `more`. Both will exit with a status code of 0.

```
xml2ag (GNU AutoGen) - XML to AutoGen Definiton Converter - Ver. 5.18.6pre15
Usage:  xml2ag [ -<flag> [<val>] | --<name>[{=| }<val>] ]... [ <def-file> ]

All other options are derived from autogen:

  Flg Arg Option-Name      Description
   -O Str output           Output file in lieu of AutoGen processing

All other options:

  Flg Arg Option-Name      Description
   -L Str templ-dirs       Search for templates in DIR
                                    - may appear multiple times
   -T Str override-tpl     Use TPL-FILE for the template
      Str definitions      Read definitions from FILE
      Str shell            name or path name of shell to use
   -m no  no-fmemopen      Do not use in-mem streams
      Str equate           characters considered equivalent
   -b Str base-name        Specify NAME as the base name for output
      no  source-time      set mod times to latest source
      no  writable         Allow output files to be writable
                                    - disabled as '--not-writable'
      Num loop-limit       Limit on increment loops
                                    - is scalable with a suffix: k/K/m/M/g/G/t/T
                                    - it must lie in one of the ranges:
                                      -1 exactly, or
                                      1 to 16777216
   -t Num timeout          Limit server shell operations to SECONDS
                                    - it must be in the range:
                                      0 to 3600
      KWd trace            tracing level of detail
      Str trace-out        tracing output file or filter
      no  show-defs        Show the definition tree
      no  used-defines     Show the definitions used
   -C no  core             Leave a core dump on a failure exit
   -s Str skip-suffix      Skip the file with this SUFFIX
                                    - prohibits the option 'select-suffix'
                                    - may appear multiple times
   -o Str select-suffix    specify this output suffix
                                    - may appear multiple times
   -D Str define           name to add to definition list
                                    - may appear multiple times
   -U Str undefine         definition list removal pattern
                                    - an alternate for 'define'
   -M opt make-dep         emit make dependency file
                                    - may appear multiple times
```

Version, usage and configuration options:

```
Flg Arg Option-Name     Description
 -v opt version         output version information and exit
 -? no  help            display extended usage information and exit
 -! no  more-help       extended usage information passed thru pager
```

Options are specified by doubled hyphens and their name or by a single hyphen and the flag character.
This program will convert any arbitrary XML file into equivalent AutoGen definitions, and invoke AutoGen.

```
The valid "trace" option keywords are:
  nothing        debug-message server-shell  templates      block-macros
  expressions    everything
  or an integer from 0 through 6
```
The template will be derived from either: * the ``--override-tpl'' command line option * a top level XML attribute named, 'template"

The ``base-name'' for the output will similarly be either: * the ``--base-name'' command line option * the base name of the .xml file
Packaged by Bruce (2015-08-21)
Report xml2ag bugs to bkorb@gnu.org

8.7.2 the-xml2ag-option options

All other options are derived from autogen.

output option (-O).

This is the "output file in lieu of autogen processing" option. This option takes a string argument file. By default, the output is handed to an AutoGen for processing. However, you may save the definitions to a file instead.

8.7.3 autogen-options options

All other options. These options are *mostly* just passed throug to autogen. The one exception is --override-tpl which replaces the default template in the output definitions. It does not get passed through on the command line.

templ-dirs option (-L).

This is the "search for templates in dir" option. This option takes a string argument DIR.

This option has some usage constraints. It:

- may appear an unlimited number of times.

Pass-through AutoGen argument

override-tpl option (-T).

This is the "use `tpl-file` for the template" option. This option takes a string argument `TPL-FILE`. Pass-through AutoGen argument

lib-template option (-l).

This is the "load autogen macros from `tpl-file`" option. This option takes a string argument `TPL-FILE`.

This option has some usage constraints. It:

- may appear an unlimited number of times.

Pass-through AutoGen argument

NOTE: THIS OPTION IS DEPRECATED

definitions option.

This is the "read definitions from `file`" option. This option takes a string argument `FILE`. Pass-through AutoGen argument

shell option.

This is the "name or path name of shell to use" option. This option takes a string argument `shell`. Pass-through AutoGen argument

no-fmemopen option (-m).

This is the "do not use in-mem streams" option. Pass-through AutoGen argument

equate option.

This is the "characters considered equivalent" option. This option takes a string argument `char-list`. Pass-through AutoGen argument

base-name option (-b).

This is the "specify `name` as the base name for output" option. This option takes a string argument `NAME`. Pass-through AutoGen argument

source-time option.

This is the "set mod times to latest source" option. Pass-through AutoGen argument

writable option.

This is the "allow output files to be writable" option.

This option has some usage constraints. It:

- can be disabled with –not-writable.

Pass-through AutoGen argument

loop-limit option.

This is the "limit on increment loops" option. This option takes a number argument `lim`. Pass-through AutoGen argument

timeout option (-t).

This is the "limit server shell operations to **seconds**" option. This option takes a number argument **SECONDS**. Pass-through AutoGen argument

trace option.

This is the "tracing level of detail" option. This option takes a keyword argument **level**. This option has some usage constraints. It:

- This option takes a keyword as its argument. The argument sets an enumeration value that can be tested by comparing the option value macro (OPT_VALUE_TRACE). The available keywords are:

```
nothing      debug-message server-shell
templates    block-macros  expressions
everything
```

or their numeric equivalent.

Pass-through AutoGen argument

trace-out option.

This is the "tracing output file or filter" option. This option takes a string argument **file**. Pass-through AutoGen argument

show-defs option.

This is the "show the definition tree" option. Pass-through AutoGen argument

used-defines option.

This is the "show the definitions used" option. Pass-through AutoGen argument

core option (-C).

This is the "leave a core dump on a failure exit" option.
This option has some usage constraints. It:

- must be compiled in by defining **HAVE_SYS_RESOURCE_H** during the compilation.

Many systems default to a zero sized core limit. If the system has the sys/resource.h header and if this option is supplied, then in the failure exit path, autogen will attempt to set the soft core limit to whatever the hard core limit is. If that does not work, then an administrator must raise the hard core size limit.

skip-suffix option (-s).

This is the "skip the file with this **suffix**" option. This option takes a string argument **SUFFIX**.
This option has some usage constraints. It:

- may appear an unlimited number of times.
- must not appear in combination with any of the following options: select-suffix.

Pass-through AutoGen argument

select-suffix option (-o).

This is the "specify this output suffix" option. This option takes a string argument `SUFFIX`. This option has some usage constraints. It:

- may appear an unlimited number of times.

Pass-through AutoGen argument

define option (-D).

This is the "name to add to definition list" option. This option takes a string argument `value`.

This option has some usage constraints. It:

- may appear an unlimited number of times.

Pass-through AutoGen argument

undefine option (-U).

This is the "definition list removal pattern" option. This option takes a string argument `name-pat`.

This option has some usage constraints. It:

- may appear an unlimited number of times.

Pass-through AutoGen argument

make-dep option (-M).

This is the "emit make dependency file" option. This option takes an optional string argument `type`.

This option has some usage constraints. It:

- may appear an unlimited number of times.

Pass-through AutoGen argument

8.7.4 xml2ag exit status

One of the following exit values will be returned:

'0 (EXIT_SUCCESS)'

> Successful program execution.

'1 (EXIT_FAILURE)'

> The operation failed or the command syntax was not valid.

8.8 Replacement for Stdio Formatting Library

Using the 'printf' formatting routines in a portable fashion has always been a pain, and this package has been way more pain than anyone ever imagined. Hopefully, with this release of snprintfv, the pain is now over for all time.

The issues with portable usage are these:

1. Argument number specifiers are often either not implemented or are buggy. Even GNU libc, version 1 got it wrong.

2. ANSI/ISO "forgot" to provide a mechanism for computing argument lists for vararg procedures.

3. The argument array version of printf ('printfv()') is not generally available, does not work with the native printf, and does not have a working argument number specifier in the format specification. (Last I knew, anyway.)

4. You cannot fake varargs by calling 'vprintf()' with an array of arguments, because ANSI does not require such an implementation and some vendors play funny tricks because they are allowed to.

These four issues made it impossible for AutoGen to ship without its own implementation of the 'printf' formatting routines. Since we were forced to do this, we decided to make the formatting routines both better and more complete :-). We addressed these issues and added the following features to the common printf API:

5. The formatted output can be written to

   - a string allocated by the formatting function ('asprintf()').
   - a file descriptor instead of a file stream ('dprintf()').
   - a user specified stream ('stream_printf()').

6. The formatting functions can be augmented with your own functions. These functions are allowed to consume more than one character from the format, but must commence with a unique character. For example,

   ```
   "%{struct stat}\n"
   ```

   might be used with '{' registered to a procedure that would look up "struct stat' in a symbol table and do appropriate things, consuming the format string through the '}' character.

Gary V. Vaughan was generous enough to supply this implementation. Many thanks!!

For further details, the reader is referred to the snprintfv documentation. These functions are also available in the template processing as 'sprintf' (see Section 3.5.32 [SCM sprintf], page 48), 'printf' (see Section 3.5.27 [SCM printf], page 46), 'fprintf' (see Section 3.5.7 [SCM fprintf], page 40), and 'shellf' (see Section 3.5.31 [SCM shellf], page 48).

9 Some ideas for the future.

Here are some things that might happen in the distant future.

- Fix up current tools that contain miserably complex perl, shell, sed, awk and m4 scripts to instead use this tool.

Appendix A Copying This Manual

You may copy this manual under the terms of the FDL (the GNU Free Documentation License).

Concept Index

Function Index

streqvcmp...................................... 142
streqvmap...................................... 142
string->c-name!................................ 54
string->camelcase.............................. 54
string-capitalize.............................. 48
string-capitalize!............................. 48
string-contains-eqv?........................... 48
string-contains?............................... 49
string-downcase................................ 49
string-downcase!............................... 49
string-end-eqv-match?.......................... 49
string-end-match?.............................. 49
string-ends-eqv?............................... 49
string-ends-with?.............................. 50
string-equals?................................. 50
string-eqv-match?.............................. 50
string-eqv?.................................... 50
string-has-eqv-match?.......................... 50
string-has-match?.............................. 51
string-match?.................................. 51
string-start-eqv-match?........................ 51
string-start-match?............................ 51
string-starts-eqv?............................. 51
string-starts-with?............................ 51
string-substitute.............................. 51
string-table-add............................... 52
string-table-add-ref........................... 52
string-table-new............................... 52
string-table-size.............................. 53
string-tr...................................... 54
string-tr!..................................... 54
string-upcase.................................. 54

string-upcase!................................. 54
strneqvcmp..................................... 143
strtransform................................... 143
sub-shell-str.................................. 55
suffix... 36
sum.. 55

T

teOptIndex..................................... 132
time-string->number............................ 55
tpl-file....................................... 36
tpl-file-line.................................. 37
tpl-file-next-line............................. 37

U

UNKNOWN.. 62
USAGE.. 131

V

VALUE_OPT_name................................. 131
VERSION.. 132
version-compare................................ 55

W

warn... 37
WHICH_IDX_name................................. 132
WHICH_OPT_name................................. 132
WHILE.. 62

Table of Contents

7 Automated Option Processing 83